MORE FUN IN
THE NEW WORLD

MORE FUN IN THE NEW WORLD

THE UNMAKING AND LEGACY OF L.A. PUNK

JOHN DOE WITH **TOM DESAVIA** AND FRIENDS

DA CAPO PRESS

Da Capo Press
Hachette Book Group
1290 Avenue of the Americas, New York, NY 10104
dacapopress.com
@DaCapoPress, @DaCapoPR

Printed in the United States of America
First Edition: June 2019

Published by Da Capo Press, an imprint of Perseus Books, LLC, a subsidiary of Hachette Book Group, Inc. The Da Capo Press name and logo is a trademark of the Hachette Book Group.

The Hachette Speakers Bureau provides a wide range of authors for speaking events. To find out more, go to www.hachettespeakersbureau.com or call (866) 376-6591.

The publisher is not responsible for websites (or their content) that are not owned by the publisher.

"Sliver of Glass" Lyrics written by Charlotte Caffey, Susanna Hoffs, and Jane Wiedlin. Published by Stridgirl Music (ASCAP), January Dream Music (BMI), administered by Universal Music Publishing and Wiedwacker Music (ASCAP).

"The New World" Lyrics written by Christine Cervenka. Published by Grosso Modo (ASCAP) administered by Applause and Encore Music c/o Concord Music Publishing.

"The Unheard Music" Lyrics written by Christine Cervenka and John Doe. Published by Grosso Modo (ASCAP) administered by Applause and Encore Music c/o Concord Music Publishing and Lockwood Valley Music (ASCAP) administered by Words and Music Publishing.

"Goin' Down Slow" lyrics written by James B. Owen. Published by Arc Music (BMI) administered by Songs of Universal Inc. (BMI).

Editorial production by Christine Marra, *Marra*thon Production Services. www.marrathoneditorial.org
Book design by Jane Raese
Set in 12-point Dante

Library of Congress Control Number: 2018968045

ISBN 978-0-306-92212-1 (hardcover); ISBN 978-0-306-92211-4 (ebook)

LSC-C

10 9 8 7 6 5 4 3 2 1

For the spirits who have left us and
those who keep the punk rock spirit alive.
We hope to honor people's memories
and inspire the uninitiated.

—Doe/Teeger/DeSavia, Sherman Oaks, California

CONTENTS

CHAPTER 1

INTRO: WE'RE HAVING MUCH MORE FUN

by Tom DeSavia

We never thought we'd be writing a sequel to *Under the Big Black Sun*.

When John and I set out to write our first book, which chronicled the birth of punk rock in Los Angeles, specifically spanning the years 1977 to 1982, we went into it with a purpose: we were intent on making sure that if we were telling the story of the roots of L.A. punk, it be told by multiple voices of folks who actually lived through it. It was important that it didn't become a tale from just John's perspective but rather an overview of a time that was noticeably becoming, at best, a victim of revisionist history. Its origin and ensuing years had been thinly documented on any global scale, especially compared to the concurrent New York and UK musical revolutions.

When we first pursued a deal to write what would become *UTBBS*, our goal was very simple: pen the history of the West Coast punk rock movement. Once we actually signed a deal to publish the tale, we realized that in order to make it cohesive, it would be best to devote the narrative, historically, to those first five years. The perfect year to end it seemed to be 1982, just as punk rock was really entering the consciousness of the US mainstream.

I wish I could tell you with confidence that we knew what we were doing when we undertook writing *Under the Big Black Sun*, but blissfully we didn't. We asked a handful of participants to write chapter-length essays on specific topics, tales that suddenly would—to our surprise and delight—evolve into mini-autobiographies that painted the feel of a city, a scene, and its inhabitants. These writers—a select group of varied architects and chroniclers of the punk scene—individually and collectively led us into this fabled underworld, where drugs and sex and violence lived side by side with art, camaraderie, desperation, quests for fame, quests for self-destruction, and, of course, self-expression. As we collected these chapters we quickly discovered that—with a little added narration and color commentary—an actual story was forming.

Jane Wiedlin, guitarist and songwriter of the groundbreaking Go-Go's, was the first person to submit her chapter for what would become the inaugural volume. Jane's chapter, "The Canterbury Tales," is an unflinching, unapologetic, honest, funny, and sometimes brutal account of living in Los Angeles during the evolution of punk culture. It made both John and me take pause and realize that we might actually be able to tell this story as it should be told. The illuminating essays began rolling in, written by musicians Exene Cervenka (X), Dave Alvin (The Blasters), Henry Rollins (Black Flag), Charlotte Caffey (The Go-Go's), Jack Grisham (T.S.O.L.), Teresa Covarrubias (The Brat), Mike Watt (The Minutemen), Robert Lopez (The Zeros, El Vez), Chris D. (The Flesh Eaters), and Pleasant Gehman (The Screaming Sirens) as well as journalists Kristine McKenna and Chris Morris. Suddenly we had a book; the chapters sequenced effortlessly into an engaging tale better than anything we had hoped for.

The book met with immediate positive reaction from both press and the public; the response surpassed our wildest expectations. *Under the Big Black Sun* spent seven weeks in the top ten on the *Los Angeles Times* hardcover nonfiction best-seller list, and even nabbed a "best spoken word recording" GRAMMY nomination for its accompanying audiobook, which featured every participating author reading their own chapter.

Still, we never figured we'd be writing a sequel.

It was toward the end of the promotion for the first book that the story suddenly felt unfinished, and it began to seem logical to tackle the next five years—closing our tale in the confines of a decade of musical revolution. We are grateful that the unexpected success of *Under the Big Black Sun* gave us the opportunity to really explore the concept of finishing what we started. With this volume we hope to contribute to the currently limited—but growing—historical documents that exist on this era. Without rewriting history, the prospect of completing the "real" story—which essentially can be summarized with "and then hair metal won the L.A. Sunset Strip civil war"—seemed depressing, if not historically accurate. Certainly the world knew the victors—punk rock didn't die, but it was seemingly relegated to the fringe, forever represented by the few who had established sustainable touring careers or moved on to some sort of mainstream notoriety.

It was a casual conversation with our mutual friend Krissy Teegerstrom that really set forth to define what this book would become. It gave us a story arc we felt we could wrap our heads around while trying to tell this tale of the second half of Los Angeles' original punk rock scene. It was Krissy's impression, after reading the first book, that the first-wave pioneers had thrown seeds and that those seeds had taken root. Watching the discussions that would unfold, she was overwhelmed to discover the influence this scene had—not only on musicians but also on so many aspects of contemporary art and lifestyle. She was the one who suggested we not craft this story as the end of a once-important regional music scene but rather let it evolve into more of a historical study of the scene's importance to international culture.

Personally, after the last book I found the majority of comments I received were from folks who related to my story of discovering punk at the end of its first five years, citing identical personal revelations. As much as any of the prose, many specifically made note to me of the book's dedication, where I thanked the members of X for altering everything my young brain thought it knew about music and art. This was—not surprisingly in retrospect—an experience shared by so many. It didn't matter if you were from L.A. or what gender you were or if you came of age in the 1970s or the 2000s—if you got a taste of the poison, it seeped in and became part of a shared DNA.

In a chapter of the first book devoted to regional punk rock art and photography, I wrote that the style of the time—captured primarily in show flyers and spearheaded by the likes of art pioneers Raymond Pettibon or Robbie Conal—most likely inspired the work of twenty-first-century icons like Shepard Fairey and Banksy. In a very kind post scripted upon the book's initial release, Fairey wrote, "I was incredibly honored when DeSavia describes the importance of flyer art and the ubiquitous flyer culture of the time and accurately points to how this untraditional art form seeped into the creative minds and souls of artists—both music and visual, and inspired the likes of me and Banksy. That's very true; I'm not sure if he's heard me mention flyer culture as an inspiration in interviews, but if the connection seemed obvious to him intuitively, he was correct."

Krissy's suggested narrative began to reveal itself as thus: along with the participants of the time featured within these pages, we asked a few select folks to write about their own bond with the music and the time, often from the experience of how it affected their own art and helped them define and celebrate their individuality. The first person we reached out to with this concept was Shepard. He is an unapologetic and vocal fan of the time and a torchbearer of the ethos of punk. Fairey enthusiastically drafted a chapter detailing his inspiration that came from punk culture and the courage it gave him to pursue the then-misunderstood/oft-criticized street art culture that helped define and establish its prominence. We're completely honored that Shepard, along with legendary pro skater Tony Hawk, acclaimed film director Allison Anders, and renowned actor Tim

Robbins, contributed essays to this volume on punk rock's influence on their art and individuality.

Seeds were thrown, for sure. What was essentially hiding in the shadows moved from a whisper to a scream in rapid-fire time. This late-twentieth-century cultural revolution—or artistic mutiny, depending on how you perceived it—aided in altering the way we looked at music, art, fashion, gender roles, authority, and almost all aspects of a post-sixties counterculture subtly and, ultimately, so significantly. In the eighties the former hippies—who generationally had laid the groundwork for what would become punk—represented a then enemy; a new establishment composed of bohemian free spirits was suddenly rapidly evolving into a bunch of Reagan-era "greed is good" stereotypes. The punks ditched the harpsichords for something decidedly aggressively melodic, if melodic at all. It was a less-discussed generation gap, steeped in both political unrest and economic uncertainty but ultimately one that historically created a wider chasm than that created by the clashing of Sinatra to Elvis. In the early days any of the minimal mainstream coverage of the West Coast's music scene primarily focused on safety-pin stereotypes and the threat of violence it seemed to promise. Now that musical uprising is culturally celebrated in museum exhibitions and coffee table art books. Pretty groovy.

By 1982 the impact the West Coast was having was undeniable, evidenced by the records released that year: The Descendents' *Milo Goes to College*, The Misfits' *Walk Among Us*, Flipper's *Generic*, Bad Brains' eponymous debut, Bad Religion's *How Could Hell Be Any Worse*, Angry Samoans' *Back From Samoa*, FEAR's *The Record*, The Circle Jerks' *Wild in the Streets*, T.S.O.L.'s *Beneath the Shadows*, Rank and File's *Sundown*, and X's *Under the Big Black Sun*, to name a handful. Around the globe suburban kids were now becoming converted to the ways of punk, thanks to The Clash, who released *Combat Rock*, their fifth and best-selling album (eventually going on to sell two million copies in the US alone). Throughout the next five years the L.A. punk landscape was splintering into a dizzying array of genres that engaged and thrilled Angelenos. Regionalism was alive and well, and we had it in spades: the press identified the scenes as "cowpunk," the "Paisley Underground," or "power pop," all sourced from the various elements that birthed punk in the Gold Rush State: country, the blues, fifties rock 'n' roll and sixties garage rock, Latin music and culture, and on and on. Bands as diverse as Lone Justice, The Long Ryders, The Bangles, The Red Hot Chili Peppers, Blood on the Saddle, The Dream Syndicate, Fishbone, and many more started to dominate and redefine the local musical landscape.

Hardcore was growing stronger and more global. It split into curiously overlapping camps that embraced violent, political, and straight-edge cultures. It grew more sophisticated and influential in the hands of local bands like Suicidal Tendencies, D.I., The Adolescents, The Vandals, The Crowd, Middle Class, China White, The Stains, and Jody Foster's Army as well as more established bands like FEAR, The Circle Jerks, Black Flag, Saccharine Trust, The Minutemen, and T.S.O.L. It was building what would eventually become punk's strongest and most enduring following.

A West Coast punk-led spoken-word movement began to rival that of the East Coast through the voices of local poets and writers such as Wanda Coleman and Harvey Kubernik as well as the emerging literary voices of musicians Exene Cervenka, Henry Rollins, and Jello Biafra, and including folks like Doe, Dave Alvin, Chris D., and many more.

A new crop of independent record companies formed, joining and/or replacing the first wave of pioneering labels. And of course, the major labels came racing to the chum in the water, hedging bets on this untapped youth culture movement. All the while, bigger and smaller bands relentlessly toured the US, developing the live audience, venues, and indie/college radio circuit that would allow the later indie and grunge-era bands to make a truly significant impact on the under-thirty crowd.

Cutting-edge pop and rock, specifically new wave, firmly took hold of the mainstream, and it took hold fast. MTV had debuted in the fall of 1981, and with it came a tidal wave of this new alternative music— most of which were pop acts branding themselves to a young generation by adopting punk style. Yeah, video killed the radio star, but it also conditioned the USA for kids sporting then-shocking dyed hair or leather spiked chokers. Sure, parents didn't like it, but they reluctantly had to accept it. An unexpected result was the beginning of the end for regional variations of new music because everyone saw the latest trends at the same time. New music, now in real danger of becoming a campy fad and stereotype, was profitable again. The end was nigh.

The early eighties fragmented our regional punk climate so much that our camaraderie of community began to crumble, while record deals and tours broke the gang apart. Punk began to splinter as the division between the hardcore kids and punk fans widened. As heavy and hair metal was taking hold, fans were drawing their lines in the sand.

Personally I was as excited about the prospect of this book as much as Doe originally hesitated: 1982 marked my first real foray into the punk scene, with my first X show at a club in Los Angeles' San Fernando Valley suburb. For John I believe 1982 not only marked the beginning of the dissolution of the community but also excitement as the spotlight was starting to shine on this disparate group of musicians, artists, photographers, and writers. The future was bright and the future was terrifying—depending on the day, I reckon.

Like *Under the Big Black Sun*, John didn't want the book to be about X or X's view of regional punk rock; he wanted it to be everyone's story . . . or at least as many as we could wrangle and fit. He fought against the photos of him and Exene on the covers—not out of a false modesty but a desire for them to reflect the community that existed. The community that eventually fell apart. The community that would remain tethered over the decades, either in celebration or brought together by loss.

Like the last book, we are incredibly humbled that so many agreed to join us on the journey of telling this tale; like the last book, we regret that we couldn't invite every single participant from the era. It has always been our sincerest hope that everyone who participated, supported, or was moved by this moment in rock 'n' roll history is compelled to take pen to paper and write of their own experiences.

We are obviously very thankful that our friend had shared with us her epiphany about the seeds that were thrown during these monumental years. This book is about those seeds and how firmly those roots were planted . . .

Oh, and sex and drugs and loud, loud music.

CHAPTER 2

MOSH PIT UBUISTS

by Tim Robbins

Plattsburgh, N.Y., 1978. The ceilings exploded as The Sex Pistols played in the shit hole off-campus apartment I shared with roommate and soon to be lifelong friend Frank Bednash. Frank had recently bought *Talking Heads 77*, Lou Reed's *Street Hassle*, and The Pistols' *Never Mind the Bollocks*. "GOD SAVE THE QUEEN" shouted out in that dingy apartment on Brinkerhoff, and our ceiling tiles, which were already precariously close to our heads, fell victim to weaponized heads and fists as they busted through the tiles above. My seventies hit parade aesthetic was shattered by the raucous, disrespectful, anarchic energy coming from these "punks" from the UK.

Punk rock was a liberation, a smashing of the dull, the mundane, the formulaic.

Two years later I'm thrashing in mosh pits in Los Angeles, seeing bands like FEAR, Black Flag, Circle Jerks, and X and feeling, in those moments, FREE from the various loads of crap I was dealing with in the early eighties, including but not limited to Ronald Reagan, paying rent, and trying to get a job that didn't suck.

These bands demanded attention. It was immediate, raw, and relevant to our lives. It made us physically ready for anything, inspired anger at things that we should be angry about, and eviscerated liars, frauds, and moral hypocrites. These songwriters were composing songs about us—our indignations, our loves, our fears. In the mosh pit, as crazy as it got sometimes, I saw more people taking care of each other than I saw people who wanted to hurt others. We were a disparate, anarchic community. There was a strange family in those sweaty clubs. There was nothing "hip" about it. Sure, there were scene-sters, but more often than not there was someone to call out the pretender, the fraud. This was an outsider movement. We were outside the culture. The real story was not being reported on. The media did not understand. They sensationalized it, made it as if it were some kind of teen dysfunction, some irrational acting out by privileged brats or homeless derelicts. On television episodics punks were depicted as mentally ill criminals.

I wonder if any of us thrashing around in a mosh pit in 1982 could have imagined the impending commodification of punk in music, fashion, and art. Expensive Warhol paintings of Sid Vicious and $4,000 designer jackets replete with safety pins and the anarchy symbol still float around us today as the men and women who made it all happen live in poverty. Punk was never going to make any of its musicians rich. It was almost as if making a lot of money was the opposite of being a punk rocker. Radio stations never played the bands I liked—the music wasn't "palatable" enough for a mass market. I believe the absence of these bands from the airwaves speaks to their importance: their music was essential. These artists were there to bend our ears beyond the mind-numbing normality of "classic rock" and hit parades. They were there to liberate us from the "palatable."

The band I followed most in the early eighties and still see today was X. John Doe, Exene Cervenka, DJ Bonebrake, and Billy Zoom played incredible live shows—and still do—that went hardcore while bringing beauty, poetry, and heart to the party. They had a touch of Woody Guthrie in them, a people's music sensibility that reached back to Appalachia and Mexican roots music as it set the standard, in my opinion, for L.A. punk rock. Everyone had "their band." And FEAR, Black Flag, and Circle Jerks all blew my mind at one time or another, but I always circled back to X.

Around the same time that I was driving my grandmother's push-button trans '64 Dodge Dart to the Masque, Club Lingerie, or the Anti-Club, I was a theater student at UCLA, studying directing. I met comrades in arms there, fellow punk rockers named Arenberg, Hinkley, Campbell, Robinson, Olivier, Schlitt, White, Bell, and Foster. We wanted to bring that mosh-pit energy to the stage. We were done with realism. We didn't want to do plays set in living rooms that had an imaginary wall where the audience was and an audience who we "cheated" toward yet never acknowledged. We wanted to bust that wall. We wanted to affect people—challenge their sensibilities, shake them up in a way that was worthy of the punk rock shows that were inspiring us.

I read a play called *Ubu Roi* written in 1896 by an eccentric (Dadaist? Surrealist? Provocateur?) and madman named Alfred Jarry. At the first performance of *Ubu Roi* in Paris the audience became so incensed at the content that a riot broke out, and they tore up their seats and threw them onto the stage.

This was the play to do. Although written in 1896, *Ubu* was punk rock. It was rude, satirically funny, and wickedly relevant. W. B. Yeats, who witnessed the first performance, viewed it as an event of revolutionary importance, saying, "After all our subtle color and nervous rhythm. . . . After us, the savage God."

We did midnight shows at the Pilot Theater in Hollywood. It wasn't as if this was a venue that was presenting new work or anything remotely related to punk rock. I was able to convince the owner, for a cut of the gate, to let me share the space with other productions that were in there. So at 10 P.M. we would take down the set of *Grease* or an evening of one-acts that were really not plays but actually unsold TV pilots, and we would put up our set, which we had purloined in a slightly illegal way in a late-night run to a scenic shop. We had no money to advertise, so to get word around that we were doing it, we did a preview performance at Janet Cunningham's newly opened CASH Gallery, put up posters illegally, did "flash mobs" by piling out of cars in front of movie theaters that were showing films at midnight to perform quick acts of brutal mimed violence for the people on line. Before anyone could figure out what was going on, they were holding a flyer for our show and we were driving away. *Ubu Roi* became a hit: we played for six months, and The Actors' Gang was born. The crowds were great—there was a sense of danger and excitement every night. We were coming at them full throttle, telling the story of *Ubu*'s vicious rise to power and his greed and avarice, bringing life to this wild play complete with scatological debrainings, slow-motion assassinations, green phalluses used as weapons, and a merciless teddy bear.

When audiences arrived at the theater on a darkened Seward Ave just off the strip from hooker land, they would notice a shady-looking man dressed in an overcoat and carrying a boom box. He was our "plant," a character we called the Ubuist. He would lurk outside, switching radio stations alternating from punk rock music to Christian radio preachers to more punk rock to sappy pop songs—in general, making the waiting audience uncomfortable. (Semi-full disclosure: we had to mix-tape this because, unlike the preachers and the sappy pop, you couldn't find punk rock on the radio.)

Eventually, when the audience was getting settled in, the Ubuist would enter the theater and sit in the back row, still playing his boom box, now annoyingly switching stations every ten seconds or so. He was the fan who had seen the show too many times and was there to take the cool out of the experience, to create a discomfort for the trendy who found their way there. By the sixth scene in the play, he was part of the show. His boom box now had Ubu's voice in it, and he became complicit with Ubu as a tax collector preying on poor peasants. Toward the end of the play there is a decapitation, which would nightly prove too much for the Ubuist to take. He would stand up and protest the brutality, and the actors would then forcibly eject him and his boom box from the theater. This was always a great moment, but there was an ulterior motive involved: it was the Ubuist's job to get to the liquor store before 2:00 A.M. so we could have cold beers waiting to get drunk with after the show. We were young, arrogant, and ready to fuck shit up. The Actors' Gang of 1982 was inspired by, fueled by, and beholden to punk rock. Punk was at the core of our energy and commitment on stage. Most of the actors in the show were no strangers to mosh pits. We were not meant to be doing tame theater. We were going to sweat hard and push beyond our physical limits. We were going to give as much to our audience as we had received from X or FEAR or The Dead Kennedys. We wanted to bring a punk rock aesthetic to theater. We wanted to communicate in this new language—independent in spirit and bold in defiance yet possessed of a conscience. We have carried this sensibility with us throughout the decades. That endurance in independence, defiance, and conscience has as its genesis and owes its life to all the West Coast punks who shared their hearts with us and changed our lives.

CHAPTER 3

IT SOUNDS TOO MUCH LIKE THE BLASTERS: 1982-1985

by Dave Alvin

One afternoon in 1984 I was sitting in the plush office of Lenny Waronker, the president of Warner Bros. Records, with Mr. Waronker and three of Warner's Artist and Repertoire (A&R) staff. We were listening to tapes of the new songs that my band, The Blasters, had recorded for the upcoming album we were making for Warners. As a song I had written called "Kathleen" came to an end, a heavy, judgmental silence filled the room. Then the newest member of the A&R staff looked at me with a smirk on his face.

"Don't get me wrong," he said, "It's a good song, I guess, so I'm not sure how to say this but, ahh . . . I mean, I'm sure it will go over great with your crowd and all, but . . . I just think, ah . . . that it sounds too much like The Blasters."

I pulled a cigarette out of my shirt pocket, but I didn't light it. I just twiddled it nervously between my fingers as my other hand gripped the arm of the chair I was sitting in. I could feel my temperature quickly rising and my face starting to burn with anger. I wanted to shout at the smug A&R man, "What the fuck did you just say, mother-fucker? What the fuck do you fucking know about anything? You dumb-fucking fucking fuck?"

Instead of screaming at him with righteous indignation and hurling myself fists first into his face, though, I timidly looked at Mr. Waronker and the other two A&R guys for any sign of support, but none came. They just stared blankly back at me, waiting to see my reaction to the provocation. After a few awkward moments of inner turmoil and mental confusion I finally muttered the only diplomatic response I could think of: "Well, um, yeah, you're absolutely right about that. Maybe that's because we are The Blasters."

No one laughed.

Yeah, we were The Blasters all right, but unfortunately I was the only member of the band present at this meeting. By this time in The Blasters' relationship with Warner Bros., things had gotten so strained that I was the only Blaster ever allowed at any A&R meetings. During the year or so after we signed with the label most of the meetings be-tween the band and the executives could be described as uncomfortable at best, with some descending into loud and ugly shouting matches.

The crazy thing, though, is that these primal-scream sessions were usually not between the Warner folk and us; most of the time it was The Blasters yelling at each other over something that had nothing at all to do with whatever the damn meeting was about in the first place. We'd all grown up together in Downey, California, and knew each other so damn well that arguing and fighting with ourselves was just how we communicated. We pushed, shouted, shoved, screamed, and punched each other whether we were seriously pissed off or simply showing sincere affection, so why should discussing artistic, career, or business decisions be any different? After one particularly incendiary showdown between my brother and me at a Warners meeting, over the pressing issue of whether or not the drummer on an old Little Willie John record kept time on the high hat, Mr. Waronker firmly decreed that I, as the band's songwriter, would be the only band member they would ever meet with again to discuss creative issues. You can imagine how well that went over.

That afternoon I was especially angry with the novice A&R man and his snide putdown because, out of everything The Blasters had recorded before or since, "Kathleen" was—and remains—my absolute favorite performance we ever did. It was often difficult for us to replicate the raw energy of our live shows in the cold and clinical environment of a recording studio, but when we cut "Kathleen" we captured the sweaty abandon of a live gig perfectly. It's a song I wrote about two blue-collar kids running away from home, and I wanted the music to sound like one of the great rhythm-and-blues tracks cut in New Orleans at Cosimo Matassa's J&M Studio back in the 1950s. Naturally The Blasters did not let me down.

"Kathleen" featured the complete Blasters "big band" lineup of my brother Phil on vocals, Bill Bateman on drums, John Bazz on bass, Gene Taylor on piano, Lee Allen and Steve Berlin on saxophones while I bashed some Chuck Berry–ish guitar. While everyone played and sang their asses off, the real stars of the track were Lee and Gene. A 1950s New Orleans tenor sax legend who'd moved to Los Angeles in the sixties, Lee Allen had been every Blaster's beloved friend, teacher, musical mentor, and lifestyle coach since we met him in the early seventies. Lee was an honored veteran of hundreds of those historic sessions at Cosimo's studio, where he blew the melodic sax solos on classic hits by Little Richard and Fats Domino, among many others, and his solo on "Kathleen" was as vibrant and playful as any of his solos from three decades before. What really made the performance my favorite, though, was that our then producer, Jeff Eyrich, instead of stopping us after the song was technically over, let the tape keep rolling as the band, led by Gene's powerhouse piano pumping, blasted happily away at full power into an impromptu boogie-woogie improvisation unlike anything we'd allowed ourselves to record in a studio before then.

I was also upset and embarrassed that I had possibly let down Lenny Waronker. He had taken more than his share of grief at Warners for signing a band that some folks at the label considered to be just a numb-skull, pompadoured, three-chord novelty act. Mr. Waronker, though, saw potential in my brother's passionate vocals and my developing songwriting. After The Blasters' first album for the sweet-talking scal-awags at Slash Records started to garner critical praise from places like *Time* magazine and then actually started selling more than a handful of copies, a few major labels began to inquire about signing us. The only label I wanted to sign with, though, was Warner Bros. because I knew about Mr. Waronker's reputation as a producer and his com-mitment to allowing his artists great artistic freedom. He'd produced records for folks like James Taylor, Ry Cooder, Gordon Lightfoot, Arlo Guthrie, Rickie Lee Jones, and The Everly Brothers, among others, but what impressed me most was that he had produced one of my fa-vorite albums, Randy Newman's masterpiece, *Good Old Boys*. I wanted to learn how to be a decent songwriter and felt that Mr. Waronker could help guide me in little ways toward that goal. Fortunately that was one thing I was not wrong about.

There was, unfortunately, one thing I was quite wrong about. All of The Blasters wanted to move up to a major label for more serious distribution, promotion, and financial support, but I also didn't want to completely desert the supposedly independent, supposedly ideal-istic rascals at Slash Records. After all, they were the ones who had originally given us a chance to record when no one else would. I mis-takenly believed that having Slash would protect The Blasters from some of the artistic and financial nightmares I was seeing other bands go through when they signed to a major label. I certainly wanted to have a hit record, but I definitely wanted any hit record to actually sound like The Blasters, and I foolishly believed having Slash with us would help that happen. Despite warnings from my skeptical brother and from our very patient manager, Shelly Heber, as well as our savvy music publishers, Dan and Fred Bourgeois at Bug Music, a unique deal was proposed. The agreement was that we could sort of be on both labels at the same time. The Blasters would officially be War-ner Bros. artists, but by generously giving Slash Records 15 percent of our earnings generated from recordings before recoupment, there would be a Slash Records logo displayed on our albums right next to the Warner Brother's logo. After many heated discussions and more screaming, The Blasters signed with Warner Bros., who immediately took over pressing, promoting, and distributing our first Slash album.

In hindsight it was a pretty silly and stupid deal for The Blasters, but it was an extremely good and profitable one for Slash. This arrangement between The Blasters and the two aesthetically disparate labels created a positive working relationship between Warners and Slash that quickly led to a permanent distribution deal in which Slash became sort of an A&R farm team for Warners. With the infusion of the major label's money, Slash went on to sign groundbreaking acts like Los Lobos, The Violent Femmes, Rank and File, The Bodeans, The Del Fuegos, Faith No More, L7, and many more. Sadly for The Blasters, though, Slash representatives weren't quite the defenders of our artistic credibility I thought they would be; instead, they merely became yes-men to the Warner's A&R staff. If Warners thought "Kathleen" sounded too much like The Blasters, then Slash thought "Kathleen" sounded too much like The Blasters.

On the positive side, while writing the songs for our second album and first full Warner Bros. release, 1983's *Non-Fiction*, was when I actually started to feel like maybe I could, maybe, kind of, maybe sort of, perhaps, truly become a real, live songwriter. Even though some of the songs I'd written previously for the band, like "Marie Marie," "American Music," and "Border Radio," have over the years become semi-standards in the roots music world, I seriously considered my writing of them to just be a lucky damn fluke. I really didn't know how to write songs like a professional. Because of that fact, I was deeply stressed out at having to come up with a bunch of new songs for the album. I quit drinking beer and ceased all my mindless late-night carousing for a while in order to buckle down with a guitar, some pens, stacks of yellow legal pads of paper plus countless packs of cigarettes to force myself to become some kind of songwriter.

As I said earlier, the main thing I got right about us signing with Warners was that Mr. Waronker gently steered me to write about more topics than simply boy meets girl or boy loses girl. I greatly

appreciated his confidence in me, but I still struggled with the pressure
to not disappoint him or let down our fans or screw things up for my
Blaster brothers, who were now depending on me to supply them with
an album of new, original songs. Late one night, while I was wrestling
with the words of some song I was working on, a very drunk Blaster
barged into my bedroom. He stared at me for a moment and then
loudly declared, "That better be a good fucking song 'cause my whole
fucking life depends on you now so—don't fuck it up!" He glared at
me after he finished and then turned and left the room, slamming the
door behind him. I was too shocked to say anything. All I wanted to do
was give up, quit the band, and go back home to Downey. After a few
minutes of imagining going back to my previous life as a wanna-be
poet and a fry cook getting paid under the table, I lit another smoke,
grabbed my guitar, and got back to work.

Eventually I started writing some decent songs, like "Long White
Cadillac," "Jubilee Train," "Red Rose," "Boomtown," and "Bus Station." These songs had bittersweet lyrics about hard times, missed
opportunities, fading hopes, and even everyone's favorite lighthearted
topic, death. I knew that these weren't the usual topics for Top Forty
hits, especially at the height of the early-eighties' neo-romantic, syn-
thesizer, dance pop, but I didn't really care. I knew my brother would
understand what I was writing and would sing the hell out of these
songs. All I was doing was adding to my songs the spirits of John Stein-
beck, Nelson Algren, and Woody Guthrie as well as the attitude of the
old picket-line songs we heard our union-organizer father sing around
the house when we were growing up. Those kinds of lyrics fit right
in with The Blasters' hopped-up mix of various shades of blues, early
R&B, rockabilly, country, Cajun, and other roots styles.

In contrast to the downbeat lyrics I was writing, the musical ar-
rangements the guys and I came up with were as rocking as anything
on our previous album. This was a trickster way of subtly conveying
a socially conscious message while still getting folks out on the dance
floor. After our first album a lot of people thought of The Blasters as a
one-dimensional good time—rockabilly revival combo—and I wanted
to put an end to such thinking. Whether I succeeded or not, I guess,
depended on how closely you listened to the lyrics. Some folks did.

Some folks didn't. Mr. Waronker seemed to get it and encouraged me to follow the path I was traveling down.

To be fair to all the folks at Warners, we were not always the easiest group of guys to deal with or to promote, even when we weren't arguing and fighting. Our ragged, jumbled gumbo of American roots music was very difficult for the Warners promotion department to market into a simple AM radio commercial product that could slip easily in between cuts by Culture Club or Soft Cell. Another problem for us was that we weren't quite blues enough for some of the blues crowd or rockabilly enough for some of the rockabilly crowd, and just forget about us being arena rock enough for most of the arena rock crowd. Another harsh reality was that none of us possessed the dreamy teen idol good looks that could land us on the cover of gossip magazines. We also made their lives difficult by demanding to produce *Non-Fiction* ourselves, just as we had produced our previous album on Slash, because we'd yet to find a producer or recording engineer we trusted to capture our sound. We were a bit shocked Mr. Waronker agreed to this demand—he apparently had some faith in us that we knew what we were doing, and we kind of did in some ways, but in other ways we didn't have a damn clue. We would have meetings with prospective producers or engineers who had grown up influenced and shaped by the complex sonic glories of *Sgt. Peppers* and *Dark Side of the Moon*, but we would show up with a bunch of scratchy old 78s by Big Joe Turner or Sonny Boy Williamson and then ask the stunned engineers if they could make us sound exactly like those.

At the same time that all the legal and business jazz was being worked out, The Blasters were transitioning from being a Los Angeles club band into being a national touring act. After the release of our first Slash album and its relative success, plus our ability to deliver a solid live show, we found ourselves on the road seven to eight months out of the year. Financially we were not making big rock-star bucks, but we were making more than any of our previous day jobs had paid us. We soon were making enough money to pay ourselves salaries, pay our bills, pay for our manager, pay a booking agent, pay for insurance, pay for a touring van, and, soon after, pay for a second van to haul our gear and sometimes keep one or two band members away from the other band members. We could afford a loyal road crew headed by our beloved road manager, Wally Hanley, and our sweet natured sound-man, Robert Tomasevski. We crisscrossed the USA playing good gigs, bad gigs, great gigs, transcendental gigs. We became a headlining act selling out shit holes as well as rock palaces. We missed our families. We missed our friends and lovers. We gave interviews and said stu-pid things and smart things. We broke guitar strings, drum heads, and hearts. We drank too much. We smoked too much. We sweated too much. We stayed up days at a time too much. We all threatened to quit but never did. We toured Britain, Europe, and Canada, making a joyous racket. We released a live EP of blues and rockabilly cover songs. We had our PBS TV special and had Willie Dixon and Carl Per-kins as our guests. We caused a few minor riots. We were banned from three cities in California. We wreaked havoc on our personal lives. We helped friends get gigs and record deals. We received praise from Sam Phillips, Bo Diddley, and Bob Dylan. We came home to sleep a couple days, then we hit the road again. We laughed with each other. We fought with each other. We took care of each other. We made some people aware of and proud of their musical heritage while making them dance and giving them a little hope for the future or, at least, inspiration to go start their own band and make their own sweet noise. It was truly an intense, amazing time, but then . . . things got weird.

Despite positive reviews and our constant touring, including a month-long US tour with Eric Clapton, *Non-Fiction* didn't sell as many copies as our first album. Some people blamed our production and the album's murky sound quality, while others blamed Warners for not promoting it enough or classic rock FM radio for ignoring the album entirely. Those reasons were all possible explanations, but in the end, I only blamed myself. I felt I had tried my best to be a goddamn song-writer but had ultimately failed. I failed our fans, failed Mr. Waronker, and, most importantly, failed my Blaster brothers.

Fortunately Mr. Waronker didn't drop us from the label. He agreed to make another album with us, but he demanded we use a producer that he and the A&R staff approved of for the next album. The Blast-ers argued about this, of course, but eventually we agreed to play ball with Warners and use a producer. Then the big bone of contention between the label and us was just who this producer would be. We'd make a suggestion, but Warners would shoot it down for whatever reason. Then Warners would offer up a candidate who we would say no to. For example, my brother refused to work with one producer because Phil was convinced the guy was in a religious cult and would try to convert him, while I wouldn't accept another producer because he had never heard of one of my favorite guitarists, Johnny "Guitar" Watson. As the two sides thrashed about with various producer options, I reluctantly went back into my sober songwriting mode with my guitar, pens, paper, and cigarettes to write the next album.

The most unfortunate, maddening, and infuriating incident involved the great Booker T. Jones, of the Memphis groove masters Booker T. & the M.G.'s. He saw us play in San Francisco, came backstage, and discussed producing our next album. In a rare moment of precious agreement, every single Blaster immediately said yes. It seemed to be the perfect solution. Well, at least it did until I told the Warner's A&R staff. Despite the fact that Mr. Jones had just produced Willie Nelson's multi-million-selling album, *Stardust*, they said he was too old and wanted someone "young and hip." I argued, begged, and pleaded with them, to no avail. Naturally it wasn't the A&R staff who had to call Mr. Jones to tell him he was too old—that terrible burden fell on me. Needless to say, I've never heard from him again, and it's a frustrating, sad memory that still keeps me awake some nights, wondering what could have been.

Eventually the A&R crew and I came up with the plan of trying a young producer named Jeff Eyrich, who had recently produced The Plimsouls' magnificent record of Peter Case's song, "A Million Miles Away." Jeff was an excellent musician who had toured with artists as wide ranging as Tim Buckley and Tanya Tucker but, most importantly, was a local guy who grew up on our side of town and went to the same high school as Phil and me. After some fast talking on my part, the guys agreed to give him a try, and we finally headed back to the studio to record what would become my last album with The Blasters, 1985's *Hardline*.

Lyrically and thematically, the new songs weren't much different from the songs on *Non-Fiction*, but musically I tried to push the boundaries of The Blasters' style further than they had been stretched before. There were still some songs in the cranked-up, classic Blasters style, like, "Kathleen," "Trouble Bound" (our ode to rockabilly existentialism). and the cynical rave-up "Rock and Roll Will Stand," but the rest of the tunes were more of a mixed bag. I wrote two slow blues grinders that dealt with intolerance and slimy politicians, "Dark Night" and "Common Man." I tried my hand at writing a straight country shuffle with "Help You Dream" and attempted a Curtis Mayfield and the Impressions–inspired soul strut called "Can't Stop Time." We also took a rock 'n' roll song I'd cowritten with my pal John Doe, titled "Little Honey," and rearranged it into a quiet, moody, folk-bluegrass ballad. For our own damn kicks we recorded a jumping version of an Elmore James blues song, "Cry For Me," but then one day Phil shocked all of us by going into the studio alone and not allowing any of us to be there. That day he cut a stomping solo interpretation of the ancient spiritual "Samson and Delilah," accompanied only by his own guitar and two fabulous gospel singers, Bobby King and Herman Johnson, from Ry Cooder's band. This track showcased my brother's best guitar playing and, perhaps, his greatest vocal performance ever. I think it was also his way of saying "screw you" to the guys at Warners and, especially, maybe to his little brother who was pushing him a bit too much in uncomfortable musical directions.

Jeff convinced us to bring in other musicians to augment our sound for the album, so we invited good friends like David Hidalgo from Los Lobos to play some accordion and mandolin as well as Larry Taylor from Canned Heat and the Tom Waits combo to play some acoustic bass, while Jeff brought in bluegrass fiddle virtuoso Richard Greene. When Phil had a brilliant idea for gospel harmony vocals on "Trouble Bound," Jeff simply said, "Cool. I'll call the Jordanaires and see if they can do it." Much to our delight and shock, they said yes! Phil, Jeff, and I flew to Nashville and recorded them on three songs in one afternoon. For The Blasters, who loved fifties rock 'n' roll and its cultural history, to have Little Richard's and Fats Domino's sax player *and* Elvis Presley's damn backup singers together on one of our records was way beyond anything we'd ever expected in our lifetimes.

I felt an enormous sense of relief. The songs were written. The recording was finished. The tracks sounded big and professional. The album was done, and it was good, plus we hadn't killed each other. Everything felt like we were on the right track. Sadly this euphoric state came to an end when I received an ominous phone call from Warners to come meet with Mr. Waronker and his A&R gang to discuss their "issues" with the album. This was the meeting where the smug A&R man made his crack about "Kathleen" sounding too much like The Blasters. To be honest, Mr. Waronker said many nice, positive things about the songs and the band's artistic growth, but I was half-listening because of my anger at his junior A&R man. But I heard him loud and clear when he said the two sentences all recording artists dread hearing: "We don't hear a single. Go back into the studio and come out with a hit record." Okay. Sure. That's easy. No problem.

Within a couple of weeks our producer was removed from the album and, sadly, "Can't Stop Time," "Cry for Me," and, my favorite, "Kathleen" were all removed as well. I went back to sitting on the side of my bed in my apartment with my guitar, pens, papers, and cigarettes, trying to figure out how the fuck do you write a fucking hit song. Before I could get too suicidal, though, our manager called and shocked the living hell out of me. Shelly breathlessly informed me that John Mellencamp, then one of the biggest rock-pop stars in the country, had called her and proclaimed that he wanted to write and produce a song for us in order to "Get The Blasters a damn hit record!" Naturally Warners loved this idea, and naturally The Blasters argued, screamed, and fought about it before we agreed to give it a try with Mr. Mellencamp.

Mr. Mellencamp's song for us, "Colored Lights," was kind of a midtempo, early sixties R&B/pop number, which was cool with us, so we started arranging it to fit our Blasters style. He quickly stopped us and, as nicely yet firmly as he could, explained that our arrangement ideas were one of the reasons we didn't have any hits. He then began arranging the song his way. I'd never seen a real hit-making team in action before, so I was fascinated watching him and his coproducer, the astute engineer Don Gehman, discussing what sort of tempo would be best for the song because of what sort of radio formats we were shooting for as well as what instruments and sounds were currently radio friendly and which weren't, and so on. After deciding on the tempo, they began building the track layer by layer, starting with Stan Lynch, the drummer from Tom Petty's Heartbreakers, and our drummer, Bill Bateman, recording a percussion loop to help the rest of the musicians keep perfect time. Then Bateman, Bazz, and I laid down our basic rhythm tracks, followed by Mr. Lynch adding more percussion and Mr. Mellencamp sweetening the whole thing with some acoustic guitar, vibes, and keyboard parts. After I finished recording my little guitar solo, the track sounded like a hit record even before Phil had sung a note. When it was time for my brother to sing, Mr. Mellencamp managed to get an uncharacteristically tender yet tough lead vocal out of him. Lastly he had Mr. Lynch sing some harmony with Phil, and that was that. We left the studio feeling like we finally had the single that Warner Bros. wanted.

We were absolutely right about that, but then, of course, the powers that be were so pleased with "Colored Lights" that they wanted us to go back into the studio and record another just like it. Unfortunately Mr. Mellencamp was no longer available, but, very fortunately, his coproducer, Mr. Gehman, was willing to do it. It was also fortunate that I had a pretty good song that I'd been writing with John Doe, a bluesy ballad called "Just Another Sunday." We recorded it the same way as "Colored Lights"—one piece at a time, building up from a percussion track. The finished version of "Just Another Sunday" had the same glistening pop-radio sheen as "Colored Lights," and Warners finally agreed to release our new album, *Hardline*.

Warners spent more money on promotion and publicity on this album than all our others combined and, because *Hardline* sold much better than its predecessor, were definitely committed to making a follow-up album in the same vein. Sadly, that next album was never made, and sadly, *Hardline* was the last studio album I made with The Blasters. After its release we went back on the road and spent a year touring the US, Canada, Great Britain, and Europe, but the mood of the band had changed for many reasons for everyone. We were still a killer live act, but offstage the fighting, the pressure to succeed, the hurt feelings, and the paranoia and suspicion had taken a toll on me. I quit the band in October of 1985 after an ugly, humiliating performance in Montreal, where we were actually fighting on stage like horrible little children. It was the last straw. Through all the years together, despite the silly arguments and crazy behaviors, I was always proud to be a Blaster. I'm still proud of that. I loved playing with my brother and my Blaster brothers. They all protected me, encouraged me to grow as a writer and as a guitar basher, and each of my Downey brothers made me who I am today. Being a Blaster was always fun for me. I could handle the good, the bad, the joys, the hassles, and the insanities as long as it was ultimately fun. To put it simply, I left The Blasters because it just wasn't fun anymore.

Three decades later I still love Phil, Bill, Gene, John, and Steve and treasure the rare times we can make some stress-free racket together. Three decades later I still miss the late Lee Allen every time I walk on stage. Three decades later I'm still pissed off that "Kathleen" wasn't on *Hardline*. Three decades later, though, I can finally admit that the smirking A&R guy was absolutely correct: "Kathleen" truly did sound too much like The Blasters, but what the fool didn't understand is that sounding too much like The Blasters is a really great fucking thing.

CHAPTER 4

SLIVER OF GLASS

by Jane Wiedlin

SO MANY YEARS SEPARATE US NOW
STILL I JUST CAN'T LET GO SOMEHOW
I WORKED SO HARD FOR SO LONG
TO MAKE YOU DISAPPEAR
STILL YOU'RE ALWAYS HERE
ALWAYS HERE
YOU'RE A SLIVER OF GLASS UNDER MY SKIN
A SLIVER OF GLASS BURROWING IN
YOU CUT RIGHT INTO THE HEART OF ME
TILL YOU'VE BECOME A PART OF ME

SILENT AND INVISIBLE
ABSOLUTELY CLEAR
YOU ARE ALWAYS NEAR
ALWAYS NEAR
YOU'RE A SLIVER OF GLASS UNDER MY SKIN
A SLIVER OF GLASS BURROWING IN
A CONSTANT LITTLE HURT
THAT NEVER EVER ENDS
AGAIN AND AGAIN
WE CAN FORGIVE
BUT WE WON"T FORGET
GO ON AND LIVE
CUZ IT'S NOT OVER YET
YOU'RE A SLIVER OF GLASS UNDER MY SKIN
A SLIVER OF GLASS BURROWING IN
A CONSTANT LITTLE HURT
THAT NEVER EVER ENDS
A CONSTANT LITTLE HURT
THAT NEVER EVER ENDS
AGAIN AND AGAIN
   —"Sliver of Glass" by Wiedlin, Caffey, and Hoffs

What the fuck just happened?

It's 1982. The Go-Go's first album, *Beauty and the Beat*, is number one on the *Billboard* charts. We're nominated for a goddamn GRAMMY. We've just spent TWO YEARS on the road. I'm so tired I think I'm going to die, but I'm still just twenty-three years old, and my body hasn't started to break down yet.

That will come. Pretty soon things will start to fall apart, and I'm not just talking about body parts. First to go will be my mind. Then of course, the band.

We've gone, in four short years, from teenage punk rockers scaring vanilla people with our crazy color hair and thrift-shop get-ups to being on the cover of *Rolling Stone* and hanging out with the ACTUAL Rolling Stones.

Things couldn't be better . . . could they?

We've gotten our long-awaited revenge on the music industry, who could never see past their own misogyny to get that The Go-Go's were a force to be reckoned with. That even though there'd never BEEN a successful female band who could make them money, there was most certainly about to be one.

The only company that saw the potential—or the gimmick factor, as President Miles Copeland often recalls—was IRS Records, at the time a TINY company with little money and no big artists.

We were disgruntled at not getting a huge deal with a goliath corporate label, but our manager, Ginger Canzoneri, finally convinced us that IRS was our last best hope. Virtually EVERYONE else had rejected us. So we signed a deal with them that later, due to our massive and surprise success, would nearly bankrupt the company. (The record contract was structured with huge increases in our royalty rate IF we sold a shit ton of records. IRS expected to sell fifty thousand, and were just as shocked as anyone when we went on to sell millions.)

And now we were living the rock-star life. Swimmin' pools. Movie stars. Only there was no time for actually savoring success because we'd become cogs in a machine much, much bigger than us and not of our making. Gone was the cozy community of Hollywood punk. No more compatriots sharing our discontent with the world, our freedom, our nurturing small world where anyone could start their own band and be cheered on by a group of kids who had become like family. Now we were . . . FAMOUS. And boy, what a bittersweet cookie that was turning out to be.

. . . YOU'RE A SLIVER OF GLASS
UNDER MY SKIN . . .

The demands on us were relentless. There was never a week, a day, or even an hour just to sit back and marvel at what we'd managed to accomplish. Nope, it was all photo sessions and interviews and video shoots and business decisions. Decisions that we were woefully unqualified to make. Suddenly the main thing we didn't know how to do went from playing our instruments to saying "no." It didn't occur to anyone in the band that we could just say, "No, we want to have time to recuperate from this last tour before the next one starts." Or, "No, we want to get away from each other for a bit." We spent 24/7 together, and the looking glass was beginning to crack. What once had been exciting and fun started becoming difficult and stressful. There was so much fighting. What should the next single be? Should there even be a next single? Should songs be chosen by merit or by who wrote them? Was our manager good enough? Was this guitar part great or lame?

There was no community anymore. There was just the five of us now, in an insular and dysfunctional marriage.

. . . A SLIVER OF GLASS
BURROWING IN . . .

I WANTED to be happy—I really did. But it seemed like any energy I had left needed to be saved for smiling for the cameras and the fans. We called ourselves The Robo-Go-Go's because you could just wind us up, and we would perform, looking like we didn't have a care in the world. Meanwhile five minutes earlier we would have all been screaming at each other backstage.

One time we were playing a gig in Washington state before we headed into Canada for a series of shows. Some fans who seemed cool invited us to a house party. When we got there we found out everyone was in the backyard doing opium . . . up their butts. Being The Go-Go's, we naturally joined in, squatting around a campfire with about fifteen kids, all of us with opium shoved up our asses! I kept waiting and waiting for something to happen, but I couldn't feel a thing. So I asked for more. And more. Eventually we came back home—to the hotel—and went to bed. Early the next morning I woke up HIGH AS A FUCKING KITE. My eyes were pinned like . . . well, like pinheads. We all crawled onto the tour bus and drove to the border. Of course, because we were in a rock band, the Canadian immigration cops dragged us out of our bunks. We had to stand in their freezing-cold office for hours while they tore apart the tour bus. I was sick to my stomach and paranoid as hell, surrounded by suspicious dudes in uniforms. Finally we were allowed into Canada, and we drove to the gig. I was still so nauseous that my roadie had to put a big trash can next to me side stage to throw up in during the concert. It was not pretty. And by "it" I mean "I." But damn, that was an epic example of Robo-Go-Going!

. . . A CONSTANT LITTLE HURT
THAT NEVER EVER ENDS
AGAIN AND AGAIN . . .

We had become "America's Sweethearts." People LITERALLY called us that. We weren't punk anymore. Now we were new wave, whatever that was. We didn't flip the bird at the Establishment—we WERE the Establishment.

The blowback from the kids still in Hollywood was swift, ugly, and final. The Go-Go's had SOLD OUT. Never mind that anyone who was in a band, punk or not, would've killed to be popular. To actually make a living making music. But we had abandoned ship. Like rats, but cuter. And it hurt to hear what our "friends" back home now thought of us.

. . . SO MANY YEARS SEPARATE US NOW . . .

I don't know that I could've stayed in the Hollywood scene for much longer anyway. When the boys from Orange County invaded Hollywood, our little punk rock hamlet completely changed, almost beyond recognition. To me it felt like an occupation. Things went from inclusive, intelligent, and nurturing to violent and stupid. L.A. punk hadn't been about punk-on-punk violence. Sure, we hated grownups and the police and the Establishment in general, but we didn't hate each other. And that's what changed. Testosterone tore apart the place we'd known and loved. That original scene was the sole reason The Go-Go's even came to be, but we'd turned into successful and famous outcasts.

. . . A SLIVER OF GLASS BURROWING IN . . .

The us-against-the-world mentality we'd always had was a lot less heartwarming when the "us" was just four other people instead of a gang of hundreds of like-minded kids. Sure, The Go-Go's had lots of fun times, but they were constantly counterbalanced by the painful times. We hurt each other again and again. We became experts at backstabbing. Squabbles about publishing money and who was getting more attention than whom were starting to eat us alive from the inside out. We always described our band as a five-headed monster. The energy we could create was palpable, but that very energy could be just as destructive as it was creative.

> ... A CONSTANT LITTLE HURT
> THAT NEVER EVER ENDS
> AGAIN AND AGAIN ...

There's an old expression that's one of my favorites: "When the only tool you have is a hammer, every problem looks like a nail."

We were living in a pressure cooker, and none of us had a clue how to deal with it. So drugs and booze became our daily—and nightly—go-tos. If you felt happy, you wanted to celebrate . . . with drugs and booze. If you were upset, you wanted to medicate . . . with drugs and booze. If you were tired . . . drugs and booze. If you were anxious . . . drugs and booze. If you needed to sleep . . . drugs and booze. If you needed to wake up . . . drugs and booze. And when you just wanted to escape when there was nowhere to run to, there were certainly drugs and booze. Nail, meet Hammer.

So postshow you'd have a few drinks, snort a few lines, and all of the sudden it's 6:00 A.M. again, and bus call is in thirty minutes. And you were fucked. My claim to fame with the rest of the band is the night in Atlanta, always the number-one city in America for Go-Go misdeeds. After the gig I invited a bunch of sketchy strangers to my hotel suite in the fanciest, most expensive hotel—I think it was the Peachtree—in the city, where I proceeded to smoke a shit ton of crack (first and last time) all night. I was still up when I slithered onto the bus the next day carrying a six-pack of beer. I felt like death but could not sleep, even with the breakfast beers on the bus. I don't even remember where we played that night, but I DO know it was a great example of Robo-Go-Going. I got out there on the stage and smiled and danced

like Shirley Fucking Temple. CRACK! No one has EVER let me live
that one down! And rightly so.

. . . SILENT AND INVISIBLE
ABSOLUTELY CLEAR . . .

Of course, with the workload we had, it was insane to be getting
wasted constantly. It surely was a vicious cycle, and the only things that
seemed to—temporarily—help were, you guessed it, drugs and booze.
I suppose it is a testament to our inner strength and fortitude that we
all survived our band experience. Plenty of our peers sure didn't.

. . . YOU ARE ALWAYS NEAR
ALWAYS NEAR . . .

I totally get that the yarn I'm spinning is in no way original. I'd
venture to say that pretty much every big rock band ends up in the position we found ourselves in. The twist was: we were chicks. And I really believe it was harder on us emotionally and physically. It certainly
became HUGE news when stories began to leak. "Go-Go's Can Party
Like the Boys!" "Go-Go's Make Led Zeppelin Look Like Amateurs."
THAT, my friends, just isn't true. First of all, at our worst, our consumption was probably HALF what male bands were snorting, guzzling, smoking, or shooting. Second of all, the one time we destroyed
a dressing room, we turned the deli tray into a piece of "erotic art" (ha
ha) and threw some stuff around the room, then CLEANED IT ALL
UP before we vacated the premises! AND, contrary to folklore, we
didn't have sex with groupies. Like I said, we were a five-headed monster, and any young man who managed to get backstage would likely
go running, tail between legs, after witnessing the five of us together
in a small room! There was a bit we'd do in dressing rooms to crack
each other up, where one or two of us would crawl around on the
floor on our hands and knees with straws in our mouths, pretending
to suck up filth. We called this the Corner Cleaners. This was one of
Kathy's brilliant ideas. Kathy is wickedly funny and has made me pee

my pants more than once from laughing so hard. Can you imagine sneaking backstage to meet the band and stumbling on a scene like this?!

There were a few aggressive girls who wanted to be groupies, but we had little interest in sex with strangers, male OR female. The Age of Aquarius was long dead and gone; now it was the Age of AIDS, and no one knew exactly what it took to get infected. So we didn't have wild sex encounters like all the boy bands had/have. We hooked up with a boyfriend or girlfriend, sometimes just for a tour, sometimes longer. And we weren't above cherry-picking a musician from the opening act or cute crew guy when the opportunity arose. It was convenient.

I fell in love with a great guy named Tim. He was talented, kind, and beautiful—so beautiful that he modeled for Robert Maplethorpe (no, not one of the gay pictures). I was crazy about him. We got matching tattoos. (I know, right? So eighties.) We got engaged, and then I proceeded to destroy the relationship by having an on-tour sex affair with one of our roadies. Granted, this roadie was a big hunky piece of man flesh and I was a sex fiend at the time, but still . . . SO uncool. Such a dick move. I was still a selfish "teenager" (close enough), but no excuses—it was hurtful and wrong.

So, back to drugs. What kind of drugs did The Go-Go's "enjoy," you ask? Well, cocaine was king in those days. Relatively cheap and definitely easy to find. People would give it to us. FOR FREE. That created a bad habit of us hanging out with people we didn't like or even KNOW just because we wanted to get high. This is probably one of my only other regrets, besides cheating on my fiancé. Life is too fucking short to hang out with stupid or annoying people.

Besides blow, other popular drugs with band members were ecstasy, mushrooms, LSD, Valium, and even heroin (for some). Heroin was actually the Forbidden Drug. In our collective minds, coke, weed, psychedelics, and prescription pills were fun "party" drugs. Heroin was crossing a line. So, unlike the other drugs, which we all did openly, heroin was always hidden. The two times I tried heroin, both on the road, were a bust. The first time I took so little (I was scared shitless) that nothing happened. The second time it was after a gig. We went into the dressing room toilet and smoked some H. I believe that's called "chasing the dragon." I'm not that good with junk slang because, like I said, I only did it twice. So I didn't really feel anything whatsoever, and I pretty much had decided that I was just some mythical unicorn creature immune to the effects—until we were driving back to our digs for the night. Suddenly I started to feel really, REALLY awful. When we finally got to the hotel I bolted toward my room. I distinctly remember the feeling that those corridors were ten miles long and no matter how fast I sprinted, I'd never make it in time. I barely made it through the door and into my bathroom before I violently barfed. Like, really violently. I laid down on the bed. The room was spinning. I started to itch. Itch like CRAZY. Itch like I was completely covered in spider bites. This went on and on. I vowed never to take heroin again. Why would I? I feel lucky that I didn't like it.

So a normal night for The Go-Go's in Anywhere, USA, was usually up all night, chopping out lines, babbling about bullshit, noses dripping, chain smoking, and drinking all the booze we'd stolen from our dressing room. Was it fun? I actually can't remember. What I do remember as being a blast were the thousands of hours we spent on the tour bus. We were pretty good about not getting high during the day, and on overnight drives we normally didn't indulge in drugs, except maybe some weed and wine. I'm not sure why. Instead, we spent countless hours creating absurdities to amuse each other with.

There was Belinda's Wise Old Curtain Woman. Babe (our nickname for Belinda) may be chic and jet set, but she is also a total crack-up. She would lay in a bunk with her head peeking through the curtains, holding a flashlight illuminating her face spookily, dispensing sage wisdom. We'd ask her a question like, "Wise Old Curtain Woman, what will tomorrow bring?" and she'd spit out the funniest advice, always in rhyme. It was so dumb, but always sent us into peals of laughter.

Trouble trouble on the bus
I smell trouble for all of us
Trouble trouble in the air
Trouble trouble everywhere.

There was the Love Canal. We would all lay in our respective bunks with the curtains closed and all the lights out. We would demand of an innocent bystander—usually our tour manager, Bruce—to make their way through the pitch-black hallway of the bus. We would proceed to grope them indiscriminately with outstretched arms and hands. Ha ha! We'd get sued for that kind of thing today, but it wasn't predatory; it was pranksterism. The ONLY reason we'd do shit like this was to make each other laugh.

We'd take colored gels from the lighting guy and cover all the interior bus lights. Someone would be stationed at the light switch, turning it off and on. We'd blare disco music (Bee Gees or Donna Summer, anyone?) and dance the night away while we hurtled down nameless highways. It was so much fun! The Go-Go's were ALWAYS a great mixture of innocent and debauched.

When The Go-Go's got nominated for a Best New Artist GRAMMY, we showed up at the ceremony wearing our fanciest thrift-store dresses. Charlotte had a brown paper bag of booze in her arms. We were all ducking down in our seats to swill out of the bottles she had so kindly provided and were running back and forth to the bathroom to do blow. When Sheena Easton was awarded Best New Artist instead of us, we all collectively thought, *Well, that's that!*, got up from our seats, and marched out of the venue to search for our limo. There was a veritable sea of long, black cars, and we were hammered. I think we ended up stealing Grace Slick's limo, if I remember correctly! We wanted to get to the after-parties as quickly as possible, where we hoped to meet big stars. We seriously thought that because our part of the show was done, there was no point in staying. Our ten empty seats (boyfriend dates) in a prime location in the auditorium stuck out like sore thumbs on camera. The GRAMMY organization was FURIOUS, and there were articles about our terrible behavior in industry rags the following day! Naughty Go-Go's!

We were flying first class by then, and when we'd travel, we'd take over the whole first-class area and treat it like a girls-only treehouse. First Class was really amazing in the eighties. Don't get me started on the service, the real champagne, and the caviar. Thems was the days. First-class menus in those days were pretty elaborate. Each one would have its own unique reproduction of a painting as the cover. One trip we ripped these out and attached them to the walls and windows of the plane. Then we started wandering around the cabin, talking as loudly as humanly possible, acting like art critics about our favorite painter, Glare Smithpocket, who of course didn't actually exist. The stewardesses (that's what they were called then) got so fed up with us, they just abandoned the cabin! We were, as usual, out of control. You could take the girls outta punk rock, but you couldn't take the punk rock outta the girls!

. . . I WORKED SO HARD FOR SO LONG . . .

So that was just some of the fun, but balancing out the pranks and the mayhem was the pressure. Musicians will always say you've got your whole life to create your first record, but only a few months to make the next one. Sophomore Slump is a real thing, and we weren't immune to it. *Beauty and the Beat* (the title was Babe's brilliant idea), our first album, ended up selling three million copies. Charlotte's iconic "We Got the Beat," propelled by Gina's powerful drumbeat, was everywhere and shot up the charts to land at number two for ages. Char is truly one of the greatest songwriters I've ever known, and "WGTB" went on to have a very long career on its own and still continues to get used for all kinds of things today.

. . . STILL I JUST CAN'T LET GO SOMEHOW . . .

When I returned to L.A., after doing hundreds of gigs, starting with tiny dive bars and escalating to stadiums, I was a zombie. I will never forget unlocking the door to my little apartment in West Hollywood and thinking someone had slipped me a mickey. The floor was writhing and moving like a scene out of *Requiem for a Dream*. I recoiled back and sent my boyfriend in to investigate. Turns out all the flea eggs that had been, unbeknownst to me, hibernating in the carpeting had come to life. It was spring, and the weather was warming up. There were thousands and thousands of them, literally crawling over each other looking for someone to suck on. Perhaps a metaphor for my new life?

I ran as fast as I could to the nearest hotel, which is where I felt most comfortable anyway, and stayed there 'till my place was thoroughly cleaned and fumigated.

I didn't have a lot of friends anymore and had no idea what was going on in the Hollywood punk scene that had formally been my whole life. I had the band and the onslaught of work that comes along with being successful. Now what happens?

Clearly, with *Beauty and the Beat*, we had achieved kind of a high bar to leap over again. We had not nearly recovered from the constant touring and self-abuse surrounding the first album when we were told it was time to record a new one. Oh crap. We were in a panic, digging through old abandoned tunes and cobbling together ideas to come up with content. We wrote new songs too, but now we thought that getting coked up and writing was a brilliant way to combine two "fun" things. Like anyone else, we'd heard the stories about how all great writers were drunks (Hemingway, Bukowski), so we thought we were on to something. The coke songs were pretty crap, btw.

We were lucky that Kathy had a song from her previous band, The Textones, that we all really liked. It didn't actually have a chorus, but Charlotte stepped in, and the two of them wrote a chorus just as catchy and compelling as the verse. At least now we knew we had a single. "Vacation." Theming the album around that song was a smart move. Our kitschy cover—a faked photo of us on water skis—and even kitschier video helped make the album a success. Not nearly the success of *BATB*, but still.

We had progressed from making $6,000 videos ("Our Lips Are Sealed") to $250,000 videos ("Vacation"). We hated making videos. We thought of them as pointless, boring exercises that we were forced to participate in. The shoot for "Vacation" went on and on and on. We were so over it that we started drinking at around hour seven. Over the next five hours we got progressively drunker until, in the finished product, you can see us boozily wobbling in front of a green screen, pretending to be water skiing, and waving crookedly at the camera. Totally cross-eyed. It was actually a repeat performance of this kind of bad behavior in the face of important events. Earlier, when we were asked to appear on *Saturday Night Live* (probably thanks to our friendship with the late great John Belushi), we were so bored that we got totally tanked while sitting around the NBC studio. We were absolutely AWFUL when we finally did our live performance. Quite recently, I saw a review of that *SNL*, recapping the "ancient" episode, that said about us: "An underwhelming performance with nothing in the way of intensity or expressiveness to offset the flimsy, amateurish musicianship and singing. It came off as a bad talent show spot." OUCH. The truth hurts. Regardless, we sold a ton of records in the following weeks.

Between 1981 and 1984 we made three albums, toured America a bunch of times and the world more than once, sold out Madison Square Garden and the Hollywood Bowl, and opened for The Stones AND David Bowie, my lifelong hero. Our signature thrift-store style became the rage across the country. Every night we'd be blinded by the sea of polka dots and stripes that our young female fans dressed up in. Our look became a mall staple. But we left our fans behind (stylistically) as we started to make money. Suddenly we could afford new clothes made by actual midrange designers.

As lead singer, Belinda's fame skyrocketed past anyone else's in the band. Soon we were getting shoved aside by fans eager to meet the charismatic and gorgeous star of The Go-Go's. Before this we'd always been a team, a democracy, a girl gang. Now we couldn't even get through a lunch without people in the restaurant wanting pictures and autographs with Babe while the rest of us might as well have been invisible. It was NOT her fault, but that didn't stop it from hurting. (These days I understand how hard it was on Belinda too.) Because I spoke out about this new reality, I became known as "the jealous one." In no way was I jealous; it's just that I still had the old mindset that we were all equals. I LOVED singing harmonies, and I thought a girl playing guitar was the ultimate in cool. I spent my childhood learning the backing vocals to every Beatles record and, in fact, every song on every record I ever owned. I thought being a songwriter was about as awesome a thing as anyone could ever be. But once we got famous, it went from The Supremes to Diana Ross and The Supremes. Our Girl Power, originally so natural and so real, started to erode—quickly. Now we had to fake our solidarity.

By 1984 I realized I was sick of drugs and sick of myself on drugs. I got into a real strict health regimen, with lots of running and the gym and no cocaine. I was still drinking, but it was super easy to drink A LOT less when you're not fried out of your brains on blow. Being around the rest of the gang got really difficult. If you've ever been stuck in a room with a bunch of cokeheads yammering on for hours about a bunch of bullshit, you can imagine just how alienated and fed up I became.

. . . YOU CUT RIGHT INTO THE HEART OF ME . . .

After finishing our third record in 1984, the final (coke) straw broke the (girl) camel's back. Gina accidentally saw one of Charlotte's publishing checks and discovered that the writers were making a lot more money than the nonwriters. Sure, the band was making a ton of money on other stuff, like the performance royalties, record sales, touring, merchandising, etc. We even had a deal that we shared a bit of our publishing money, but it still didn't change the fact that there was an income disparity within the band. Gina was/is a kickass drummer, and when she joined the band in 1979 she instantly elevated our sound. She was also a stickler for professionalism. With her behind the kit, we began rehearsing a lot more and started taking our musicianship more seriously.

. . . TILL YOU'VE BECOME A PART OF ME . . .

Anyway, Gina told Belinda, now the de facto Queen of the Go-Go Kingdom, about the money thing. A meeting was called. A demand was made: all publishing income must be split equally. I made the point that songwriting is a separate skill, one that takes a lot of time and effort on top of all the other band obligations. In my mind that warranted it being paid separately. They made the point that we were in this together. But it didn't feel that way anymore. They insisted we split the publishing on our upcoming record, *Talk Show*, equally. I tried to come up with a compromise. I said I'd be happy to split the publishing equally on the NEXT album—THIS one was already done. That idea was rejected. I had the lion's share of the songs on *Talk Show*, while Charlotte, the other main writer, was dealing with her own stuff and didn't speak up. So I was on my own. I was really over it by then. Between the drugs, the way four of the musicians had become the worker bees, and now this ambush about publishing, I blew up. I told them "I quit." That I'd rather be a failure as a solo artist than a success in this band. Be careful what you wish for, girlie.

... SILENT AND INVISIBLE
ABSOLUTELY CLEAR ...

The band told me I could do what I wanted but that I had to wait until after the *Talk Show* promotional tour was finished. I really, really did not want to stay, but I didn't have much choice. That final tour was the worst. I was still off drugs, and now I wasn't really even in the band anymore, so I felt totally alienated and shunned. The low point of the tour was when we stayed in this weird hotel in Chattanooga, Tennessee, that was made out of train cars. This was before cell phones. While using the landline I noticed the lines were somehow crossed. I could hear other peoples' conversations, and of course I heard the rest of the band talking shit about me. It was enough to make a gal heartbroken and paranoid. Yuck.

YOU ARE ALWAYS NEAR
ALWAYS NEAR ...

I was quickly replaced. There was a reshuffling of the players because Kathy wanted to play guitar, which was her first instrument. In 1985 The Go-Go's went on to play one last place: Rock in Rio, an enormous festival in Brazil that drew over a million people. From what they tell me, it was a harrowing trip filled with new heights of excess. Rod Stewart commented after witnessing The Go-Go's in action that "The Go-Go's could snort the varnish off a coffee table." Post-trip there was a change of alliances—always the changing alliances—and Belinda and Charlotte dismantled the band. Babe went on to a huge solo career with Char by her side for the first years, continuing to be the awesome songwriter she'd always been.

I, on the other hand, was on my own. A few days after I stopped being a Go-Go, I went to see the newly released movie *This Is Spinal Tap*. I was horrified how accurately it portrayed being in a band—well, my band anyway. I cried through a lot of it. It was embarrassing. I knew it was a comedy, but at that moment it was just too close to reality for me. Remember when Nigel Tufnel is freaking out in the dressing room because the bread is square and the deli meat is round? You probably think that that was nowhere close to real life, that it was a wildly exaggerated scene. I would argue that it is no more than a tiny bit exaggerated. I wept for what was, for my part in it, for the unknown future. I was alone. Nobody to lean on anymore. No constraints either.

A lot of times what makes a band great is what they DON'T do. Think of The Ramones—no guitar solos, no more than three or four chords in a song, no flashy drum fills, no emotive singing. Just amazing, kickass pop songs. The Go-Go's had a lot of restrictions that made our sound. Gina hit hard as hell with precision timing, but there were no drum solos, no fancy jazz-time signatures. Charlotte was a trained musician . . . in PIANO. So her guitar parts were minimal but so damned ear-wormy. I think our harmonies were great, but we didn't go over the top with them. When the vocal layers started getting too thick, we'd say, "You have been accused of the crime of barbershoppery. HOW DO YOU PLEAD?" There was a stupid good joke for most every occasion, even when we were at each other's throats.

. . . SO MANY YEARS SEPARATE US NOW
STILL I JUST CAN'T LET GO SOMEHOW . . .

As a solo artist I got a new manager and well-known producers. I was still signed to IRS, and they gave me free rein to create what I wanted. I made an album, one that I later grew to hate to this day. It was just too soon for me to know how to work outside of a band structure. Growing up in a big family, I'd always been a team player, a collaborator. Now, adrift, I made an album in a bubble. A crappy bubble, I guess! Critics, who were still pissed that I'd had the nerve to leave The Go-Go's, were merciless. They said my voice was worse than Yoko Ono. They said a lot of stuff. I sold something like seventy-five thousand copies and declared myself a total failure. (I'd kill to sell seventy-five thousand records today!) My claim that I'd rather be a failure on my own than a success with the band came back to bite me in the ass.

> . . . I WORKED SO HARD FOR SO LONG
> TO MAKE YOU DISAPPEAR . . .

I was really on my own now. These were the days when I had to grow up, to toughen up, and to take responsibility for my actions. I pushed aside my punk roots and made some purely pop records. Some of them did okay, but I continued to wallow in obscurity. I changed labels to EMI because one guy there believed in me. I was sent on promotional tours, now without a band to at least commiserate with. Those promo tours were pretty much my definition of Hell on Earth. Meeting radio people was harrowing. Besides the payola, which was rampant at the time, you really had to suck up to everyone. Radio people held ALL the power then, and they knew it. It was 100 percent the rule and the norm. I'd get insulted, get hit on, and tolerate long boozy dinners with men who considered music and musicians to be products. I'd cry myself to sleep every night after another torturous day of humiliation. I never felt more like a whore than in those days.

> . . . STILL YOU'RE ALWAYS HERE
> ALWAYS HERE . . .

I don't think I learned anything from being rich and famous, but being broke and a used-to-be—otherwise known as the proverbial School of Hard Knocks—was extremely informative.

I continued to make albums that have sold less and less to this day. The good news is that I also came to care less and less what people think of me. I stand behind a lot of my music and, more importantly, keep making music because I HAVE TO. So I am happy and fulfilled just to write a song or record an album that I think is cool.

> . . . WE CAN FORGIVE
> BUT WE WON'T FORGET . . .

I do think all of us have PTSD from the hurt we inflicted on one another the last forty years. Imagine being in an intense marriage with four other people for that long! Kinda crazy when I think about it. I did a ton of therapy in the last several years (ha ha, SO L.A.!), most of which revolved around resolving my feelings about the band. I see so many things I could have done better and so many ways I could have been kinder. I guess we just did the best we could at the time. Looking backward I am happy to see, so much more clearly, how special a group we were. I am really proud to have been part of it. And, weirdest of all, the story still isn't done! We are lucky enough to all be alive and to continue to be presented with amazing opportunities, like the new Broadway musical that uses our songs.

> . . . GO ON AND LIVE
> 'CAUSE IT'S NOT OVER YET . . .

The Go-Go's, a band of girls with NO experience, came to be because of the nurturing environment of the early Hollywood punk scene. I became, against all odds, a lifelong songwriter and musician. Maybe there were times I didn't appreciate what was happening to me, but I sure as hell am grateful now for every day of the life I've had and the life I am living today. The Go-Go's reunited in 1990 and have remained a band since then. Our forty-year marriage. These days we play a few gigs here and there, and I like to think all five of us realize how special and lucky our particular situation is. I don't think any of us will ever get 100 percent right/clear in our relationships with each other, but at least now we are trying to love, honor, and appreciate each other, like the good wifey-poos we are!

CHAPTER 5

UNDER THE MARQUEE

by W. T. Morgan

Screamers
X

I am standing under the marquee of the Whisky a Go Go—on broken pavement stained with gasoline, beer, bubblegum, and puke, face bathed in sickly neon-white light—transfixed by the black runes staring back at me.

It is 1978, mere days after returning to my hometown. The last time I stood on this spot I turned away, late for a date with a woman I just met—an actor and force of nature named Alizebeth Foley.

Since then, much water has (not) run down the concrete canal called the L.A. River. I've moved in with Alizabeth. And just returned from Paris, where I'd been writing, holed up alone in a friend's vacant apartment, listening over and over to the only two records there: Bob Dylan's *Blood on the Tracks* and *Never Mind the Bollocks, Here's the Sex Pistols*.

Ah, if only there was this hybrid fantasy band that fused the sonic fury and mocking humor of The Sex Pistols with the street poetry of Dylan . . .

Then I walk into the Whisky and see that band.

On the surface X embodies the pulse-racing, ear-splitting punk onslaught that blows your hair back. But there's hidden currents beneath the choppy seas. John Doe and Exene brood and howl into their microphones in a dark duet between Orpheus and a beautiful banshee. DJ Bonebrake thunders on his drums like a manic one-man marching band. Then there's Billy Zoom: posed still as a statue, grinning like a deranged marionette, Apollo in a silver leather jacket and bright blonde hair bathed in golden light, effortlessly tickling torrid licks out of a silver-speckled Gretsch guitar.

Their music contains multitudes: punk minimalism, hard-rock backbeat, rhythm-and-blues roll, rockabilly swagger, off-kilter homespun harmonies—all wrapped in a unique, category-smashing sound.

I stay for The Screamers—radiating their own inimitable Carnival of Souls glory—but I leave that night with my head spinning with X's performance. I have to do something with these people—though I have no idea what.

I found a two-story tower corner office in Ocean Park, which I shared with my college buddies Christopher Blakely and Everett Greaton, who were working on a documentary about the L.A. music scene.

We bathed in the L.A. punk music/art/cultural scene, which was rampant with free radicals burrowing down to the roots of every music genre, art style, and societal norm. Despite the occasional bloody nose, robbery, rape, or drug overdose, the scene itself felt like an artistic safe space. No fear of failure, just freedom to experiment.

We were a tribe of vampires: dreaming by day, out all night. We'd see lineups that confounded and inspired us. X, The Blasters, and Los Lobos. Dwight Yoakam opening for The Minutemen. Germs, Alley-cats, Black Flag, Circle Jerks, FEAR, Cramps. Tom Waits and other idiosyncratic geniuses. Hybrids like The Flesh Eaters and Top Jimmy and the Rhythm Pigs, featuring guest stars and the ubiquitous Steve Berlin. On and on, at different venues—Hong Kong Café, Club 88, the Starwood, Anti-Club, you name it.

But the Whisky became a favorite haunt. Two shows stood out: the first time we went as a group to see X, Alizabeth, enthralled, made her way to the front of the stage to get a closer look at Exene, whose jacket read "Society's Outcast." And the fateful night when X—in a heroic and healing act—came out to play a second set minutes after learning that Exene's sister had been killed in a car crash en route to the show.

Despite the media-fanned caricatures of punk rockers as gob-smacked suicidal spikeheads—or, in the wake of the hardcore invasion, South Bay Nazi skinheads—the scene was refreshingly diverse.

Male and female were equally nurtured, most famously in the part-nership between John & Exene. Women fronted The Bags and Go-Go's. The love-child of Jimi Hendrix and James Brown emerged in the young funk of Fishbone. Lee Allen brought South Central to Holly-wood by joining The Blasters, and many of us returned the favor in treks to rhythm-and-blues clubs to soak up living legends Etta James, Big Joe Turner, and Roy Milton. The Plugz and Los Lobos—who billed themselves ironically as "just another band from East L.A."—raised the roof for lily-white westside crowds with their unique blend of Latin, blues, and rock.

And it was DIY. You really did have to do it yourself. There were no barriers between band and audience; audiences were jammed with other bands. X did their own artwork. Band flyers and handbills were works of street art. Local fanzines and mags—*Slash*, *LA Weekly*, *The Reader*, *Wet*—highlighted the cross-pollinating currents.

But it wasn't just musicians making the scene. Artists, actors, pho-tographers, comedians, writers, lawyers, students, dropouts, activists, plumbers, carpenters, surfers, filmmakers—it takes a village.

Alizebeth and I lived next door to a motley crew of artists, and our office hood was turning into a hotbed of independent filmmakers. One night we wandered over to a nearby parking lot to see friends make a car levitate—for the movie *Repo Man*.

Another night we wandered into a cramped theater to see the play *Ubu the King* by a new company of renegade actors called The Actors' Gang. Wearing a grotesque fat suit, Tim Robbins, lead actor and director, careened around the stage like a manic pinball, slam dancing the other actors and invading the audience's space as he sprayed his lines in a guttural rap. He reminded me of D. Boon, the rambunctious lead singer/guitarist for The Minutemen, and I went up afterward to tell him so. Tim got the reference—and loved X, one inspiration for The Actors' Gang's brand of anarchic punk theater.

In April 1980 the album *Los Angeles* came out. I rushed down to Rhino Records and plucked the record from the rack. Within days Alizebeth and I had literally worn out the grooves and had to return to buy a second copy.

Every song on that album was a powerhouse. And for the first time we could make out the lyrics, which displayed the witty artistry of John & Exene. This was wordplay on a par with Dylan, Lennon, Tom Waits, and Jim Morrison, coupled with the boho, neo-beat edge of Bukowski and the searing L.A. noir of Raymond Chandler. They were writing about real life in a real city—my city—not the clichéd sun-drenched lotus land depicted by New Yorkers looking down their noses on the far coast but true, blood-soaked snapshots of life lived in the here and now.

Then there was "The Unheard Music," with its spectral melody and lyrics about being "locked out of the public eye":

> We set the trash on fire
> And watch outside the door
> Men come up the pavement
> Under the marquee

My college thesis was on "The Waste Land"—a touchstone for "The Unheard Music." So the resonant title's reference to "Burnt Norton," another T. S. Eliot poem, caught my eye:

And the bird called, in response to
The unheard music hidden in the shrubbery,
And the unseen eyebeam crossed, for the roses
Had the look of flowers that are looked at.

We decided to turn our accidental office-sharing arrangement into a partnership to produce a film about X. Chris, aided by Everett, spent the next few months negotiating with X's management.

There was one potential hitch: I had just completed a directing class with Lee Strasberg, and he had invited me to New York to join a new Shakespeare unit. Just then Chris walked into the office, signed X contract in hand. Shakespeare in New York or X in Los Angeles? Good night, sweet prince.

We filmed X at Golden Sound Studios cutting a new single—a catchy punk ballad, "White Girl"—their first recording since *Los Angeles*.

You could tell it was our first day of production—carefully shot, lighting inspired by Italian Renaissance *chiaroscuro* (thanks, Stanford-in-Italy!). Pretentious reference for a punk rock film? Of course. But I knew we'd found our director of photography when, instead of shrugging it off, John Monsour asked what I meant ("chiaro-huh?"), and then made it look that way.

Having blown all our cash in one day, we cut "White Girl" into a reel to present to backers for our next shoots—a process we would wash and rinse repeatedly in the coming years. MTV did not yet exist, and conventional wisdom held that no one—I mean no one—was interested in seeing music "ruined" by visuals. After tapping our own resources and testing the boundaries of risk with close friends and family, we turned to outside funding, which proved to be a bust. Though we did find one potential investor who said he'd come up with the money for a "new wave *Rocky*."

The following months we captured X in their native habitats:

Billy Zoom as dry-wit virtuoso of Vespas, guitars, and clarinet. (Chris brought his own instrument to the interview and Billy blew us away with his supple and delicate play.)

DJ as the polyrhythmic rhythm king.

Exene in her studio breaking up her life into fragments, then rebuilding it into colorful collages.

John noodling and storytelling, writing songs on the bass.

John & Exene inside their tiny West Hollywood duplex, singing country songs and working up harmonies.

Then Ronald Reagan was elected president. Well, that happened.

In December 1980 we planned to accompany X on a winter tour, but funds fell through, and at the last minute we had to cancel. I called John to break the news to him, and he seemed bummed out beyond proportion—which is when I learned that Darby Crash had just died. Shit.

We provided X with two 8mm cameras and some film to document themselves on tour. Luckily Michael Hyatt was also tagging along to shoot black & white stills. Using vintage postcards and tongue-in-cheek stop-motion animation, we later assembled a better cinematic version of the tour than planned, cut to a song not yet written: "Motel Room in My Bed." The home movies also came in handy for the "word-sea" sequence, with all four members narrating how they came together as a band.

That night we were still in the office, drinking generic beer and commiserating, Monday Night Football on a tiny rabbit-ear TV in the background, when Howard Cosell broke the news that John Lennon had just been shot and killed.

Months later Mayor Bradley and various mucky-mucks unveiled a statue of John Lennon. A clown sang "Happy Birthday" as I stood next to a Lennon impersonator. This surreal and disturbing scene made the perfect segue in the film from a commercial radio ode to "songs that make people feel good" to the *Twilight Zone*–inspired "I Must Not Think Bad Thoughts."

We embraced the Mack Sennett School of Filmmaking. Creator of the Keystone Kops, Sennett was famous for rushing out to shoot a burning building, then figuring out later what to do with the footage.

We were similarly opportunistic. One of our first "camera tests" was outside the Starwood, where we captured an ambulance crew responding to a drug overdose, which we'd later incorporate into the "Johnny Hit & Run Paulene" sequence.

But the best example of right place–right time was the house-moving sequence.

Did I mention the vampire hours?

As usual, Alizabeth and I were up late one night, enjoying an unhealthy but delicious meal at Fatburger in Westwood.

All of a sudden a house drove by.

Which is not the strangest thing we ever saw, but close.

I was dead tired and went to bed, but Alizabeth grabbed our 8mm camera and charmed her way onto the moving house. Days later we screened the footage on our kitchen wall and made plans to film it for real in glorious 16mm.

We rushed over to the Wilshire Boulevard location where the apartment buildings were getting torn down, and I shot Alizabeth as an emotionally destroyed "Paulene" wandering through the ruins by day and, later that night, illuminated by candlelight in her temporary squat.

Then with John Monsour and our Angel City colleagues, we chased half an apartment building around Los Angeles for two nights, getting dangerously low to the asphalt with an extremely wide-angle lens to capture that Titanic-sinking effect.

At the end of the first night the tow company parked on an empty lot overlooking downtown L.A., which enabled us the next evening to capture a bravura shot of the house pulling away to reveal City Hall and the rest of the L.A. skyline. We liked the location so much that we shot "Paulene" living in her car on the same lot. As luck would have it, there was a bar nearby called "Johnny's," which provided a neon arrow pointing directly to our eponymous character.

Some people call *Wild Gift* X's masterpiece. I prefer *Los Angeles*. Though it's like arguing whether *The Godfather* or *Godfather II* is better. They're both masterpieces.

Wild Gift provided the soundtracks for radically different stylistic approaches to sequences, each of which began with a different challenge:

How to compress the history of L.A. punk into three and a half minutes? Assemble photographs (by Ed Colver, Gary Leonard, Ann Summa, and other artful image catchers of the underground scene), flyers, crude cut-up animations, and vintage film into a cubist collage and set it to X's kinetic syncopations to create the "We're Desperate" sequence.

On May 4, 1981, we shot X live. John & Exene decorated the stage in an Easter motif, and we used dramatic lighting and deployed three cameras—our biggest shoot.

It was a long day. Beers were consumed. Tensions arose. A mirror was shattered. But we got the shots—including an unleashed rendition of "World's a Mess" that, in my book, is one of the greatest, most bone-chilling live performances in rock 'n' roll history.

Days later Alizbeth and I eloped to Mexico.

In 1982, interviewing Bob Biggs of Slash Records, we could tell something was off. Turns out he had just heard that X was leaving Slash to go to Elektra Records.

We attended the formal signing at Elektra, onetime home of The Doors, and interviewed Elektra/Asylum's president, legendary music exec Joe Smith, who compared it to signing The Grateful Dead to Warner Bros. in the 1960s.

Under the Big Black Sun featured a batch of powerful new songs shimmering with the lingering repercussions from the death of Exene's sister. The cover was moonlit and somber, eerily rhyming with interior shots in the house-moving sequence. One song featured Billy Zoom on sax, a shift in tone and rhythm that would provide an emotional underpinning to the "Come Back to Me" sequence, which explored Exene's artistry and motivations.

The Whisky announced they were closing their doors (it's still operating, folks). Touring backstage, Exene pointed out the broken glass still out there on the air conditioning unit from the window John broke when he heard the news about Exene's sister's sudden death. Heartbreaking at the time. Still is.

That night we shot X performing what we all thought would be the last two songs ever played on the Whisky stage: "Johnny Hit & Run

Paulene" and, with Ray Manzarek, "Soul Kitchen." The energy was apocalyptic, even if it wasn't really The End.

Michael Blake was a long-suffering writer and stubborn denizen of the nineteenth century with a hearty laugh whose pathways in the early eighties often crossed ours. We hit it off, and before long Alizabeth was attending an acting workshop in Michael's downtown loft, along with John, Exene, Frank Gargani, Chris D., an aspiring actor named Kevin Costner, and various other friends of Michael.

X named their quasi-social club the Wolves. For *Under the Big Black Sun*—hopped up on their own relationship, Howling Wolf, the book *Of Wolves and Men*, and the Native American worldview—John & Exene wrote a song called "The Hungry Wolf."

We pitched an insane plan to film a live wolf wandering the streets of downtown L.A. as X played out of various dark corners and inside an art-directed "den" of "Wolves." The insurance policy cost alone shot this plan down. But we did find a place in *Unheard Music* for "The Hungry Wolf"—playing a loop of the drum break/guitar feedback "howls" over images of wolves descending from the hills into the City of Angels.

Michael Blake was similarly taken by the song and—also inspired by *Bury My Heart at Wounded Knee* and the story of Cynthia Ann Parker (fictionalized as "Christine" in homage to Exene)—gestated a project around the theme of wolves and wild men. He'd call it *Dances with Wolves*.

As the years wore on, X was understandably starting to get a little sick of us getting all up in their business and openly wondered when—and if—this fucking film was ever going to come out.

By the time *More Fun in the New World* came out in 1983, we were running on fumes.

We could no longer afford any other crew, so it was down to just us. We'd all made sacrifices to get this far. Chris, who carried the primary fundraising burden, put up his heirloom Porsche as collateral for our rent and lost it to a creditor who gleefully drove it up to join the Rajneesh commune in Oregon. Everett acted as our production manager and full-time sound guy. Alizabeth had to dance backward in combat boots to earn the right to join our original sausage party. And, because we were drawing no salaries, we were all broke. Who was it who said, "When you work for yourself, you work for an idiot?" They were right.

There was one silver lining: "I Must Not Think Bad Thoughts," a song that—along with "The New World"—signaled a new, more socially conscious (and semi-acoustic) direction.

By this time there was little chance of dragging X back to do another shoot—nor was there money to pay for it—so our sequence would be band-free.

El Salvador was the war *du jour*, and a couple of friends—Glen Silber and Tete Vasconcellos—risked their lives to shoot hair-raising footage on the front lines for their documentary *El Salvador, Another Vietnam*. They graciously allowed us to use outtakes.

We couldn't afford to take it to a lab, so we borrowed a print and reshot it off a white wall in our office on our hand-cranked Beaulieu 16mm camera. The DIY technique looked cool, though the shutter was out of sync, which created a strobing effect. Weirdly, when we set the footage to the beginning of the song, the strobe hit the beats right on time, creating the perfect hypnotic effect.

For the flurry of sound and vision at the very end of the song I kept Alizabeth up all night changing channels while I used the camera's plunger to shoot single-frame images off the TV to create a kaleidoscopic climax. By the time "Los Angeles/All Night Movie" appeared on the television screen, I knew we were done.

The final shoots for *Unheard Music*, four years after we began, were for the "Paulene" sequences.

"Paulene Clairvaux" is the one fictional character in the film (if you don't count the personae adopted by the band members and other scenesters).

The original inspiration for the character goes back to one of our earliest shoots, with Exene in her studio off Hollywood Boulevard. Amid the creative clutter on her desk was a handwritten letter from an overidentifying fan who claimed X's songs were all about her.

When I saw the letter I asked Exene if we could work it into a pan across her inspiration wall. She impaled the letter to the bulletin board with a green glass shard, and we shot it.

From these fragments was born the character of "Paulene," who loved X and lived in her car. She would become our audience surrogate, a lens through which to see the story of X and, yes, an actual character in an X song. Paulene's arc provides thematic harmony for the melody plot line of X going up against the world. And the fate she meets in the film was drawn from real life.

Once again our nighthawk lives were responsible. Alizabeth and I were sitting in a window seat at Johnnie's Pastrami in Culver City late one night when we witnessed an actual hit and run: A car screeches to a halt. A woman is shoved out into the middle of the street. A second car runs her over. Yet: "She was still awake." Life imitates art in the most horrible way.

On Bastille Day 1984 we had a raucous midnight screening of *Unheard Music* as a work-in-progress for the Olympic Arts edition of Filmex. Posters plastered all over the city for the festival looked like an ad for our film—a stark black & white strip of film and a big X. Just a meaningful coincidence—but we'd take it.

It was the most nerve-wracking and best screening we ever had. The theater was packed, with ticketless hordes outside pounding on the doors to be let in. The room was dripping with anticipation.

The film was still unfinished, so we screened it "double system"— projecting the same scratched and battered workprint we'd been running back and forth over the Steenbeck heads day after day, accompanied by a separate mono mix track. Fingers crossed it would all stay in sync.

A bigger worry: the film would break midscreening. We double-taped the print, back and front, which held it together but created an unanticipated special effect.

The thick tape slipped in the gate, creating a blurred transition between cuts. Not sure what was happening, I raced up to the projection booth and poked my head in. To my horror, I saw film spooling upward toward the ceiling, while the heroic projectionist yanked it back through the gate, keeping it in sync. It was a sight to behold. Realizing there was little I could do, I slipped back into my seat and sweated it out until the end. It was live film, baby!

The reaction was explosive. People came up afterward and asked how we created that cool blurring effect.

Still, it took another year to land a distributor: Skouras Pictures. The advance barely covered our costs to blow up the film to 35mm, do a stereo mix, pay off all the licensing and legal fees, and so on. In the end we were still broke, but at least our film was going to be released.

Skouras hired Chris Morris to do publicity and asked where we'd like to have the cast & crew premiere. I was stumped. Dream Big, they urged. I don't know . . . the Cinerama Dome? Never in a million years thinking that would happen.

Weeks later I'm sitting in the control room, working with a Dome technician to tune the thirty-seven—or however many it was—sur-round speakers. What was I thinking? This film was shot in 16mm and barely in stereo, and we're screening in the room where 2001 happened?

Rodney Bingenheimer and other scenesters showed up, many in vintage cars. All it lacked was the red carpet and the klieg lights. An-thony and Flea of The Red Hot Chili Peppers plopped down front-row center. We sat in the back of the balcony with the band and friends.

We had a party at the Roxy afterward, which was swell, then on the way home Alizabeth and I were rear-ended by a drunk and belligerent dude who later became a big-time movie producer. Perfect.

We had our official world premiere at Sundance. Robert Redford shared that watching relics of his old hometown drift by the windows of the moving house evoked powerful childhood memories.

The Unheard Music started its theatrical run in March 1986. The re-views rocked. But for all the hype and critical love, we were still a bare-bones independent film about an acclaimed but obscure cult band, so the theatrical release would be extremely limited. As in: five release prints worldwide, shuttled around from city to city in weekly rollouts.

In Los Angeles we unspooled at the cavernous Four Star Theater, which, at eight hundred seats, was too big for us. We'd sell four hun-dred tickets per show, but instead of generating critical mass, it'd feel

. . . half empty. We had been booked into a hundred-seat theater at the new Westside Pavilion, where the same numbers would have created a sensation, with sold-out shows and long lines clamoring to get in. But Westside Pavilion got cold feet, fearing punks rampaging through Nordstrom's, so we ended up in the middle of Nowheresville, losing the perception game.

The film played well enough in different cities. But there was one amazing anomaly: Seattle. Skouras had to keep extending the original one-week run due to sold-out houses and rave reviews. At the time our reaction was: Seattle? In those pre-Grunge days, we had no idea what was going on up there. Years later Kurt Cobain told me he and some friends saw the film three times. Ah ha.

The Unheard Music was five years of blood, sweat, and "96 tears in 24 hours."

By the time it was released, John & Exene had broken up. The band parted ways with Ray as producer and released *Ain't Love Grand*. Billy left the band. Dave Alvin of The Blasters (and Knitters), then Tony Gilkyson of Lone Justice joined X in an awesome twin-guitar attack. Then Dave left just as the band released *See How We Are*. This should have been the record that finally broke X through to mainstream acceptance. It didn't.

I went to Japan with a Sundance delegation headed by Robert Redford, where we screened *The Unheard Music* in a movie palace in Tokyo—on the fourth floor of a fancy department store. Go figure.

Late in 1987 John Doe called to say X was signing off. But they were going out in style, performing a last stand at the Whisky a Go Go. Elektra was recording the shows for a live album, and the band wondered if I would film it.

Hell yes, I would.

Only . . . I was up in San Francisco prepping a new film. I would need to take an extended Xmas break to come down, shoot the concerts, and cut something together for a valedictory music video.

There was no budget, as usual. So, reaching into the DIY bag of tricks, I asked friends planning to be there anyway to become 8mm camera operators. Along with Alizabeth and me, they would include Exene's new husband, Viggo Mortensen, by whom she was now nine months pregnant; screenwriter Nick Griffin; and Michael Blake.

The farewell Whisky shows were powerful, poignant, unforgettable.

In the middle of editing, on January 28, 1988, John & Exene and their respective spouses had their first children: a son and a daughter, born on the same day in the same hospital with the same doctor—twins by different parents. Just the way you'd expect with wolves.

We chose "Devil Doll" for the video and put the finishing touches on it—a freeze frame of hands, band, and fans in a final clasp, which would become the back cover of the album—with Viggo and Exene, nursing Henry, sitting in the editing room.

It was X (ten) years to the day since I first stood on the corner staring up quizzically at the Whisky marquee. Full circle.

Ending and beginning. The gyre turns, the *karass* abides, the pack survives.

It was a new world.

But that's another story.

CHAPTER 6

THE NEW WORLD

by John Doe

honest to goodness
the bars weren't open this morning
they must have been voting for a new president or something
"do you have a quarter?"
I said, "yes" because I did
honest to goodness the tears have been falling all over this
country's face
it was better before, before they voted for what's his name
this is supposed to be the new world

flint ford auto mobile, alabama
windshield wipers

buffalo, new york, gary, indiana
don't forget the motor city
baltimore, d.c., now all we need is
don't forget the motor city
this is supposed to be the new world

all we need is money
just give us what you can spare
twenty or thirty pounds of potatoes
or twenty or thirty beers
a turkey on thanksgiving
like alms for the poor
all we need are the necessities and more
it was better before, before they voted for what's his name
this is supposed to be the new world
don't forget the motor city this was supposed to be the
    new world

It was as if the blood of the Midwest was slowly leaking out. All the people and buildings and rivers and corn fields remained, but all were slightly shrunken or withered. Even though we would see the Mighty Mississippi flood its banks a couple times and run its waters fifty feet over its banks, right up to the steps of the Mississippi Nights night club, this whole swath of land and its people were sad, sitting in a corner with their head drooping. The "trickle down" economics were trickling somewhere else, if at all. Manufacturing plants closed or laid off most everyone. Steel mills had refused to modernize back in the mid-seventies. Some workers at the remaining auto plants and parts suppliers avoided losing their jobs when senior union workers took vacation leave or cut their hours so that junior members could keep working and keep the plant open. Yes, there were more and more people coming to clubs to see us, but they were sad and had lost their jobs, and so we tried to keep our ticket prices low and give them a night off when they didn't think about their problems.

In a poem Exene used the phrase "smokestacks & steeples" to describe these cities. We tried to make it a song but never quite could.

She loved the working class. Her dad, Lou, worked as a carpenter most of his life and kept their family just on the lower edge of the middle class. He was a tough Chicago bohunk who gave her the work ethic all of us knew from the forties and fifties. Somehow we applied that "head down," "nose to the grind stone" method to our band. We took the opportunities we were offered and toured and wrote songs as if our life depended on it—because it did.

At this point in time we saw those broad shoulders slumping and farmers were losing their homes like one of our heroes, Woody Guthrie, sang about. Now a major shift was happening right before our eyes, and since we crisscrossed the country several times in just a few years, it couldn't be ignored.

I didn't much care for Ronald Reagan. He didn't strike me as very smart or connected to people working for a living, even though they were the ones who elected him. Maybe for the first time we thought that someone else pulled the strings on the commander-in-chief. Maybe now you couldn't figure out who or what was responsible for everything going to hell. Exene and I protested the 1980 presidential election by taking a train to Guadalajara, Mexico, because it seemed evident that this straight-laced, movie cowboy was changing the whole deal in Amerika.

By 1983 many of those changes had taken effect. He busted unions, and the middle class didn't see much reason for celebration. Even now this economic debate continues, but the general morale in the country, especially the Midwest, seemed at an all-time low. We noticed that we didn't know many people who belonged to unions like the ones our parents were a part of or had known.

After the release of our second record, *Wild Gift*, we toured at least four to six months a year. My International Travelall couldn't stand all that mileage, so from 1980 through early '84 we toured in a white, Chevy step-van. Back then people called them "bread trucks," but nowadays a UPS truck would be the best description.

Billy Zoom had a vision of how to convert this white shell of a vehicle, and the final result was certainly that. He said country-western bands that couldn't afford buses would convert a step van for their version of a tour van. We decided that being able to stand up as we rolled down the road warranted having a truly original vehicle. Why should we settle for some old Ford or Dodge fifteen-passenger van? So, in the parking lot behind Billy's second-floor apartment near Melrose and La Brea, we converted this 1979, sixteen-foot box delivery van into our tour dream on wheels. I believe we bought it for around seven grand, which was quite a bit then, but it was almost new with very low mileage. We changed the rear differential so it drove smoother & faster on the highway. These trucks were set up for city driving only. I'm not certain why Billy was so motivated to tackle this grand project. This was not his general demeanor, but he/we attacked it with a kind of manic intensity & determination. Maybe small amounts of "medicinal" speed helped? I know that we were dedicated to making this band the most grand adventure, and we were going to do it in style. This whole conversion connected with our DIY spirit and we didn't mind being shade-tree mechanics. We rented a Milwaukee Sawsall to cut out hunks of the side panels & put in sliding bus windows. We built a couch out of two-by-fours, made foam seats, installed a passenger seat from the junk yard, screwed in sound insulation covered by plywood siding, which we Varathaned with a clear resin. Exene contributed by walking over to Pink's for chili dogs before it was so popular that a gargantuan line of tourists prevented the local disciples from going there. Billy designed & built a back compartment for our gear that, on the inside of the van, made a platform for a queen-sized bed/loft just behind and above the couch. We also wired a couple of speakers above the front windshield with a lead to plug in a cassette player/boombox. Even with the carpet, beanbag chair behind the driver's seat, six to seven people, coats & assorted clothes, etc., it was still pretty damn loud rolling down the highway, practically too loud to hear the stereo we'd installed. So what we played was like natural selection—quiet country or blues didn't stand a chance. We opted for the Sun Records mix tapes Phil or Dave Alvin made us, James Brown, Little Willie John, or other mix tapes of fifties, sixties & seventies rock 'n' roll and garage bands.

We watched the state of things in the whole United States through these windows as the landscape rolled slowly past. We saw the flooded Mississippi when The Replacements opened for us. We ran off the road in Oregon, pitching Exene and me out of that loft bed—our biker roadie Kit Miara got an endless amount of shit for that one. We had to install a second gas tank because west Texas didn't have twenty-four-hour gas stations close enough together for us to drive through the night. The night we learned that, we stayed in a fleabag motel in Balmorhea instead of running out of gas on the side of the road. When I asked the desk clerk with curlers in her hair for a wake-up call, she reached under the desk, plopped an alarm clock in front of me, and said, "Here's yer wake call."

We noticed the decline and decay of the US and a general shift in the mood of its people. Exene connected so deeply with this situation, possibly because of her dad or because she saw the rural Midwest that she loved disappearing along with its working class, which was being ignored, soon to be forgotten. She and I identified with the sturdy, no-BS Midwest since we both knew that from when we were kids. She wrote all the words to the song "The New World" in one sitting on one page of her journal. As happened several other times, she wrote a piece that had its own rhythm, sometimes rhyming, sometimes not, but from top to bottom it was a complete song.

I had begun playing more acoustic guitar, using it as a writing tool, and learned the traditional rock 'n' roll "dun-da-dun-da-dun" like almost every early rock 'n' roll song. In the key of A all you have to move is one finger & you're playing that signature Chuck Berry or blues lick. Since I always looked for a way to turn things upside down or at least sideways, I thought, "What if I started with the second note and then went down to the first note 'da-dun-da-dun'?" This became the main musical figure for the verse of "The New World."

There might've been some editing, but the song's lyrics start with the story of a bum trying to get his first drink of the day. Years ago bars were closed on election day, and this old-timer couldn't figure out what had happened to close his local bar. Recently Exene told me that this was the key to the whole song. The concept that "nobody knows what's going on," just like we had, this hobo had checked himself out of society and had no way of understanding what was going on. At this point we all had an intuitive feeling that there might not be any way of truly knowing who or what caused this change and decline.

The difference was that this time the whole country began to have the feeling that strings were being pulled, that manufacturing was going away / overseas & it probably wasn't coming back. Little did we know that thirty-five years later, long after global corporations had decided this issue of manufacturing, this would be a campaign promise that would help elect the forty-fifth President of the United States.

"it was better, before they voted for what's-his-name.
this was supposed to be the new world"

CHAPTER 7

ANOTHER STATE OF MIND

by Mike Ness and Tom DeSavia

For me, since I was a kid I had always been searching for art that inspired and informed me. I'd been intensely listening to music since I was five years old, maybe earlier. I was listening to the radio and was really shaped by what was coming through and digging the rock 'n' roll records my uncles gave me. My background was in sixties and seventies rock as well as the music around the house: my dad's tastes were really rootsy and ran from Johnny Cash to The Dillards to Buck Owens; my mom liked The Rolling Stones and a lot of the rock 'n' roll of the sixties, and she had this great Smithsonian Folkways Revival box set I devoured. Real cool stuff.

In junior high I became a huge Bowie fan and a huge KISS fan and generally loved the whole glitter/glam-rock scene. By that time I had naturally gravitated to songs that had more guitar and deeper or odder lyrics than was what was coming through the Top Forty, and I liked stuff that just screamed individualism. There was that point in time when some of the tunes from the glam scene somehow became bigger and snuck in through the radio and showed us that, indeed, there was something else out there. The only real exposure or proof that a musical underground was happening was from the photos I would find in the back of magazines like *Creem* or *Circus*, where they would show scenes from far-off clubs like CBGB in New York, which was a whole world away for me. These cats all looked cool, but I didn't know where to buy these records. Hell, I didn't know what they sounded like—they definitely weren't playing *them* on the radio. But I was transfixed by the images.

Punk rock, for a lot of kids, was a natural evolution from glitter. The people I was hanging out with didn't expose it to me, though . . . no one I knew had those records. It wasn't until I was a junior in high school in 1979, when Dennis Danell entered my life, that it became real. Dennis was one year older than me and from the other side of the neighborhood. I kind of knew who he was from growing up in the same town, but we didn't know each other at all in any kind of real way. It was on the very first day of school when I remember looking at him . . . he had cropped hair, baggy pants, and a punk T-shirt, and I was, like, "Man, this dude looks hip." I thought I was hip, but this dude *really* looked hip. He looked *modern*.

I sought him out, and because I had a passion for music and he obviously did too, we pretty much hit it off instantly. He turned me on to the whole world of punk right away, and I started to finally hear what all those bands sounded like . . . in came The Sex Pistols, The Ramones, and a bunch of other stuff from New York and London. But it was actually Dennis's older brother, Gunner, who was the key to this underworld, as he worked lights at the Starwood on Tuesday nights. Dennis had already been going to shows there, and he invited me one night to head out to Hollywood with him, and that was it—it was all over. I cut all my hair off and tossed my Led Zeppelin records out the window and replaced them with records by bands like Generation X and The Clash.

It was otherworldly going to Hollywood and going to the Starwood. It was real, and there was pretty instantly that feeling of "This is where I belong." I pretty much immediately started to branch out and head to other clubs that were happening. The second Masque was still operating, and places like Hong Kong Café and Madame Wong's were drawing us all in. One of the first shows I went to was The Cramps, The Go-Go's, and The Simpletones at the Masque. However much money you had in your pockets—a couple of dollars—that was the admission. You'd stuff your leather jacket with Budweiser cans for the show or you bribed your way in with the doorman with a couple of brews. There were no rules. That's what attracted me too, obviously.

What I loved about the scene is that you could go see Levi & the Rockats or The Gears or FEAR—some nights on the same bill. You didn't leave there any night going, "Wow, the Blasters didn't sound very punk tonight" or "FEAR didn't sound very rockabilly, did they?" That's what was very attractive—that embracing of uniqueness, of identity. I mean that was, of course, what the whole punk scene was supposed to be about: individualism.

So we were going to the Starwood every week and diving into this world of FEAR and The Blasters and hearing Rodney Bingenheimer DJ. We were underage, but back then security was pretty lax—you just brought colored pens to fake a hand stamp or rubbed off someone else's ink onto your hand. What was cool is you could see whatever band, and when the set was over Rodney would be playing in the disco and all these new wavers would be dancing on the dance floor and leaving their long island ice teas on the tables, which Dennis and I would swiftly move in and swoop up.

Now the Orange County scene was already underway, with bands like The Middle Class, D.I., and The Adolescents already making a name for themselves in this subregional scene in Orange County. There was no musical rivalry at this point, or at least not one I was aware of. What did exist a bit was the city kids versus us suburban ones.

Sometimes we would get shit from the Hollywood kids simply because we were from suburbia. People don't realize that there's a different kind of angst that comes from suburbia, and it really was way more dangerous being a punk rocker there than on the streets of Hollywood—freaks were accepted in Hollywood. Always. But if you walked down the street in suburbia in a leather jacket, jeans, and dyed hair here in 1979, you were gonna get into a fight. Pretty much guaranteed.

Specifically, I was from Fullerton, and even though The Middle Class—who were from Santa Ana—had been around and gigging since 1976 or 1977, I wasn't aware of them. The only thing I had in Fullerton was a local band called The Mechanics, and I thought they were the coolest thing ever, but in Hollywood they wouldn't have been accepted because a couple of the guys had long hair and the guitars would have been way too "rock" for that period. But they were like The Stooges—they would play all the high school parties and cause a scene; they would come out and say, "Hey, we're The Mechanics, and we don't play any fucking slow songs" and just tear into it. They were a huge influence on me.

Being that we lived in this sort of small-town environment, there weren't a lot of places we could hang out. Or places that would let us hang out. The Mechanics' warehouse was the main place everyone would meet. I also remember these two girls who had a house way out in Yorba Linda, and they would have blowouts and invite everyone down. Parties were really what helped the scene grow and how the camaraderie formed. I had an apartment for a while that was famously dubbed "the Black Hole," and that became an infamous party pad.

The Black Hole was a one-bedroom apartment, appropriately filthy, and covered with graffiti. It served as a mainstay of the growing scene, and it wasn't unusual to have a hundred people in there at one time. It was filthy, and there was spray paint all over the walls. It was a meeting place. I let all my friends move in to help pay the rent—it was a crash pad. There was a guarantee of drugs, fights, arrests, bonding, and whatever else was establishing the reality of being teen punk in this new world.

The circle of punks started to grow. You made friends with people from different areas because you had to. If you were riding the bus and there was another kid with cropped hair and peg-leg pants, chances are you were gonna talk to them because you wanted to find out where the parties and shows were in their area. It was a sense of unity and, I suppose, a feeling of strength in numbers.

I started Social Distortion because of The Mechanics and my pal Dennis's influence. The Mechanics opened up for (legendary San Francisco punk band) Crime one night, and I was, like, "Oh my god, these guys look so cool with their slicked-back hair and their ties," and they even had roadies that looked cool. And some older punk rock chick with an eye patch was trying to pick up on me, and I thought, "This is fucking awesome." From that point on I knew I had to be a part of this. I had to start a band.

I was a guitar guy. I liked The Gears, The Blasters, X . . . I liked the bands where there was a certain amount of showmanship that I felt—and still do—was so important. If you didn't know how to play, act like you did. And honestly, most didn't know how to play that well, especially in the beginning . . . but they played with intensity and passion. That's what mattered. Over the years some really great musicians developed with real, unique style. Everyone was learning from this giant melting pot of influences and from watching each other.

I was self-taught. I learned to play "Michael Row the Boat Ashore" when I was in seventh grade and kind of figured out and felt really comfortable on guitar. I already wanted to be a rock star since I was five years old. I knew that much. So guitars came naturally.

The first show that I sang was actually at a wedding at a Marina Del Rey skate park. We had a singer who I think was tone deaf. I was writing these songs and giving him melodies, and he just couldn't do it—it just wasn't working. So that night I just drank seven or eight beers and thought, "I'm just gonna do this myself." From that point on I became the singer; it just became obvious.

It took a little while for us to be ready to really break into L.A. I had an early incarnation of Social D with some of the guys from The Adolescents, and I really wanted my friend Dennis to be in the band, but he wasn't a musician. I literally taught him how to play guitar. Up until then he was a cool fan guy who knew a lot about the scene, but he was not a player. I figured I could teach him how to play and we could be in a band together. I needed friends to play with—I wasn't necessarily looking for accomplished musicians.

Everyone in our scene was really encouraging and pushing us on. Locally we'd play the Galaxy; Costa Mesa wasn't that far, and they had the Cuckoo's Nest. But I wanted in to that Los Angeles scene.

It took a minute for us to get serious. It was bands like The Middle Class and Eddie and the Subtitles who helped us. They were playing shows in L.A., and they would have us open for them. That was the genesis of our regional scene—all those guys were so great and supportive. The Adolescents were our contemporaries. They just inspired me in a good way; they were around a couple of years before us. "They're doing it. I can do this"—that was a real motivation.

Further acceptance in the L.A. scene happened in 1981 when Rodney Bingenheimer started to spin the single we just recorded on KROQ. That year we were also included on the now-infamous SoCal punk compilation *Hell Comes to Your House*, which also featured tracks from Redd Kross (then "Red Cross"), 45 Grave, Christian Death, Rhino 39, and The Super Heroines, among others.

We would go to L.A. two to three nights a week—the drive for us was nothing. We would get six or seven of our friends and a cooler full of beer and just drive out there. There were shows all over L.A.—it wasn't just Hollywood. We'd go to the Valley to Downtown L.A.—wherever. Then it wasn't long before the beach kids got into it . . .

Punk started to get popular. When something cool becomes popular, it becomes uncool. People started coming for the wrong reasons, mainly an excuse to trash something, which I was guilty of too. I had a lot of anger inside, but it started to become a scene where punks were fighting punks. I never understood that. That's where the OC vs Hollywood thing really started to crystalize. It was dangerous enough as it was, but these clubs and parties were supposed to be a place we all came together.

I was one of the only guys from Fullerton, and Fullerton was considered a little more "arty," I suppose. No one was looking for conflict, and my friends didn't really like to fight—I don't know that I did either. But I just didn't like to back down. I didn't like to take shit. So that got me in a lot of trouble.

I remember one incident in L.A. when there were a bunch of beach punks, and they caused a big scene at a show that was shut down—I think it was an X gig, actually—and the Hollywood kids were pissed. They were screaming, "Go back to Orange County, you rich kids," which a lot of them were: a lot of them were beach kids who were all tan and healthy and had all the proper attire, but not the thrift store wardrobe—they wore the expensive shit. You felt that class warfare begin to grow among the kids.

We finally got to play the Starwood; we started to get real gigs and were developing a decent following in L.A. The growing popularity of the band was tempered by my increasing drug addiction and alcoholism, something that at first I didn't realize—and later didn't care—how much it was interfering with and affecting the band.

I had started real young with alcohol and other drugs, but then heroin entered the picture, and—as it does—everything changed.

It was one of the older kids in Orange County who got me started on heroin, one of the older musicians who turned me on to it. It was at a rehearsal space where musicians would congregate, and these were guys I looked up to, and that's what they were doing. That's what I had always done—hung out with the older guys and followed their example. I didn't want to do what kids my own age were doing—I had no interest. I did my first shot of dope . . . at that point I'd need to drink five hours to get drunk, where just $10 worth of heroin—I weighed 140 pounds then—did everything it was supposed to do. I was addicted immediately.

Locally we loved playing with The Circle Jerks; they were always a fun show. You were going to see all your friends, and the band was so entertaining. Bad Religion, The Weirdos—one of my favorite bands— only played now and again. Geza X would always have us to his parties. Exene would see us hanging outside of the Hong Kong Café, broke, and she'd let us into their gig. She did that a lot. It was awesome.

The Another State of Mind tour was 1982, marking the first time the band really hit the road in a real way. I was also deep in the bowels of my growing addiction. But we went out and it was cool; people kind of knew who we were. The early years helped: the fanzines and Maximum R&R helped build a foundation for us—and the fact that we never toured beyond local stops kind of built a mystique around us. We were just some band out in California, and suddenly we'd find ourselves playing to a couple hundred kids each night.

Up until then we'd just do San Francisco, San Diego, Las Vegas, Arizona. We didn't have any managerial skills, so we were just making up the business side as we went along. We had a manager who was a mechanic—literally a car mechanic. But he could buy us beer.

By 1984 we had a real solid following in L.A., but my addiction was so bad that people were walking out of shows. We were suddenly losing what fan base we had. We couldn't do a show until I got drugs or we couldn't do a show because I pawned all the gear or I was arrested or I was in some failed version of detox. We definitely couldn't tour.

I remember New Year's Eve 1984 we did a show at the Cathay de Grande, and we were guaranteed $500. We could fill the place at that point, easy. I remember the promoter pulling me aside and saying, "Hey, I've got some white heroin, so I can just pay you in that," and I was, like, "Hell yeah!" Well, that was the night my rhythm section quit the band. They were, like, "Now this guy is taking our money. He already stole our gear—fuck this!" That wasn't a catalyst to get clean, though: I figured I could replace them. I did replace them.

The catalyst to finally get clean was when the band was in limbo at the end of '84/beginning of '85. I was alone. I had burned every bridge. Dennis's mom—who had always been there for me, always opened her home, fed me when I was hungry, made me feel cared for—suddenly wouldn't allow me in her house because they were afraid I was gonna steal something.

When you're living in someone's tool shed in their backyard you are aware you're all alone, no matter how fucked up you get.

When you're roaming the streets of Santa Ana and even your drug connection doesn't want you around because you're such a pathetic mess, you're short on money, you're sick, you're fucking bawling like a little baby, and you got nowhere to go afterward.

That's a very lonely existence.

At that period I was also overdosing and was afraid of dying. Even in the darkest period of my life, when I would get to feeling that maybe I should just end this, I would always think, "Well, what if

I came into some money tomorrow?" I would have missed out. So there was always a little bit of optimism, a little bit of hope, as odd as that sounds.

I wanted to be a musician more than anything. I wanted to be a musician more than I wanted to be a junkie. But I became a junkie. Somehow, in the throes of addiction, I thought that's what I wanted.

I was kicking cold turkey in the county jail, and I knew there was no one who was gonna bail me out and I was gonna be sick for a long time. I was in lockup and surrounded by two things: one was those guys who were just so proud to be a fucking convict, an inmate. White dudes with no shirt on who had clearly accepted that reality and were enjoying it. That was their life, their identity. I was, like, "This is fucked. That's not what I want."

The other was the old veteranos, dope fiends, guys in their fifties, puking and laying on the floor, dope sick. Here I was thinking the older you got at this, the better you got. I figured I would be a dealer. The reality was I was gonna be one of these dudes. Dealing didn't work for me anyway—I did all the profits right away.

I remembered seeing Dennis Danell on that first day of junior year of high school. I remember how struck I was by him. I remembered I wanted to be a rock star. I had places to go, people to see. Instead, I went to jail for burglaries and dealing drugs.

How did this happen? It didn't happen to Dennis. He wasn't waking up with stitches in his head or going to jail. I just took this lifestyle and ran with it.

There were a couple of false starts, but in 1985 I changed my reality. I still didn't know if I would be a rock star, but I wasn't going to die like this. I quit cold turkey.

It was October 1985 when I got cleaned up. I really started to really acquire some sort of a work ethic. I realized if I wanted to do this for the long haul, I should treat it like a job. That was also around the time I started to listen to a lot of American music.

And that, in turn, was the epiphany for me: "*This* is what I could do to differentiate myself from hardcore." We weren't a hardcore band, but because of the time ("Mommy's Little Monster" came out in 1983), the singles before it, and the name of the band, people just thought we were a hardcore band, but we weren't. I didn't fight it. I just knew we really didn't fit into what that world was becoming.

It really changed when I started seeing racism at shows. It's when I needed to leave the hardcore scene completely. I remember once I had to get a police escort out of Florida because these skinheads were beating up these college kids, and I would call it out from the stage, and then, naturally, they wanted to kill me.

By now I consciously wanted to distance myself and the band from hardcore. Because that was where the majority of the violence was happening. I always preferred songs with melodies and some song-writing ability. I'd always rather go see D.O.A. in the era when suddenly the high school quarterback could become the singer of a band just because he had a bunch of testosterone. I was always more into style and the look and the sound.

There was great hardcore, but we were different. The scene was getting dumber, and we were getting smarter.

Remember, I also got clean off drugs.

When I got clean I was basically like, "I'm gonna have to give this up." It had become such a lifestyle for me. At first it was sex, drugs, and rock 'n' roll, and then it became just drugs. I was twenty-three years old. My first gig sober was opening up for Nine Nine Nine at the Santa Monica Civic. I was scared shitless, but a minute and a half in, I was fine.

I didn't make any declaration—I didn't want to be a flag waver for sobriety or anything—but obviously the backstage environment had to change, and I demanded a work ethic from the band like we'd never had. It had to change. The audience knew because the shows were better; we weren't fucking up. For a couple of years I was the only sober guy in the band, which was horrible. The other guys drank like fish for years into my sobriety, and so on nights off I would just stay in and write. That's when I wrote the songs that would become 1988's *Prison Bound*.

That period squashed the fear that my recovery would change the art, not improve it. I feel we really restarted the band in '85. That was when things really started to happen because I had all this energy now to put toward that. I still had to have a day job—I had to have a day job for five years; I was a house painter. But, you know, that allowed me to

travel and set us on our way to become a national touring act. We got
in the van and actually came home with some money.

American roots music had completely taken hold of me at this
point. I latched on to that part of my youth of soaking up the music
my parents exposed me to. That Smithsonian Folkways box set of my
mom's had everything from Leadbelly to The Carter Family. When I
heard the Carter Family as a kid it resonated with me. It sounded so
authentic and had so much emotion. That music now engulfed me.

There was a period in the early punk scene when I couldn't listen
to a five-minute blues song—I didn't have the attention span. By 1985 I
was rediscovering Chuck Berry and all these pioneers of rock 'n' roll,
the melodies. I really liked the primitiveness of it all. It was so primi-
tive, and I just saw a direct connection.

We weren't the only ones. It was The Stray Cats. It was X. It was
The Gears. It was The Clash. All these bands were drawing from similar inspirations. Billy Zoom grew up listening to Chuck Berry as a
teenager, so of course it was going to influence his music.

Musically what we were doing wasn't hardcore, wasn't even very
punk by standards then. But it was the same rebellion; it was the working class writing about working-class issues. I was writing about real
life. I took a lot of flak, even though I saw Johnny Cash and Waylon
and Hank Williams as real rebels. And they were the punks I wanted
to emulate.

The first wave of NY and English punk was very blues-based
rock, just a little faster. *Gen X* was a very pop record, just with blazing
guitars. Billy Idol was singing very melodic. These continued to be
inspirations.

It was definitely a little rough. I call it the era of the punk rock
police. All of a sudden there were all these rules. Rules??? I remember
telling people I wanted to play Johnny's "Wanted Man" live or record
"Ring of Fire," and people were, like, "Why the hell are you doing
that?" Why? Because it's fucking cool and it was my fucking band.

I found that the true music fans were accepting. The ones who
were there for the right reasons were along for the ride. To the others:
there's the fucking door.

CHAPTER 8

HOLLYWOOD SHUFFLE

by Keith Morris and Jim Ruland

The eighties were some of the best years for The Circle Jerks, but they were also some of the hardest. We had just recorded our third album, *Golden Shower of Hits*, and were waiting for it to come out. So there wasn't much creativity going on.

For me this was the period of the beerbonic plague when I was on a cocaine leash and drinking a case or two a day. I was trying to cram as much fun into a twenty-four-hour period as humanly possible, and there was a lot of clubbing and partying going on, even though I never had any money.

In spite of all that, it was a period of growth for the band. Our crowds were getting bigger. We'd play a sold-out gig, and afterward there would be two hundred kids on the sidewalk who couldn't get in. We had to find bigger venues, and we did. We started playing at places like the Olympic Auditorium with FEAR, Uniform Choice, The Dickies, The Vandals, Sin 34, Detox, Youth Brigade, D.I., and occasionally bands from the UK. We could have up to five thousand people show up, and that was a pretty big deal.

But when we played big shows like that, we weren't allowed to play any of the smaller venues in Southern California. We couldn't play the Music Machine and then two weeks later play the Olympic Auditorium. The promoters were smarter than that. We had to spread out the shows. Because of that, in order to survive we had to go out on a rock 'n' roll adventure and see the world. Bands like Black Flag were already doing it. They would be out on the road six, eight, ten months out of the year, just wearing out the asphalt. But it was new to us.

When it came to California, we'd been to San Diego, Riverside, Pomona, Sacramento, and San Francisco, but we hadn't done much beyond that because we didn't have the wherewithal to go out there and see what was past the California border. Was the earth flat and were we going to drive off the side? We had no idea. We had to go find some new places to play.

We pointed the van toward Phoenix or Las Vegas or Portland and from there would head in whatever direction. We'd go anywhere. We were on the road for a minimum of two months, but usually it was three or four. We would bring our black book and Rolodex and the corporate credit card for long-distance phone calls. We would pull up to a phone booth because if we used the credit card number at a friend's house, somebody could get busted. "Hey, we're in Cincinnati! Can we play at your place on Friday night?"

One time we played a sausage factory in Wisconsin that had a dance hall for Oktoberfest. We drove ten hours in ten feet of snow from wherever we were to play the punk rock polka for 250 people. We were just getting our road legs under us and trying to figure out where we were popular. That was the most attractive option at the time, so we did it. Sometimes we'd fill in the blanks as we went along. Sometimes we'd arrange things in advance, but it was hit or miss. Sometimes we'd drive sixteen hours to a gig, and there would be nobody there, just a handful of people who didn't know anything about us and didn't care.

These tours were long and grueling. This was a period of time when there weren't many all-ages shows, so it wasn't unusual to play two sets a night—one for the underage kids earlier in the evening and then again for the main event after they opened the bar for all the alcoholics. Anything to sell a few more tickets, a couple of more T-shirts. Even if it was only twenty kids.

It was a case of the blind leading the blind, just hoping for the best. It felt like we were throwing darts at a map of the United States, and wherever it hit we'd go. We were barely making any money. If we got a guarantee, it would be for $100 or $200. On a good night the guarantee would be $250 and we'd play for a percentage of the door. So it was shaky times, sketchy times.

When we came back to L.A. it wasn't much better. Three or four months would have gone by, and it would be a different place. Times changed. Clubs shut down. People fell out of the scene to go back to school to become lawyers, dentists, scientists at the Teledyne Rocket Factory, and members of religious cults. It was easy to lose touch.

A perfect example was my friend Jeffrey Lee Pierce. He was one of my best friends, but it was hard to keep up with him and the people he was hanging out with because we'd be gone for so long. At one point he got a dual-citizenship and moved to Shepherd's Bush outside of London. A lot could happen in four months.

When we came back we usually didn't have any money. We'd need to look for a new couch to crash on and scramble to pay bills. Most importantly, we had to find new places to play because clubs like the Roxy and the Whisky had changed their policies and turned into hair-metal havens, which bugged me. I wasn't down with the pay to play because the bands who did weren't worth paying to see.

There were all these smaller venues in Los Angeles and the outlying areas where we'd play just to keep some kind of cash flow going. We would play places like Cathay de Grande. It was like the men's room at a Texas truck stop, but on Monday night you could see Top Jimmy and the Rhythm Pigs and rub elbows with John and Exene of

X, Buster Batemen and the Alvin Brothers from The Blasters, the guys from Los Lobos, and a smattering of friends from other bands. It was a wild, well-rounded scene.

We would play Club Lingerie, where our friend and favorite Scotsman, Brendan Mullen, who was responsible for the early L.A. punk rock scene at the Masque, was the main booker. We'd go downtown to Al's Bar or to the Music Machine on the West Side or to Raji's on Hollywood Boulevard or to Godzilla's out in the Valley.

We'd go see our friends play at these places and get the royal shit-hammer going. We needed to have party favors. There were a lot of people in bands we ran with who would deal drugs. That's how they paid their rent. I'm talking about guys who were in pretty popular bands that could draw a thousand people and had put out major albums, really well-received albums—they still weren't making enough money to pay their rent. A lot of these guys were in the same situation I was in. Back then it seemed like I was always short $100. I owed the coke dealer some money or rent was coming up or my car was out of gas or I needed something to eat. I was always scrambling to find the dimes to rub together to make nickels.

But one of the great things about those days was the club circuit. If a friend's band was playing, they'd put you on the guest list, and if you couldn't get on the list you'd do the back-door shuffle. We knew all the guys who worked security and watched the back door. The back door was basically the front door as far as bands were concerned. The van would pull up, and everybody would jump out to load in. I'd pick up a guitar and walk in with them. Whoever was working the back door would recognize me as a member of The Circle Jerks. "Hey, you played here last week—I can let you shuffle through here . . ." There was Johnny Snot, who worked the back door at Club Lingerie. Bernie and Clint worked at Raji's. If English Frank was promoting a show down at the Music Machine, he'd be at the back door, charging people to get in after it was sold out.

"Hey, what's up? What's going on? Any chance we can slide on through here?"

It worked nine and a half times out of ten. We knew the drill. We knew the places where we wouldn't be able to get on a list or weasel our way in. So we would pretty much avoid those places. But we would pull all kinds of stunts to slip in through the back door. Sometimes it worked. Sometimes it didn't.

At the Troubadour and the Roxy I would come in through the back window. Both places had windows that faced the back alley. Being only 118 pounds, I could easily hop onto a dumpster, shimmy up the water pipe, and climb through the window. The Palace on Vine was even easier to sneak into because the guys at the back worked for Goldenvoice. On one occasion I was making my way backstage when the Peterson sisters of The Bangles asked me to escort their parents to their seats.

I said, "Sure!"

Vicki played guitar, and her younger sister Debbi played drums. I had a crush on Debbi, even though she was built like an amazon. She could have been a striker for the UCLA Bruins women's volleyball team or a center for the USC Trojans women's basketball squad. I would have had to stand on stilts to ask her out.

I met a friend at the show, and we sat with the Peterson's parents. I was basically the usher. "This is where your seats are. Would you like something from the snack bar?" That sort of thing. Since I got in for free, that was my assignment, but it didn't end well.

I was just hanging out, enjoying the show, and The Bangles were pretty rocking. At some point me and my friend went to find the men's room. We went into one of the stalls and latched the door so we could huff up some cocaine. We were doing our thing when there was a knock on the stall. We opened the door, and it was the biggest bouncer in the Palace.

"Time to go, fellas. You can't do that here."

Normally the security would just tell you to put it away and go back to the show. But no. This guy had to be more like a narc and was kicking us out.

I said to him, "Can I tell my friends' parents I'm leaving?"

"No. You're gone."

That was kind of a drag.

I somehow managed to wave to the Petersons' parents as I was leaving. They saw their escort being escorted off the premises. I was trying to make a good impression, and there I was, getting busted.

That's not a good scene. That's not a good way to put your best foot forward. We don't want *him* as our future son-in-law . . .

Goofy stuff like that would happen now and again, but I didn't get thrown out of very many places, even though I was always finding my way backstage and swiping whatever booze I could swipe. It wasn't really stealing; it was just the common thing to do. For example, if The Plimsouls were playing, I'd go backstage, grab a beer, and say hello to my friends. That's how we were able to survive doing the Hollywood shuffle. It was about being bold and brave enough to step up and say, "I belong here." What were they going to say? "No!"?

One time our bass player Roger Rogerson did just that and regretted it almost immediately. We were playing a show at the Music Machine, and some of the guys from Suicidal Tendencies managed to sneak back into the trailer. They thought they were going to swoop on our beer. Roger was sitting there, and he was, like, "What the fuck is up with that, man?" First of all, you don't tell the guys from the Suicidal Tendencies what to do or where they can go. We were down in West Los Angeles, a couple of miles from the beach, so it was basically their turf. Second, that's what the beer backstage was for—party favors! Welcome to the fiesta! Grab a beer! We could always get more. We could go to the promoter or bartender and say, "Hey, bump us down another case of beer." That was the procedure. We weren't getting paid a lot of money anyway. We needed to get paid with something. Might as well be free beer.

I wasn't there, but Roger must have popped off to the wrong guy, because this dude grabbed a beer and busted the bottle over Roger's head. Wham! When I came backstage Roger was sitting in the chair and rubbing his head. He was embarrassed and had a headache. Luckily it wasn't a concussion. He just said the wrong words to the wrong guy.

I'm not a confrontational person. I had a knack for avoiding trouble and being in the right place at the right time. That's how the Hollywood shuffle worked: you had to keep your eyes and ears open because you never knew when the right opportunity would present itself.

On another occasion I went to see Siouxsie and the Banshees play at the Santa Monica Civic. Goldenvoice was doing big shows with a lot of these English bands that none of the other promoters in the US wanted to deal with because of the expense of flying them over from the UK and the rigmarole of securing work permits. So Goldenvoice would have them play a couple of shows in San Diego or Riverside or San Francisco in addition to the L.A. gig. What was interesting about this show is that Robert Smith from The Cure was playing guitar as a member of the Banshees. I was there because of my old roommate. Jeffrey Lee Pierce's band, The Gun Club, was the opening band. It was a great show. I've always liked Siouxsie and the Banshees. Now, The Cure is a whole different thing: I can only take The Cure in bits and pieces.

Siouxsie was all gothed out, and I was excited because I got to meet a former member of The Mothers of Invention, who was managing The Gun Club. I had seen The Mothers of Invention perform at the Hollywood Palladium the night Frank Zappa played inside a cardboard refrigerator box.

After the show The Banshees wanted to party. Those English bands were always looking for a good time. There was a warehouse party in Marina del Rey. It was owned by the grandfather of the Stern brothers of Youth Brigade and served as a prop house. Like, if you needed a couple of fake palm trees for your movie or soirée, you would go down to Marina del Rey and rent them from this warehouse.

The last time I'd been to this place The Beastie Boys were playing, and it got ugly because the Suicidal Tendencies guys showed up and ten guys beat the fuck out of one guy in the middle of the floor. I'm not dissing them—that was their gang mentality. I've run into Mike Muir on a couple of occasions, and he was nothing but a gentleman and a sweetheart. But the night of The Beastie Boys show I remember sitting out in the parking lot on one of those concrete parking dividers, smoking a cigarette, drinking a beer, shaking my head, and thinking, "What the fuck? Why does this have to happen?" A minute later Carlos, the drummer from Suicidal Tendencies, was sitting next to me. "Why did those guys have to behave like that?" I asked him. "Why do they have to ruin everybody's fun?" He told me he really loved playing in Suicidal Tendencies, but he wasn't down with the gang thing. He was kind of downtrodden, knowing he was probably on his way out.

But on this particular night with Siouxsie and the Banshees we were at their van after the show, and they wanted to go party at the warehouse.

"I know where it is!" I said.

"Let's go!"

So we all piled into the van, and off we went. Everybody was partying and having a great time. At about two in the morning the Banshees were ready to go to wherever they were going next, but they couldn't find their bass player, Steve Severin. For whatever reason I was the most sober member of the crew, which was kind of unusual. So I went looking for him all over this warehouse like I was on a scavenger hunt. I looked under replicas of royal thrones and behind giant stuffed polar bears. I finally found Steve passed out under one of the tables. He was totally unconscious. Being a good Samaritan and an ambassador for the city of Los Angeles, I grabbed him by his feet and dragged him across the floor so he wouldn't get left behind. Eventually Jeffrey helped me get him propped up on one of the benches, but he was completely out of it. We got him in the van, and it was off to the next adventure.

The Circle Jerks weren't turning down many gigs in those days, even though there were a few we probably should have. Someone at Goldenvoice came up with the insanely brilliant idea to put together a show with a lineup of punk, funk, and heavy metal. Sounded good to me, but what were they gonna do with the crowd? Keep them separated with red velvet rope? Erect a chain-link fence? That wasn't going to work. Funk and disco people weren't going to bang their heads along with the metal guys, who weren't going to pogo in the pit with the punkers.

The idea got run by somebody and they decided, "Let's just do punk and metal and see what happens." The show was out at Perkins Palace in Pasadena and featured Alcatraz and Leatherwolf, with The Circle Jerks sandwiched in the middle.

It was a total disaster.

Perkins Palace held about twelve hundred people, with another four hundred if they opened up the second floor, which they never did for punk rock shows because they didn't need anybody spitting or pissing or high-diving off the balcony. This was where Wendy O. Williams blew up a car on stage during a Plasmatics gig. I saw some amazing shows there, including The Cramps and New Order, but I witnessed a once-in-a-lifetime performance that has never been repeated and I'll never forget.

One of the roadies for The Circle Jerks was a guy named Dream, who also worked for Goldenvoice. It was 1984, during the summer Olympics, and we were going to see Saudi Arabia play Brazil in a soccer match at the Rose Bowl in Pasadena. But first we were going to hit the kegs at Perkins Palace while Dream set up the stage for Public Image Limited, who were auditioning bass players.

We were kicking back, having some beers, and watching these auditions, hearing the same songs over and over again, which didn't bother us because we loved that first PiL record. Sometimes a guy would get up and start playing, and we could tell almost immediately that he wasn't the right fit for the band. Then who should come up for his tryout but our friend Michael Balzary, a.k.a. Flea from The Red Hot Chili Peppers. Flea plugged in, and it was clear that the rest of the band didn't know who he was, but in those days not many people did. But Flea meant business. He was really into the songs and nailing every note. A couple of minutes into the tryout the members of PiL started looking at each other like, "This is it! We found our bass player!" By the time they finished their last song it seemed like they'd made up their mind to invite Flea to join their band, but he beat them to the punch. "That was really fun!" Flea said. "You guys are great, but I can't join your band!" It turned out Flea just wanted to jam with them! They didn't like that at all, but we thought it was hilarious. I got to watch John Lydon storm out of the building, and I didn't get the feeling I'd been cheated.

Anyway, I think about five hundred people showed up for the Punk and Heavy Metal Experiment. The headliner was Alcatraz. Their claim to fame was that Yngwie Malmsteen was their guitar player. He did what felt like a two-hour guitar solo for sound check, which nobody appreciated. What a load of garbage that was.

Goldenvoice had done shows with Anthrax and Megadeth and Slayer, thrash-metal bands that were closer to the punk rock thing, whereas Alcatraz was one of these big pompous operatic deals. We tried to keep an open mind about it. "Let's just see what happens . . ." Leatherwolf was the opening band, and they were pretty decent guys who were up for playing with us: "How's it going? This is kind of odd. Let's see if it works!"

There was no egotistical bullshit attached to these guys. I mean, they could have been in *The Decline of Western Civilization Part II: The Metal Years*. They could have been regulars on the Sunset Strip in Hollywood. But they were really good guys. So I watched them and thought, "Wow, I kind of like this band." I wouldn't run out and buy any of their music, but if they were playing in town somewhere and I could do the old slip and slide, I'd go see them.

But as soon as The Circle Jerks hit the stage, it was obvious the crowd was there to see us, which was a nice boost for the ego. This was back before they cracked down on stage diving, and pandemonium broke loose as soon as we started to play. We had a three-second rule: get on stage, wave to your friends, and dive off the front. We didn't need any new members. We didn't need any of our equipment rearranged or cords stepped on or instruments knocked over. For the most part everybody was on their best behavior.

While we were playing a couple of the guys from Alcatraz popped their heads out from backstage to check out what was going on, and they saw all these punker dunkers running around, slamming and stage diving. I don't think they'd ever been to a punk rock show before, because they freaked out. They had this look of horror on their faces, like they couldn't believe what was going on. Maybe they were used to everyone in the audience sitting down and clapping between songs.

We finished playing and were drying off and having a chilled adult refreshment or two when this whole scene unfolded between Alcatraz and the promoter.

"We're not playing!"

Gary Tovar, the head honcho for Goldenvoice, wasn't having any of it. "You gotta give me a reason," he said. "I've already put up half your guarantee," which was probably pretty astronomical.

"Those punks are gonna hate us! They'll destroy our equipment! They'll kill us!"

I thought that was pretty messed up. The punks didn't kill Leather-wolf. And what about *their* fans who came to see *them* play?

"That's no excuse!" Gary said. "You signed up to do this gig. I paid you a ton of money up front!"

He was pretty heated, and I didn't blame him. These guys in Alcatraz received the red-carpet treatment. Each member of the band got his own hotel room, limousine, and deli platter, which was pretty arrogant. I like a nice deli platter as much as the next guy, but you only need one per band. I was watching all this, and I'll never forget it because I love Gary Tovar for what he did next. As Alcatraz was running out the back door, Gary started flinging the deli platters at them, pelting their limos with salami and cheese and ham and the occasional pickle. It was basically a scene out of *Spinal Tap*, which was ironic, because Perkins Palace had been featured in the film. Maybe that was the point. Maybe Gary went into it knowing he was creating his own version of *Spinal Tap*.

The Circle Jerks did its share of oddball shows. Sometimes we'd get asked to do an acoustic gig, and we'd say, "That makes no fucking sense whatsoever. Why not?" Everybody knows about our acoustic performance in *Repo Man*, but it wasn't our first, and there were plenty more to come.

The first time The Circle Jerks played acoustic was when our friend Tomata du Plenty from The Screamers was doing some whacky talent show at the Whisky that included Tito Larriva from The Plugz. It made perfect sense for Tito to play an acoustic show because he was an accomplished musician. But for The Circle Jerks it was very far-fetched. Punk rock bands don't play acoustic guitars. We toss them into fireplaces and hit people over the head with the El Kabong. But for some reason we got talked into playing the Whisky. I remember Lucky Lehrer, our drummer, playing marching cymbals. We also had friends who played the viola and stand-up harp with us that night, if you can believe it. Whenever The Circle Jerks were invited to do an acoustic performance, we played under the name Spanking Monkeys. We probably played a dozen acoustic sets over the years, with *Repo Man* being the most famous. The funny thing was that we didn't actually play while on camera. The acoustic version of "When the Shit Hits the Fan" was previously recorded.

But one of The Spanking Monkeys' more memorable performances was at a club called Power Tools with T.S.O.L., Soundgarden, and Guns N' Roses and took place in 1986 when Guns N' Roses had become a pretty big deal. It was me, Keith Clark, Zander Schloss, and Greg Hetson, and we were all wearing the tuxedos that we bought for the *Wonderful* album cover. Maybe we thought we had to impress The Beastie Boys or Fishbone or Madonna, who all hung out there. I don't know, but it was a big gig and a pretty weird night. The guys from Soundgarden and Guns N' Roses didn't seem like they wanted to be there, kind of like, "Why are we playing this show with the fucking Circle Jerks?" I don't really blame them. We were playing an acoustic show and were not an acoustic band. These were guys who probably wrote all their songs sitting on the couch with an acoustic guitar or while playing a piano. That's not how we did things.

We hung out and partied with T.S.O.L., who were our friends, but the guys from Soundgarden and Guns N' Roses wanted nothing to do with us, which was kind of disappointing. We'd hung out with Izzy Stradlin on several dozen occasions. He was into the scene because he had been in a band called The Atoms that were regulars at Cathay de Grande. And Duff had also played in punk rock bands in Seattle. So you would think they would want to step up and be a bit friendlier.

"Hey guys how's it going? We just got back from Japan. What are you guys doing? We just played the Great Wall of China. We just played on the moon."

But no. They seemed a little aloof. They weren't there for the camaraderie.

On a scale of one to ten, I'd give our performance a five or a six. But Soundgarden was outstanding. Chris Cornell (R.I.P.) had a voice that could peel paint off the walls, and I mean that as a compliment. That guy had a voice that didn't stop. There have only been a handful of guys like that, and he was one of them. Place him alongside Ian Gillan of Deep Purple, Steve Marriott of Small Faces and Humble Pie, Arthur Brown of the Crazy World of Arthur Brown, David Byron of Uriah Heep, and Little Richard. Chris Cornell had that kind of voice. He wasn't fucking around.

By the end of the eighties the wheels of the party bus had fallen off. I got sober in '88, and many of the people I ran with were dead or in jail or doing something else with their lives. All of the old clubs are gone now, and new ones have taken their place. But as long as there are broke musicians trying to make ends meet, the Hollywood shuffle will go on . . .

CHAPTER 9

DELIVERANCE

by Charlotte Caffey

I watched myself get into my car, turn the key, and start to drive along Los Feliz Blvd., making my way to Pasadena. I got off at Fair Oaks and made a left. I drove for a while, past wilting palm trees and cracked sidewalks, with the haze of the California sun in my eyes. I turned into the parking lot of a nondescript building, parked my car, and walked in. I was quickly surrounded by people who looked to me like they were in a fish-eye lens and spoke with what sounded like muffled words. I was escorted down a long hallway, passing room after room that looked exactly the same until the woman escorting me said, "This one's yours." There were two twin beds, mustard-yellow curtains, a brown rug, and beige furniture. As I sat down on one of the beds, I came crashing back into my body. Oh yeah—I just checked myself into rehab. It was January 30, 1985.

I come from a very large family of thirteen kids. I am number four. When I was a young girl, I wanted to be an actress, a waitress, or a nun—I thought any one of those would be really cool. Being a drug addict and an alcoholic was definitely not among my aspirations in life. As a kid I remember feeling insecure and not as smart or pretty as some of my sisters or girls I knew. I felt lost as I was overlooked in the crush of kids in my family, and this sparked a nervousness and profound anxiety that has always lingered within me. My dad was a workaholic via being a TV director, and my mom was at home with the chaos of all the kids. My older brothers teased me endlessly, and I was expected to babysit my younger siblings all the time. I am not blaming my parents—they absolutely did the best they could with their circumstances, but there was a limited amount of guidance to go around. My mom and dad never drank, but my dad—rest his soul—tried to explain to us about "the curse" in our family. It was more conceptual and less tangible, so I never understood it until it became my own experience.

Every weekend my mom and dad dropped us off at my paternal grandparents house. My grandfather, Poppy, was a Hollywood producer and my grandmother, Peggy, was a sensitive, beautiful woman who dressed in shades of beige and wore Joy perfume. We were out-of-control kids, ranging from toddlers to teenagers. Peggy would open the door with a big smile on her face and her arms wide open, hugging each of us as we walked in. What I didn't know at the time was that she—God love her—had the family "curse" and was a pill-popping, hardcore alcoholic just trying to cope with her life. On my mom's side of the family, who were 100 percent Irish, there was also a lot of untreated alcoholism. I learned in rehab that this was a "double-whammy," and man, did I get double-whammied.

I went to Catholic schools throughout my childhood and teenage years. The Catholic school system in the 1960s was very oppressive and extremely strict. I tried my best to be a good girl and follow all the rules. One day in sixth grade my teacher, Sister Assumpta Maria, pulled me out of class for laughing. She proceeded to repeatedly hit me in the face and the head as she backed me down the stairs with brute force. (FYI: this type of abuse was totally acceptable at that time.) I was left stunned and hysterically crying. To add insult to injury, I told my parents when I got home, and they sided with my teacher. They thought that the nuns and priests could do no wrong. That is the day, I believe, that I turned a corner. I was a good, devout Catholic girl up until that moment, when I experienced my first profound sense of disillusion, so I started to rebel. Initially, it was in really small ways, and then things escalated: by the time I was fifteen I was drinking and started experimenting with drugs, eventually progressing to acid, mushrooms, and speed. When I was under the influence I felt more relaxed, confident, sassy, and, most importantly to me at the time, not so awkward around boys. A couple of years later I enrolled in Immaculate Heart College, a music and art school. This was at the same time that I started writing songs and playing in bands. Music opened up my mind and my world.

I was fortunate enough to be living in Hollywood, CA, when the underground punk rock music scene started. It was a small group of artists, misfits and weirdos, where everyone was welcomed and encouraged to express themselves. In April of 1978 I was asked to join an all-girl band that was just taking shape, The Go-Go's. It was one of those moments in my life—and there were many—when I just blurted out "Yes!" . . . a pure gut reaction. Shortly after that, I went to England with my boyfriend, who, at the time, was Leonard Phillips of The Dickies. I missed playing The Go-Go's first gig at the now-infamous basement club The Masque. Meanwhile I was gallivanting around England getting myself into all sorts of trouble.

Up until this point it was all innocent partying—fun on the weekends, nothing more than a happy-go-lucky high. But while abroad I tried heroin for the first time. I remember vividly that I snorted something the size of a matchstick tip, thinking, "Oh, it's not much—I probably won't feel it." I was wrong, and that one fateful decision changed the direction of my life. I instantly became addicted, and I spent the next seven years trying to hide it from myself, my band, and everyone else in my life.

The Go-Go's started to play and practice more frequently. I continued writing songs while struggling with my growing drug and alcohol dependency. In spring of 1981 The Go-Go's signed a deal with Miles Copeland on his label, IRS Records. Things started moving very quickly. We went to New York for six weeks and recorded our first album, *Beauty and the Beat*. (That six weeks is a whole chapter by itself— maybe some other time!) One thing I can say is that I thought going to New York to make our record would keep me out of trouble—you know, away from L.A. and my drug connections—but I quickly discovered Alphabet City in the East Village. It was THE place to score. Even though those were some of the scariest streets in the city, my need to get high was so strong that any fear, logic, or sense of self-preservation went right out the window.

In the summer we were touring the States doing tons of press, visiting radio stations every day, promoting the hell out of our record. We said yes to everything because we didn't know how to say no. "Our Lips Are Sealed" was our first single, and we were stoked when we found out it entered the Billboard Charts. We continued to tour nonstop, and then we were asked to open for The Police. We went on The Ghost in the Machine tour that started in November and continued through January of 1982. We were now playing huge venues rather than small clubs. We played two songs on *Saturday Night Live*, and to this day, when I watch those performances, I can see the terror in my eyes as I was trying to maintain and act normal after spending the day drinking and doing cocaine. I physically remember the fear I felt right before we took the stage, when someone on set said to us, "Remember, you are playing LIVE in front of fifty million people!" Our album was rapidly climbing the charts, but after *SNL* aired, against monumental odds, it landed at number one on the Billboard Charts, where it remained for six weeks.

As our success continued to skyrocket, my personal life continued to be a train wreck. I could not sustain any meaningful relationship. I had been living with Peter Case, who I was so crazy about, but The Go-Go's and my using took precedence over everything. Though, while on the road, I would have a tour fling (or two or three), but no real relationships.

The Go-Go's got nominated for a GRAMMY for the notoriously jinxed Best New Artist category. Fortunately Sheena Easton won that year, and we were able to continue our trajectory of success. We were selling millions of records, and our second single, "We Got the Beat," was a massive hit, selling a million copies on its own. Right in the middle of all of this insanity our record company said we needed to make another album. I panicked, and the pressure started to build. I had written or cowritten eight of the ten songs on *Beauty and the Beat*, and I had written our biggest hit, "We Got the Beat." How was I going to top all of that? Was the first record just a fluke? Will our next record be a failure?

Our producer, Richard Gottehrer, suggested we record this time in Malibu at a studio at the top of a hill. We landed at Indigo Ranch, at the old Barrymore estate. It's located off of Pacific Coast Highway, about a ten-minute drive up Corral Canyon Road. The idea was that we would all live in the bungalows and record in the studio on the property. I thought that being sequestered might deter me from getting into trouble, but that didn't happen. I still had to maintain my equilibrium with a cocktail of drugs and alcohol. I would drive up and down the treacherous canyon road in all states of consciousness. A lot could have happened on the 2.4-mile drive each way, but I was spared. Once again, my need to get high was stronger than any thought of consequences for driving under the influence. Even though by that time I started to realize I was in trouble, I kept thinking I would figure it out and that I had it handled. That was my denial talking to me.

Everyone, including Richard, knew there was a lot at stake with this album. This was our sophomore effort and, historically speaking, should flop. But fortunately Kathy Valentine played me a song that she wanted to work on. She had written it for her former band The Textones. It was called "Vacation." I listened and instantly liked it but heard how I could make some changes that would lift up the melody in the chorus. Kathy was open to my ideas, and "Vacation" became the first hit single and the title of the record. It couldn't have been more perfect. The cover art was inspired by the song—a picture of the five of us water skiing in formation. It was actually a picture of five girls in a water show in Florida, with our heads superimposed, and it was classic.

By the summer we were headlining our own tour and selling out places like the Hollywood Bowl and Madison Square Garden. While in New York The Go-Go's shot our first cover of *Rolling Stone*. Legendary photographer Annie Leibowitz persuaded us to pose in our underwear. When the magazine hit the stands we were horrified to see the caption "Go-Go's Put Out." Regardless, I was extremely excited to see us at every newsstand on every corner, our faces on the cover of *Rolling Stone*!

But as big as my life looked on the outside was exactly how small it really was. As my addiction began to escalate, I began to isolate. I lived by myself, so it was really easy to disappear when I wasn't touring. I would wake up every morning around eleven, go to Chi Dynasty restaurant down the hill from my house, and have a martini for breakfast. I then would come home, call my dealer, and maybe try to write a song, but I would always end up blacking out by the end of the day. By this time I started to realize that things were NOT normal. But I would convince myself that I was doing great because I was always on time for rehearsals and press obligations and never missed a show. For a long time I could push through withdrawals, hangovers—anything. Meanwhile I would start my mornings with a six-pack and a bunch of vitamins, and then I would map out my drugs for the day.

On tour I tried to blend in while everybody else was partying—to put it mildly—but I was always singled out as the bad seed. Booze, cocaine, and pills were sanctioned, but heroin was not. It was a BIG taboo. I tried to hide my addiction, but the focus was always on me. The girls would plead, beg, cry, yell at me to stop and get some help, but I couldn't hear them. I would try to make sure that no one could tell that I was high. I have light hazel–colored eyes that always gave away what drugs I was on, as my pupils are very visible. I devised a plan that seemed foolproof to me at the time to conceal my drug use, and it would go something like this: I'd have a drink and become a little too tipsy. Then I would need some coke. "Oh God, my pupils are way too dilated. I feel too jittery, and everyone is going to know—I need something to calm me down, maybe some valium? No, heroin will do." Now my pupils are pinned. "Some more coke will even it out." This cycle was never ending. I was totally bonkers. It wasn't until a few years later when I went to Rio de Janeiro, practically falling apart on-stage as I played in front of a quarter of a million people, that I would have my first moment of clarity.

By the end of November 1982 we were at the peak of our career, having just gotten home from a hugely successful six-month world tour. I was out with a friend, and we decided to buy some dope. As we were leaving the dealers' house we were stopped by the cops and pulled into the Van Nuys police station. Here I was, one of "America's Sweethearts," with track marks on my arm and pinned pupils. I thought I was totally fucked as an older cop sat me down. I started lying my ass off, saying that I had had blood tests that day and that I had taken too much codeine cough syrup. But he wasn't stupid—he knew what was up. But for some reason he gave me a fatherly lecture and let me go. As I walked out to my car my heart was beating out of my chest. I was shaking, felt like I was going to throw up, and then drove myself home. But even with the risk of being thrown in jail at the top of my career and ruining my life, that still wasn't enough to make me stop using. And so I carried on.

We were on a much-needed hiatus at the beginning of 1983. I made a New Year's resolution to make some big changes in my life. I thought I would try to wean myself off all drugs and clean up my act. We had a long summer tour planned, and I figured if I started early in the year, I would be in good shape by the time we left. I made a chart that would help me cut down my dose each day until there was nothing left. Well, that certainly didn't work. The minute I was out of drugs, I simply just got more.

We started writing songs for our third album and began rehearsals for the upcoming summer tour. Gina had not been feeling well for a while. A series of tests discovered a hole in her heart, a birth defect. You could have knocked us all over with a feather. She was pounding those drums for years completely unaware of this. She was told that she had to have open-heart surgery. It was scary at first, but then we decided to stop rehearsing (unheard of) and drive down to Palm Springs before her operation. I gathered as many drugs as I could get my hands on, preparing for a full-on party blowout. It was just the five of us in two rented convertibles, careening down the 10 Freeway, side by side, hooting and hollering before checking into the Two Bunch Palms Resort. I remember the weekend being so insanely fun yet so out of control. Again, it was classic Go-Go's. Gina recovered very well from her surgery, but I was still struggling with attempting to portion-control my drugs. It seemed like the more I tried, the worse it got. I was also painfully aware that my writing was suffering. I started writing a new song that had this great piano part, but after six months of not being able to finish it, I asked Kathy to help me. She loved what I had written and jumped right in, came up with a great title, "Head Over Heels," and we got it done. I was blocked, but it did not occur to me that my drinking and using had anything to do with it. And even though I had only written three songs for the upcoming album, somehow I still managed to come up with another hit song.

In September we did a short tour of Texas and ended it opening for David Bowie at Anaheim Stadium on his Serious Moonlight tour. So, in true Go-Go humor, we called ours "The Serious Barbecue tour." This was a huge honor to be able to play with one of our heroes who had inspired us so much. Several months before, I started having pain and numbness in my left wrist and hand. I went to a doctor and was diagnosed with carpal tunnel syndrome. I wore a brace on my wrist and, knowing that we had some dates looming, asked ex-Rockat Tim Scott (Jane's boyfriend) to be on call in case I couldn't play. I did end up playing the show, but my health was deteriorating at a rapid pace. My passport picture memorialized this: I was down to a hundred pounds and looked a hundred years old.

Finally in November we started recording our third album, *Talk Show*. We chose Martin Rushent to take the helm, who had produced The Human League, The Rizzillos, and The Buzzcocks, among others. He had a studio in Redding, England, which is about an hour outside London. I remember thinking that THIS time, I'd REALLY be far away from the reality of temptation, and I made the transatlantic trip with every intention of keeping my partying to a minimum to focus on recording. What I didn't know was that Martin worked very methodically and wanted to work with each of us separately, so there were long periods of idle time when we had to battle our boredom. One day I decided to take a train into London and go to Miles Copeland's house in St. John's Wood. He wasn't home, but his assistant Hazel was. We proceeded to get rip-roaring drunk. I then somehow persuaded her to give me the keys to one of his cars, and we went driving. Mind you—I'd never driven a car with the steering wheel on the passenger side or driven on the left side of the road in my entire life. I was doing a pretty good job until I got to the roundabout. I entered it and just kept going around and around, not being able to find a way to get out of it.

"Head Over Heels" was released on March 15, 1984, and the next day our third album, *Talk Show*, came out. We started doing the usual avalanche of press as we prepared for the tour. We had to make a decision about who would open for us. We were at our manager's office when they showed us a picture of INXS—a really cute band from Australia who were just starting to break in the States. We looked at the picture and jokingly said, "Mmmm, there are six of them and five of us—that ought to work!" It turned out to be one of our most outrageous tours. We were like-minded in our twisted senses of humor, and they partied as much as we did! There were definitely liaisons and entanglements galore, but it wasn't all fun and games. Right before the tour started, Jane told us that she was quitting the band. I didn't really believe her, thinking she would change her mind.

About a month in, we did a gig with The Bangles opening for us at Caesar's Palace in Las Vegas. Our rooms were in the Fantasy Tower. I got to my room and laid down on the bed. I looked up, and there was a mirror on the ceiling, which normally would have made me laugh, but instead I just stared at myself, knowing that I was so fucked and so far gone. How did I get here? Is this it? Is this the way I will be for the rest of my life? I had no idea how to help myself. Jane was on her way out, the band was crumbling, and I was so ill that I should have been checked into a hospital instead of a fantasy suite at Caesar's Palace.

One night after a show I went to the bar in the hotel. Jane was hanging out with some of her friends, laughing, so carefree, and I was feeling so betrayed and sad about her quitting that I just kept doing shot after shot of tequila. The next thing I knew, I woke up on the floor of my hotel room. I got up and saw my face in the mirror. I had a black eye and bruise on my cheek. Apparently I made my way back to my room, blacked out, and hit my face on the corner of the coffee table, then passed out. Wow. Really? And wouldn't you think that would make me want to give up drugs and alcohol? Not me—I just kept going. We performed our last gig with Jane in San Antonio and then reshuffled the band, hiring a new bass player, Paula Jean Brown, while Kathy took over rhythm guitar. It felt really weird.

The Go-Go's played the first Rock in Rio festival for 250,000 people with Queen, Rod Stewart, AC/DC, Yes, and The B-52's, to name a few, in January 1985. We were in Rio de Janeiro, where cocaine was super cheap, with cuba libres flowing freely and "Girl from Ipanema" playing everywhere I went. We checked into our hotel and, of course, immediately started being loud and totally obnoxious. We made our way down to the pool, where all the bands were. It was a total scene, with tons of rock stars, groupies, managers, and hangers-on, a little bit thrilling and a little bit creepy. Later that day or maybe the next Paula Jean came to my room and wanted to talk. We chatted about set list stuff and how wild it was to be in Rio, and then she started talking about my drug situation. She said a really good friend of hers was a recovering heroin addict and knew a place where there were people going through the same thing as me and that she could help me get in. I think I said, "Wow, that's really cool." The magnitude of this information seemingly went in one ear and out the other.

We then received an invitation from Rod Stewart to have dinner with him because he wanted to meet us. We vacillated between disbelief and giddy excitement. The dinner was a bit of a blur for me, but I came out of my fog when Belinda managed to score some cocaine. I went to her room, and there was a mountain of it on a table. We eventually worked our way over to Rod's room, where we stayed up all night. He was really upset because he had to play that evening, and he said he had never pulled an all-nighter and what was he to do? I was SO confused. He's a huge rock star—didn't he know just to drink more and do more drugs and that he would be fine? That's exactly what I did. It must have been 100 degrees on stage that night. I was looking out onto a mass of humanity, barely going through the motions of playing, and my body felt like total shit as my mind was racing with Paula Jean's words playing over and over again. That was the tail-end of my three-day self-demolition derby, where Rod was pissed, I don't exactly remember what I did, but The B-52's were avoiding me, and Ozzy Osbourne kicked me out of his dressing room. About a week later I returned to L.A. and checked myself into treatment.

In the mid-eighties rehab wasn't "a thing." The hills of Malibu were not dotted with hundreds of treatment centers. There were no TV ads for recovery. The "fancy rehab" was the Betty Ford Center located near Palm Springs, but I was in South Pasadena, which at that time was low rent and littered with drug dealers. Being in rehab was an intense culture shock and also a relief from my chaotic life. There were just fifteen of us in the facility. We would wake up every morning at 6:00 A.M. and have every minute of every hour filled with some group activity or therapy. A couple of days into my treatment I arrogantly thought, "I'll stay here for a week, get clean, and then leave." I felt good enough about that decision that I would walk around the facility with a big smile on my face until one of the counselors said, "What are you grinning about? You are in a DRUG rehab." That was a fucking buzzkill.

The Go-Go's visited me. They sat in on one of my group therapy sessions with some of the other patients. I knew the girls so well that they didn't have to say anything—I could see they were mortified. At the time real feelings were cropping up because I wasn't anesthetized for the first time in years, and it felt like I was on an acid trip. I was angry, scared, confused, humiliated, and hopeless. And there I was, trying to navigate my thirty-one-year-old-self with the emotional maturity of a fifteen-year-old. You can imagine how fun that must have been. All the while, in my group meetings, I kept hearing the word "surrender" over and over and over again. I could not wrap my mind around the concept. How do I "surrender"? Shouldn't I be learning how to control my addiction? I was a fucking mess, but I stuck it out for the full thirty days.

I was very nervous leaving rehab, but there was one thing I knew: I never, ever wanted to be a prisoner of addiction again. I sought out meetings of like-minded people who had years of sobriety. I heard the words "shut up and listen," and that's exactly what I did. I showed up no matter what and soaked up everything I could learn about the disease of addiction. The years of pain and confusion started to make sense to me. I heard people talk about their lives, their recovery, and how they were staying clean. I wanted to become accountable, so I started telling everyone I was sober. I told my doctors, "I am a recovering drug addict and alcoholic" in a loud enough voice to make sure it was louder than the voices in my head that would say, "Wow, you could get some Vicodin or Valium or something. It will be okay." Yeah, right. I was fighting for myself every single day.

In April we started writing and rehearsing for the fourth album. I was only a few months out of rehab and was very raw emotionally as I walked back into an extremely dysfunctional situation. The songs being written were horrible except Paula Jean's "Mad About You." A rift was deepening: Belinda and I were on the same page, and Kathy and Gina were on another. The dynamic had drastically changed for many reasons—one of them being that I was no longer the bad seed. As much as I loved The Go-Go's, in May 1985 I made the decision to walk away from my band in order to protect my sobriety and preserve my newfound sanity. Belinda left as well. We had reminded each other of the pact we had made when we first started the band in 1978: when it stops being fun we will break up. And it had definitely stopped being fun.

Belinda asked me if I wanted to work with her on her solo record. I was so grateful to her for this. But I still felt like I had a writer's block, so I talked to some of my sober friends. The myth I told myself was that I needed drugs and alcohol to be able to write. But my sober friends told me to just put pen to paper and stop trying. It sounded impossible to me, but I did it anyway. And guess what? An entire set of lyrics flowed right out of me. I finished the music and played it for Belinda. She recorded it and put it on her record.

Shortly after I left the band I met Elizabeth, another clean and sober person. She was only twenty years old—eleven years younger than me—and was so smart, had such a twisted sense of humor, and was filled to the brim with wisdom. She told me that her mom had died a few years earlier from a long battle with cancer and her dad dropped dead nine months later from a heart attack. I couldn't understand how a person could be so grounded, happy, and full of life after experiencing such trauma. We became instant best friends—still are to this day—and she became my mentor. She helped me build my self-esteem, of which I had none, always told me the truth, kept me laughing so hard every day, and cheered me on in my sobriety as days turned into weeks, weeks into months, months into years.

In 1986 I went out on tour for the first time since The Go-Go's. I was nervous, but I felt very strong about going because I needed to know if I could stay clean and sober in that world. One of the stops on Belinda's tour was Riva del Garda, a resort in northern Italy, decorated with winding cobblestone streets, medieval and baroque structures and located on Lake Garda's northern shore. We were playing a festival with some of my favorite bands, like The Pretenders and Crowded House. After the gig all the bands went to this beautiful restaurant where, of course, a wild, drunken party ensued. I was THE ONLY person in the place not drinking. People were laughing, shouting, and dancing on tables, having a grand old time, and my mind started playing tricks on me. I heard, "It's okay. You've been clean and sober a year and a half—you can handle it. Just one drink." I was frozen with fear as I felt myself starting to give in to the thought. But then I remembered what some of my sober friends said: "If you are uncomfortable, get up and leave." I stood up and got the hell out of there. Outside, on the cobblestone street, it started to rain and I started to cry. I made my way back to my room and fell on my knees and began to pray. The next morning when I woke up the obsession was gone, and it never came back.

I recently asked Elizabeth how she saw me back then. "You were a complete lunatic, but at the same time you were so willing. You became utterly teachable. You adopted a belief system with guidelines and tools that were a gateway into another way of thinking. You were not a follower—you were a learner." And one of the most important things I learned was the day that I surrendered was the day of my deliverance.

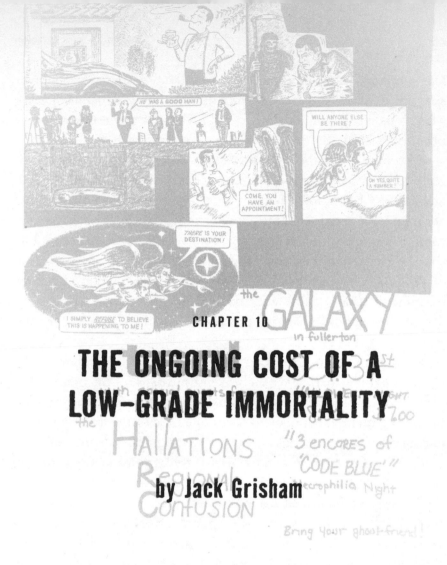

CHAPTER 10

THE ONGOING COST OF A LOW-GRADE IMMORTALITY

by Jack Grisham

The first cool cut I ever caught was a crescent-moon slash below my right eye. I was eight or nine years old, and I'd been hit with a rock in a dirt-clod fight—the delinquent volley had been tossed without regard to the conventions of acceptable childhood warfare. I was momentarily blinded: stunned, but then . . . light blue stars exploded like meth-addled embers in a pagan fire. I was alight. I stood in silent pride on a child's dirt stage, the blood running down my cheek, the tears refusing in shame to appear while that badge of dark-red honor dripped like summer heaven onto my shirt. I remember my fellow combatants standing like dirty-faced varmints in the oncoming lights of a car. They couldn't or wouldn't move until my reaction to the wound had been established. My reaction. I knew at once that that cut was cool. It was tough. It was the kind of cut that made kids in the schoolyard realize that you didn't go down easy—that you weren't going to take any of their little monkey-bar bullshit. I smiled as that small crowd admired me. I could sense the envy clutched in their I'll-never-be-anything hands. I bent down and picked up a rock, lovingly caressed its sharp corners, and then I casually said, "Let's go." In the space of a black eye I had an audience and a vibe and the beginning of a wonderful reputation. I didn't want that cut or that rep to ever go away. Toward the end of the healing process I'd pick the scab to reopen the wound.

I'm older now, and I reside in the body of a middle-aged man. The chest that I once marked with a broken-heart tattoo—my pinned-skin protest to a romantically cruel world—well, it still displays my unending crisis with love, but now that flesh billboard of my failed romantic encounters hangs on a sagging pair of man tits. It's hideous. And that cut, that beautiful crescent-moon slash—well, I've spent my whole life trying to keep that blood flowing and that adoration coming.

You see, you fuckers sit around wishing you could be somebody—a rock 'n' roll contender with a big rep and a marquee cool—but you don't know what it takes to swing in this game, to become even a low-grade immortal . . . the kind of immortal who's recognized at the gas station or the supermarket on a Wednesday afternoon.

My band barely had a name, but fuck, man, even a little bit of noise will cost you. And the thing is, when I say cost, you squares think that I'm talking about hard work, about putting in your dues: excessive practicing and long uncomfortable road trips smelling the stink of some fucker you hated before you even left town. No, that ain't the cost—that's the pleasure. That's the expectation of stardom and fame—the feeling that you've got an agenda and you're gonna change the world with your stickers and your T-shirts and your melting in the heat of a Midwestern-sun vinyl. That's the hustle you put in to get somewhere, but that ain't the price you pay for arriving.

Rock 'n' roll fame is like a credit card with an interest rate that climbs past prime—your prime. However, the bill doesn't come due until the lights go out, until the last drunken groupie has wandered away from the dressing room, until nobody gives a fuck that your eye is cut, and no matter how many times you pick the wound or leap from the stage or drunkenly stagger up to the mic to do your best Kris Kristofferson impersonation of a used-up old rock 'n' roller, they no longer stare at you with admiration in their eyes. They've wandered off to another younger model hero who is willing to bleed and to dance and to sing and to pick his wound for their love.

Now you pay.

I remember an evening when I stood and watched a young man perform—a boy barely twenty-one with jet-black hair and a junk-ied-out Elvis face. I was standing backstage—an honored guest hanging in the wings—and throughout the night many semifamiliar strangers had cowered up and paid their respects to me. I was floating on a stage of past glories and, until then, still-future promise. Even the boy himself had come by and given me my propers. As I watched him saddle up to the mic I saw the low translucent buzz of the crowd lifting over the barricades and onto the stage, wrapping its way up his legs until the buzz was clenched like impassioned stardust in his hands. All eyes were on him, and not one, not even the backstage selfie-snapping clowns had their eyes on me. I was overlooked, passed by, shadowed. I was becoming the old limp dick in a three-way, the husband who thought it would be cool to have a young stud come over and bang his wife until he realizes as the romp progresses that his wife's eye is no longer his and it's only a matter of time before he loses her and he can't get it up.

Every so often you hear one of these so-called enlightened rock 'n' roll cunts say he's only in it for the music. What a load of shit. If that were true, he never would've turned you on to his "download." He never would've walked on stage or went on tour or released anything meant for ears other than his. He would've got himself a job, a little nine-to-five, here-until-I-die role at servitude, and at night or on the weekends he'd sit around in his shit-stained underwear and thrill himself with his rock 'n' roll licks and his Bobby Dylan lyric-writing expertise. If you ever hear a song or see a band or buy a record, know that there's only one reason you're receiving it: because those fuckers want you to look at and to love and to admire them. They want more than laying down those tracks can provide—they need more. They just won't admit it.

My old buddy, the drummer Hunt Sales, once told me that success was playing on a Saturday night, and he was right. A weekend gig means they still care and you can still fill a room and the booze will still be bought and the money will still flow. A weekend gig means your shit still stinks of rebellion and teenage sex. A weekend gig means they still love you and your last check-me-out antic is still holding true. A weekend gig means the price of stardom hasn't yet come due.

Fuck, man, I remember when the first installment of my rock 'n' roll immortality came knocking on my door. It was as if that hard-hitting fucker Sales had thrown a premonition in my direction. It was a Saturday night, and a big show had rolled into town and my band hadn't been asked to be on the bill.

Cha-ching.

Who ever said, "Better to have loved and lost" wasn't no rocker. He wasn't no give-me-a-taste-of-that-and-now-give-me-another. The bitch who wrote that line probably never even had it good—good young when it still worked, when you're still strong and you can take on the world. He probably never stood on stage or commanded a crowd or walked into a room where the awe-flash cannons its way to the cheap seats as you kick in the fucking door and your voice rings like great gothic bells thundering across a landscape of upturned faces. He probably never felt adoration and then had it trickle away like an enlarged-prostate piss on the bathroom floor of a rented studio apartment. He didn't know what it was like to have been loved and to remember what it was to rule . . . and now you don't.

Oh man, I wish you fuckers could feel how much it hurts to lose.

When I was young I'd supplanted God. What use was there of a deity when my body was lean and my mind, although misguided, was cocked and firing and the words that spewed from my mouth were the words of a warrior? When I walked on stage there were those who were willing to follow even my most absurd whim because what I gave them in return, more so than this new punk rock sound, was my soul in sacrifice. I gave them the honor of watching me bleed.

The other day I was in the grocery store. I was standing in the organic produce aisle. A man walked up to me. He was fat and old and dressed like his mother had laid out his things.

"Hey, bro!" he said. "You're Jack, yeah?"

I lit up like a bitch.

"Yeah," I said. "What's up, dude?"

"Oh man, all right! I used to really dig your band. What happened? Do you still play?"

"Do I still play?" I said.

I climbed onto the produce stand, the sweet potatoes and the onions rolling and scattering onto the floor. I'd show him what I still had. I deserved his love.

"Yeah, man!" he said. "Get it, bro!"

I prowled like a caged supermarket tiger. The clean-and-brite sale on aisle fourteen slogans spat from my mouth with black-leather fury.

"Yeah!" he cheered. "Get it, DUDE !"

I delivered hard, recalling each twist and turn, my hips gyrating, my hand fist-pumping at the fluorescent ceiling bulbs.

One of the checkers ran up screaming, "You can't stage dive here!"

Fuck him. I needed this. I leapt from the counter, and all 250-some odd pounds of used-to-be-somebody hit the sparkling linoleum floor like a spilled container of past-the-expiration-date pudding. The fat man cheered, and then he pushed his cart on down the aisle.

The show was over.

I lay there, spent, useless on the ground—still bleeding, hoping he'd be back.

PRINCESS OF HOLLYWOOD

by Pleasant Gehman

Hollywood in the 1980s was a ghost town from a bygone era. Though the name had international mystique, it was more like a concept than a destination—there were no tourists there ever. The grand movie houses on the Walk of Fame were shuttered; the ones still open had threadbare carpets and broken seats, showing B movies to an audience who were there to sleep off hangovers. Once-opulent art deco apartment buildings were inhabited by elderly movie hopefuls on Social Security, pimps, drug dealers, and rock 'n' roll kids. In this weird historic dead zone *anything* could happen. Completely under the radar, we ruled the streets.

As dusk fell and the neon twinkled on Hollywood Boulevard, I sat on the stoop of Disgraceland, rocking gently on the pastel-pink porch swing. Resplendent in a 1950s emerald-green satin strapless ball gown I'd gotten for three bucks at a studio sale, I was an empress surveying her domain. Disgraceland was the most infamous punk rock crash pad in Los Angeles, if not North America . . . or maybe even the world. In the shadow of Frederick's of Hollywood on a slummy side street called Cassil Place, Disgraceland was owned by Mr. Universe 1955 Mickey Hargitay, an actor who entered showbiz as a muscleman in Mae West's revue before marrying Jayne Mansfield. The constant parade of local and touring bands was endless, and there was always an outstanding balance due on the rent. On this evening a raging party was going on inside, but that was normal.

What was not normal was feeling immobilized by the layers of petticoats sewn into my dress while noticing with an odd fascination that the empty Mickey's Big Mouth beer bottles littering the porch matched my gown perfectly. The green glass glinted, and I realized my hair was the color of pearls and felt like gossamer.

That afternoon, in homage to the blonde bombshells of the cinematic golden age, I'd had Connie Clarksville chop off my henna-orange mane to above the shoulders. Against her professional judgment, I forced her to bleach it three times in as many hours. My scalp was so full of thick scabs that it felt like a skull cap made of solidified lava. A toxic cloud of peroxide surrounded me like an industrial disaster, and if a match had been lit, I probably would've exploded. Miraculously, my hair was still intact and was now the perfect shade of vintage starlet platinum. Also, I was coming on to the three hits of acid I'd ingested the moment my hair was done. In fact, I was fuckin' blazing.

Levi Dexter and author, from the author's private collection.

I heard footsteps on the sidewalk and realized they were getting closer—suddenly Mickey Hargitay came to an abrupt halt and we locked eyes.

It was shocking: I was staring at Mickey's Big Mouth bottles, and out of thin air Micky Hargitay materialized. He never came to the house—it was always the manager, who seemed perpetually wasted on Valium, collecting the rent. Had we even paid it this month? The party noise came into focus; it was deafening. I considered employing the usual act-normal mode reserved for when cops busted our parties, but I was so high that I wasn't even sure if verbal communication was actually an option.

Staring at me like the proverbial deer in the headlights, he stuttered in a guttural Hungarian accent, "Uh, excuse me . . . but . . . has anyone ever told you that you look exactly like Miss Jayne Mansfield?"

This surreal turn of events unnerved me; my mind raced into full panic mode. Why was he here after dark? And exactly what the fuck is the etiquette when your landlord, to whom you owe hundreds of dollars for several months of back-rent, announces that you're his dead movie star ex-wife's doppelganger?

After what seemed like an eternity, I gave what I hoped was an appropriate answer—not that there even was such a thing as protocol for this . . . rather unique situation.

"Thank you," I whispered, the words reverberating in my head like an echo chamber.

He nodded nervously a few times, turned swiftly on his heels, and left.

I never saw him again.

For me and many others, the transition from the insular late-seventies scene to the underground mayhem of the eighties was swift, drastic, and necessary. Our slice of punk heaven had been shattered by violence from the same testosterone-fueled assholes who'd crash gigs for the sole purpose of starting fights. The diaspora began with the women—we weren't safe at shows any longer—and eventually spread to the guys, who were fed up with the relentless aggression and dumbing down of what had once been a thriving creative community.

Lots of us got into roots music, later to be termed "Americana." The shift got its start as early as 1978, when English band Levi and the Rockats moved into the Tropicana Motel and started playing around town. Most of us hadn't heard of rockabilly before, and The Rockats were adorable, lifestyle Teddy Boys still in their teens. Several punks jumped on board the neo-rockabilly train early on. By the 1980s there was a vibrant subscene composed of newly formed rootsy bands and their fans, record collectors, and older local musicians who also adored—and in many cases, played on—the vintage records everyone was listening to. A world of ancient blues, backwoods country, obscure western swing, psychedelia, surf, and sixties garage bands opened up. Nowadays people might not see this shift as a logical progression, but it made perfect sense to everyone involved.

Though we detested mainstream AM radio, we'd all grown up listening to Art Laboe and Huggy Boy's oldies shows, aimed at Lowriders and "The East Side Sound," doo-wop hits and vintage soul. Almost everyone in the punk scene was obsessed with the all-night border-blaster station XPRS from Baja California. Wolfman Jack would play two or three songs, and then there'd be twenty-five minutes of call-in dedications from listeners to their incarcerated homies: "This one goes out to Lil' Puppet from Shy Girl in South El Monte . . . I still love you, baby!" XPRS was immortalized in The Blasters' song "Border Radio," and it was the Alvin brothers, along with Phast Phreddie and Don Waller of *Back Door Man* magazine, Levi Dexter, Los Lobos, and a pre–Gun Club Jeffrey Lee Pierce who started influencing everyone's musical taste. Some punk bands started integrating genres and getting back to their roots, but X already had that in the bag: Billy Zoom had also been Gene Vincent's guitarist.

Several bands formed and started playing out, including Tex and the Horseheads, The Red Devils, Jimmy and the Mustangs, Blood on the Saddle, Rank and File, and my own band, The Screaming Sirens.

The music had a huge influence on the way we looked. Leather jackets and fishnet stockings remained constant, but that was where it ended. Punkettes swapped out tattered black slips for pencil skirts with tight cardigans worn backward over bullet bras, or square-dance fashions like the rick-rack trimmed, circle-skirted "squaw dresses." Guys had their hair cut in DA's by hairdressers Marty Nation or Miss Mercy, formerly of The GTOs. Women got the same cuts or started growing their hair long enough to make a ponytail. Padlock chains gave way to bolo ties; Army shirts and motorcycle boots morphed into fifties tweed suit jackets worn with pegged trousers and Brothel Creepers. Thrift stores all over L.A. were raided for vintage cowboy boots. Classic cars weren't considered collectible and could be had for a hundred bucks. Several scenesters had incredible wheels: Bill "Buster" Bateman of The Blasters drove a white 1959 Cadillac, Iris Berry's lipstick-red '57 T-bird broke down all over town, and punk photographer Ed Colver rolled in a vintage hearse with palm fronds etched into the rear window and bud vases in the back where the coffins were loaded.

We'd hit the Capital Records Swap Meet on Saturday nights after last call. Once reserved for serious record collectors, it became a six-hour after-party as everyone searched for 1930s blues on scratched 78rpm vinyl, small-label rockabilly, and novelty 45s from the musical wack-jobs Omo the Hobo or Nervous Norvus.

We'd gather at Phast Phreddie's pad to play records hootenanny style, dancing the Watusi or jitterbug jiving. The apartment was tiny, on Sunset near Bronson behind Uba's Creations, a fetish shop owned by Phred's landlady, the corseted, bouffant-sportin' Mistress Uba. Guests included Top Jimmy, Levi and Smut from The Rockats, James Harman, Steve Berlin with Little Richard's sax player Lee Allen in tow, Colin Winski and Jerry Sikorski of Ray Campi's Rockabilly Rebels, Gary Stewart of Rhino Records, and, if they were in town, Lux and Ivy of The Cramps. We'd spin our latest swap-meet finds, discussing the records and artists while they played. Nights at Phred's were like an education on the history of American music as well as an uproarious hoedown. But as far as parties went, none held a candle to what was happening around the clock on a daily basis at Disgraceland.

> Usually, when I wake up, I don't know where I am. But when I wake up at Disgraceland, I always know where I am . . . the question is: how long have I been here?
> —Matt Lee, The DIs

I lived at Disgraceland from 1978 to 1988, when we finally got evicted. It was a decade-long reign of pure rock 'n' roll insanity, but it was always congenial, creative, and fun. I moved in with Kid Congo of The Gun Club—and later The Cramps—and our pal Marci Blaustein, but Disgraceland really came to prominence during the 1980s.

My bail bondsman boyfriend, Billy Persons, bass player with The Falcons and The Gun Club, dubbed it Disgraceland because of the Tijuana plaster bust of Elvis—with Alice Cooper makeup that I added on with Magic Marker—on the mantelpiece, surrounded by empty fifths of booze.

"DG Land" was ideally located. It was blocks from several formerly elegant "movieland" apartments where our friends lived. To the east was The Screamers' Wilton Hilton and Dangerhouse, where the record label of the same name was founded. South was Malaga Castle, an ivy-covered fortress that had fallen into neglect but was still magical; north was the Fontenoy, the Ojai, La Leyenda, the Cliffwood Manor, the Lido, and, of course, the Canterbury Arms. We were within stumbling distance of several dive bars and all the Hollywood nightspots— Club Lingerie, Cathay de Grande, after-hours club the Zero Zero, Janet Cunningham's C.A.S.H., and Raji's. My brother Chuckles called this Bermuda Triangle–like location the "Circle of Death."

Disgraceland residents all shared a bullet-riddled communal convertible dubbed the Pink Cadillac From Hell. The doors were stuck shut—to get in and out, you'd vault over the side. Technically my roommate and Screaming Sirens' bassist Laura Bennett owned it, but everyone at Disgraceland had a set of keys. The PCFH was originally a hard-top Caddy sedan that had belonged to Laura's brother, who modified it . . . considerably. He took it to Earle Scheibe for a paint job, with a *Hustler* magazine. Opening it to the centerfold, he displayed it to the shocked painter, using the inside of the model's pussy as a color reference. He succeeded in chopping the roof off but accidentally set the backseat on fire. Then he drove it up to Angeles Crest Forest, using it for target practice before gifting it to his sister. Roz Williams of Christian Death added the hood ornament: a dead rattlesnake he'd found in Griffith Park. The PCFH was a cop magnet, but it'd show up with a carload of crazies every night at gigs and parties, always vanishing when a different roomie would commandeer it, driving somewhere else.

Anyone visiting DG Land had to step over passed-out bodies, records, band equipment, a wheel chair with a Suicidal Tendencies sticker on the back, a craps table, a miniature school desk stolen from Selma Avenue Elementary School, a Christmas tree stolen from Club Lingerie that stayed up for the better part of a year, piles of petticoats, and dozens of empty beer bottles.

Skateboard pro "Alabamy" Jay Haizlip, Iris Berry, and Limey Dave of Tupelo Chainsex at Disgraceland. Photo by Robert McClellan

Disgraceland was so notorious that in 1985 MTV did a special on punk hangouts—all clubs, except for Disgraceland. Art Fein wrote about us in the *L.A. Musical History Tour*; it was the subject of a feature article in *Rolling Stone* and on the *Tanqueray Gin Rock 'n' Roll History Map* and in the 1982 film *The Boost* with James Woods—the exterior was used as a crack house. Because of this and the rock stars who lived or stayed there, Disgraceland, much to my disbelief, wound up on the *Hollywood Maps to the Stars Homes*. As of this writing, decades after we got evicted, it's still on there!

Several people called Disgraceland home: Belinda Carlisle of The Go-Go's; Mike Martt of Tex and the Horseheads; Limey Dave and Joey Altruda of Tupelo Chainsex; Ruben Blue of *Scratch* magazine and, later, *LA Rocks*; artist Clam Lynch; Ann McLean of The Lame Flames; and Jenny "F-Troupe" Berry. Levi Dexter and I were married some of that time, so he lived there; members of his band the Rockats were constant roommates. Later, when I married soundman Hutch Hutchinson, the bands he toured with such as No Means No or D.O.A. crashed there too. I was writing for *Thrasher* magazine, so there were always skateboard champions hanging out: Tony Alva, Steve Olson, Christian Hosoi, Jay "Alabamy" Haizlip, and many more. Late skater/musician

Gerry Hurtado, aka Skatemaster Tate, referred to Disgraceland as the "Hollywood Harem."

My longest-running roomie was writer and Lame Flames singer Iris Berry; we formed our band The Ringling Sisters in the living room. Due to both of our social lives, the phone never stopped ringing, *ever* . . . unless, of course, it was shut off. Iris and I were such telephone abusers that when she got her own line, we'd lay in bed calling each other's bedrooms collect, having half-hour-long conversations even though we were literally fifteen feet down the hallway from each other.

Iris's boyfriend, artist "Mad" Marc Rude, was always there, as was Bill "Buster" Bateman of The Blasters, who was seeing me . . . until I gave him to Belinda—but more on that later. I'm probably forgetting several people who actually legit lived there, because, literally, an ever-changing cast of thousands slept—or passed out—at DG Land. Almost everyone on the scene partied there; the only ones who didn't were too scared to because of the stories they'd heard—most of which were true. Germs drummer Don Bolles lived in the driveway in a van with the license plate Unit 666, extension cords going through a window into outlets in Iris's room. After he left, Poison 13 from Texas occupied his spot in their broken-down touring van. The late Brendan Mullen of the Masque and Club Lingerie routinely offered the Disgraceland floor to touring bands as a motel alternative—*without our permission* . . . but we never turned anyone away.

People would show up for a party and stay for weeks. I'd randomly bump into Jeff Drake, singer and guitarist of The Joneses, on the street and ask if he wanted to come to a party. After the first few times it was a given that "the party" would turn into a marathon binge, but he never declined. Once we wound up in Tijuana, unsure exactly how we got there.

Sometimes we'd wake up to complete strangers cooking breakfast for us, but more often they were asleep beside us. A confirmed libertine and out as a bisexual since my early teens, I was always having simultaneous multiple affairs with boys and/or girls or sharing boyfriends with my Sirens bandmates. Nowadays I'd be called *poly*, but back in the eighties everyone just used the term *slutty*. Sirens' bassist Laura and I had so many mutual boyfriends that Keren "Raggirl"

Sachs called what we were doing "Going Plaid." Many times I woke up between two people; there was the delicate task of finding out if you'd *slept* with him or her or just innocently passed out together. After one particularly depraved night, I awoke cuddled up with my roommate Mike Martt, guitarist of Tex and the Horseheads; both of us were half-clothed.

"Hey," I ventured as casually as possible, "did we have sex last night?"

He looked at me with a sunny smile and answered, "That's funny . . . I was just about to ask *you* the same question!"

All the girls at Disgraceland had boyfriends who'd arrive late at night, entering or exiting Romeo style through our windows. Hollywood was safe enough to leave ground-floor windows open all night—and usually we were so drunk that we'd have no idea where our keys were, so it was convenient. Belinda always said they got lost "somewhere between the Hong Kong Café and Club 88." I'd attach my keys onto my garter belt, but they'd still disappear. The amount of men arriving or leaving on the same night—without using the door—was like a French farce. Unbeknownst to the guys, we often entertained more than one "gentleman caller" in a single night. Years later New Orleans musician Carlo Nuccio of Laughing Sam's Dice and several other bands, told me, "I remember how at home I felt when you said, 'Carlo, you're about the nicest thing that ever crawled through Iris Berry's window.'"

Whether we were seducing hapless menfolk or being Hollywood Hostesses, the parade of people through Disgraceland was endless. Just some of the touring or local bands crashing there were The Red Hot Chili Peppers, Social Distortion, T.S.O.L., Matthew Ashman of Bow Wow Wow, Fishbone, Reverend Horton Heat, Detox, R.E.M., The Vandals, Tales of Terror, The Modifiers, Junkyard, Dash Rip Rock, The Big Boys, The Gears, Billy Idol, The Polecats, The Scoundrelz, B.Y.O., Teenage Jesus, The Hickoids, Hard as Nails Cheap as Dirt, The Dicks, Stiv Bators, Candye Kane, The Daggers, Red Scare, The Replacements, and Guns N' Roses.

Most weren't even considered well known at the time, but those who were already in the limelight—and, often, exalted—came a-callin' too. On many occasions we hung with people who were icons. Screamin' Jay Hawkins usually came over after the bars closed. He was always dapper in a sharkskin suit while guzzling cheap-ass Lucky Lager, sharing his beloved "rock-star weed."

Another fixture was rock photographer Leee Black Childers, who'd been instrumental at MainMan, the company representing David Bowie, Mott the Hoople, Iggy Pop, and Lou Reed, among others. Leee had toured with Bowie and was managing Levi at the time, so he was usually around, dashing in his embroidered vintage Nudie's Western Wear suits. Leee's longtime pal, producer Tom Ayers, who'd worked with everyone from Gene Vincent to The Sir Douglas Quintet, once allowed me to put him in drag. Appropriately enough, I hauled him into the hallway *closet* to make him over. A dead ringer for Waylon Jennings, he stumbled into the living room wearing lipstick, a black cocktail dress, and the largest pair of heels I could find, wailing in his thick Louisiana drawl, "Pleasant . . . I dunno *how* you women walk in these things!"

Don "Sugar Cane" Harris, of R&B duo Don and Dewey fame, recently joined Tupelo Chainsex, so he was constantly hanging out. A terrific musician, he was also a longtime junkie. Once he terrified a bunch of New Romantic girls who'd crashed our party. They happened to walk into the bathroom while he was shooting up in our shower stall . . . wearing one of Iris's gaily printed vintage housedresses.

Musician/producer Al Kooper—who, among other things, played the iconic organ on Bob Dylan's "Like a Rolling Stone"—visited so often that he actually gave us a couch that took up half the living room. It was the only piece of furniture we hadn't taken off the street on garbage day. When people asked where it came from, we'd say it was a gift from Al Kooper—they were duly impressed. Once I pretended to reveal A Big Secret, whispering in a confidential tone that Bob Dylan had farted on it. The rumor stuck: for years guests would inevitably ask which cushion "belonged" to Bob Dylan!

Around midnight on a Christmas Eve the Godfather of Psychobilly and Doctor Demento favorite, the Legendary Stardust Cowboy, appeared on our doorstep like a wacked-out prodigal son. The Hickoids were crashing with us, and we were all on mushrooms. The Cowboy obligingly signed my copy of his hit single "Paralyzed" before serenading us with a guitar borrowed from Mike Martt.

At one of our garage sales Iris and I set up a bar for Plain Wrap Margaritas. The plan was to get our customers shit-faced so they'd buy our stuff. Our shock was genuine when Jayne County—fabulous drag queen, punk singer, and star of Andy Warhol's *Pork*—turned up with Angela Bowie. Graciously accepting the luke-warm margaritas we offered in Dixie cups, they shopped among the plethora of stained crepe 1940s party dresses and scuffed vintage Spring-O-Lators. Next thing I knew, Angie and I were tipsy and giggling, lying on my unmade bed, and spilling drinks all over each other. Our legs up in the air, each of us was wearing one of the pairs of gold Frederick's of Hollywood spiked-heeled mules she'd just purchased when Jayne walked in. Rolling her eyes, she quickly walked out muttering something about "whores."

Things rocketed to a new level when Belinda *became* a Famous Person while living at Disgraceland. By the time she'd moved in during spring of 1980 The Go-Go's had been around for a couple of years, and we'd already been close friends for ages. Both rock 'n' roll groupies and party gals, we shared an ironic sense of humor, loved Old Hollywood, and were obsessed with all things occult. We'd shop at the Panpipes for witchcraft books,

(L-R) author, Belinda, and unknown person, from the author's private collection.

candles, and amulets and play with my Ouija Board. During one session, as the planchette whizzed around the board, it spelled out:

HOUSE DIRTY

We looked at each other in amazement—this was *definitely* proof there were spirits around us.

"That's pretty fuckin' rude!" Belinda said as I yelled, "Fuck you!"

Then the planchette spelled out:

SHUT UP SLUTS

It spooked the hell out of us, and we promptly put the board away and didn't touch it again for ages.

Another time we saw *Dallas* star Charlene Tilton on the *Mike Douglas Show*. We knew she'd lived at Disgraceland in the not-too-distant-past because we always got her mail, so we watched. The interview was bland until she said something like, "I lived in a crappy, roach-infested dump in Hollywood." Though her description was spot on, we both got so indignant that we turned off the television.

The Go-Go's were about to go to New York to record their first album. Belinda was stoked but apprehensive about leaving her boyfriend, Bill "Buster" Bateman, behind. He was a catch—talented, handsome, and *nice*. So much so that when Levi was on tour, I began seeing Buster on the side. Too great of a man to let go, I "gave" him to Belinda in the same way I'd "given" Marty Nation to my pal Lydia Lunch. Levi and the Rockats were going to be in New York at the same time as The Go-Go's, so I had an idea. Girls were always after Levi and Buster, and I proposed that we swap, fucking each other's boyfriends as a safeguard so that no " boring normal girl" could lay claim to either guy. Belinda agreed wholeheartedly, and it worked like a charm, happening seamlessly. We switched back when everyone returned to California, and I don't think the guys ever knew what happened . . . until *now*, if they're reading this.

Belinda was still living at Disgraceland when "Our Lips Are Sealed" went to number one and shit, as they say, got cray. A family lived above us, and their teenage daughter would play the same 45rpm on repeat for hours. We'd fight back by blasting The Stooges, but it never deterred her. One day she switched from Donna Summer to "Our Lips Are Sealed." After five straight hours Belinda was rolling around on her bed, outright weeping with a pillow over her head. To our roomie Ann McLean and me, it was perfectly obvious that the teenybopper upstairs would never believe that the pop star who sang the song lived in the downstairs apartment! The three of us had a meeting on how to handle the situation when Ann suggested sarcastically, "Maybe you should put some cold cream on your face, wrap a towel around your head, go upstairs, and tell that bitch to stop!"

Though it made Belinda laugh, the problem wasn't solved. Soon kids at the schools near Disgraceland discovered that Belinda lived there. Every morning we'd wake up to a scenario straight out of *A Hard Day's Night*. Junior high kids from Blessed Sacrament pressed their faces against the windows, and younger children from Selma Avenue Elementary clustered on our porch, their hands constantly flapping through the mail slot. Belinda was literally a prisoner in her own house. After a few days Go-Go's manager Ginger Canzoneri whisked her away, and next time I saw Belinda she had a bodyguard. We went to dance at the Seven Seas on Hollywood Boulevard, and the poor guy had to wait by the ladies room every time we went in there to do blow . . . we did so much that evening that he was practically parked there.

As the scene changed rapidly and I entered my twenties, my life expanded in a wonderful way. Obsessed with rock 'n' roll since the age of twelve, I was now making a living off that obsession. I wrote about music for several mainstream and indie publications, was the club booker and/ or bartender at all the legal—and illegal—hot spots, and was cutting an album for Enigma Records with my all-girl band, The Screaming Sirens.

Lobotomy, the fanzine I'd created in 1978, thrust me into professional writing. *LA Weekly* founder/editor Jay Levin saw my handwritten 'zine and asked me to write for them, publishing my weekly nightlife column, *L.A. Dee Da*, which ran for years. In a punk paean to 1940s gossip columnists Hedda Hopper and Louella Parsons, I billed *L.A. Dee Da* as "The Place to Dig If You're looking for Dirt." But if I'd really spilled even a fraction of the scandals I'd been privy to, I never would've lived to tell. The way I wrote *L.A. Dee Da* was: I'd go out every night, sometimes to three or more places, scrawling a few notes in eyebrow pencil on a flyer. At the end of the week I'd spend five hours on a stream-of-consciousness one-fingered hunt-'n'-peck on a battered manual typewriter I'd gotten at a garage sale.

Simultaneously I became the booker at Cathay de Grande, a punk club in the basement of an old-school Chinese restaurant, hence the name. Among numerous other legendary bills, I gave The Red Hot Chili Peppers their first gig and put together a super-group of local musicians to play a comeback show for western swing icon Rose Maddox, of The Maddox Brothers & Rose.

In his pre–Thelonious Monster days, Bob Forrest came to me with an idea called the Sunday Club. He envisioned an afternoon event— basically a hangover party—showcasing our scene's musical diversity. The debut featured the incongruous bill of Black Flag and The Bangles . . . and, remarkably, went off without a hitch. The Sunday Club became a fixture, with everyone gathering for music and the cutthroat, co-ed softball games going on in the vacant lot across the street. They were organized by the Loyal Order of the Water Buffaloes—based on the lodge in *The Flintstones*—musicians, skaters, and ne'er-do-wells whose main occupation was day drinking. The games got so intense that often bands lost track of time, and the entire show ran late. Everyone came in their clothes from the night before, and chicks slid into the flattened beer carton functioning as home plate in thigh-high spiked-heeled boots, fishnets, and miniskirts. Club Lingerie waitress Pinky Braithwaite, who'd been Boy George's bestie while in London, always played in her customary Kabuki makeup, Victorian hoopskirts, and dainty bonnets, her Bo-Peep curls flying as she ran the bases.

The Cathay was owned by Michael Brennan and managed by Danny "Dobbs" Wilson, both of whom later ran the infamous Raji's, and I was the band booker at both places. The Cathay was run in such a lackadaisical way that it was miraculous it stayed open as long as it did. Before I started booking there Iris Berry and I were hired as the bartenders, which was a complete joke: we guzzled Jack Daniels straight from the bottle and knew nothing about mixing drinks. Texacala Jones, of Tex and the Horseheads, was the waitress. We all gave drinks away constantly, but Michael never said a word. Once, in the middle of a Social Distortion show, he noticed that nobody was tending bar. Somehow he tracked us down in the parking lot. Iris and I swilled bourbon from a bottle kyped from the bar that still had the pour-spout on. Tex lounged on the cement, tray on her stomach, head propped up on a parking curb, as we all shared a joint. Even that didn't get us fired.

Top Jimmy and the Rhythm Pigs had a weekly residence at the Cathay on Phast Phreddie's Blue Mondays. A prodigious drinker, Jimmy came up with an idea to help finance his habit. He decided to rob the postage-stamp machine in the lobby of La Leyenda, where Bob Forrest shared an apartment with Flea and Anthony of The Chili Peppers. But he mixed up the days—when he pried open the machine, instead of the month's cash he expected, there was a brand-new roll of stamps. Always pragmatic, Michael saw nothing odd about accepting stamps for Jimmy's Jack and Cokes, instructing us to charge him four stamps per drink. This went on for weeks until the whole roll was gone.

Because I had a master key to the Cathay and lived blocks away, I was drafted to deal with an assortment of problems. The most memorable was the time Michael called me frantically at 8:00 A.M. because some guy was locked in the club. Evidently the dude finally located the bar phone and called all his friends until one finally reached Michael. Ridiculously hungover myself, I headed to the Cathay all tragic and sans sunglasses. Descending the steep stairs into the basement, I heard the guy go, "Ohhh, thank God you're here!" Evidently the club's janitor, El Duce of The Mentors, hadn't noticed the guy passed out in a booth at closing time. When the dude woke up, he'd crawled to the bar, opened the beer cooler, and, to pass the time, drank as many bottles as he could until I rescued him.

Concurrently all the gals at DG Land worked at the Sound Check, a bar on Sunset just east of Vine. We weren't hired for our mixology skills—in fact, they advertised us as "The World's Worst Bartenders." Baba Soltani had started a Sunday jam night; she hired us to attract musicians because we knew everyone. She said we could give away free drinks as long as we kept track by writing them down on a pad. By 8:15 on our first shift, the pad was full. Afraid we'd all be fired, I admitted our transgression. She took one look, and said, "Just write smaller!"

The Sunday Jam Nights, as they were called, became so popular that anyone who was in town stopped by—Charlie Sexton, Peter Buck of R.E.M., and music-biz assholes like Bob Seger, who drank for free all night and left a single quarter on the bar. Even "real" celebrities stopped by—one night two famous men happened to be there at the same time. One made a beeline for Iris, the other for me. Years later Iris and I got into an argument about it, nearly getting thrown out of

Angelo Moore and Jane Wiedlin, IRS Records party. **Photo by Lisa Johnson.**

The Go-Go's (from L to R): Jane Wiedlin, Kathy Valentine, Belinda Carlisle, Gina Schock, and Charlotte Caffey. Photo by Ann Summa.

Parking lot behind the Florentine Gardens on a typical Friday Night. Photo by Lisa Johnson.

Texacala Jones of Tex and the Horseheads and Keith Morris of The Circle Jerks at the *LA Weekly* Music Awards, Wiltern Theatre. **Photo by Greg Allen.**

Mike Ness of Social Distortion. Photo by Greg Allen.

Social Distortion at the Whisky a Go Go (from L to R): Mike Ness, Derek O'Brien, Dennis Danell, and Brent Liles. **Photo by Ed Colver.**

The Adolescents performing at a skate park during a photo shoot for The Circle Jerks' *Group Sex* album. **Photo by Ed Colver.**

The Unheard Music premiere at Cinerama Dome (from L to R): Alizabeth Foley, W. T. Morgan, DJ Bonebrake, Rodney Bingenheimer, Exene Cervenka, John Doe, Everett Greaton, and Christopher Blakely. **Photo by Ed Colver.**

The Circle Jerks with their drug of choice (from L to R): Greg Hetson, Roger Rogerson, Lucky Lehrer, and Keith Morris. Photo by Laura Levine.

Jack Grisham of T.S.O.L., 1982.
Photo by Brenda Perlin.

Billy Zoom of X at Rissmiller's (Country Club), Reseda, California, 1982.
Photo by Greg Allen.

Early photo of Rank and File (from L to R): Alejandro Escovedo, Tony Kinman, and Chip Kinman. **Photo by Laura Levine.**

X at the Peppermint Lounge, New York City (from L to R): Billy Zoom and Exene Cervenka. **Photo by Laura Levine.**

Phil Alvin of The Blasters. **Photo by Laura Levine.**

FEAR (from L to R): Philo Cramer, Spit Stix, Derf Scratch, and Lee Ving. **Photo by Frank Gargani.**

The Blasters live at Cathay de Grande (from L to R): Phil Alvin, Dave Alvin, John Bazz, and Bill Bateman. **Photo by Gary Leonard.**

Top Jimmy and Luci Diehl, happily married couple. Photo by Gary Leonard.

Top Jimmy and the Rhythm Pigs, backstage at the Cathay de Grande (from L to R): Gil T, Tony Morales, Steve Berlin, Carlos Guitarlos, Joey Morales, Dick Aeilts aka Dig the Pig, and Top Jimmy. **Photo by Michael Hyatt.**

Jeffrey Lee Pierce, self-styled photo shoot, West Hollywood. **Photo by Greg Allen.**

Live taping of IRS: The Cutting Edge featuring Willie Dixon and The Blasters at Windows of Hollywood (from L to R): Alex Dixon (grandson), Willie Dixon, Dave Alvin, and John "Juke" Logan. **Photo by Greg Allen.**

Backstage trailer at the Music Machine, the night X and The Blasters backed Bo Diddley (from L to R): John Doe, Bill Bateman, Bo Diddley, and Dave Alvin. **Photo by Gary Leonard.**

Los Lobos, Santa Monica Civic Auditorium, 1983 (from L to R): Louie Pérez, Steve Berlin, Cesar Rosas, Conrad Lozano, and David Hidalgo. Photo by Michael Hyatt.

The Blasters on *American Bandstand*, 1982 (from L to R): Steve Berlin, Dave Alvin, John Bazz, Bill Bateman, Phil Alvin, and Gene Taylor. Photo by Michael Hyatt.

Dave Alvin, The Blasters, 1982. **Photo by Michael Hyatt.**

the quiet restaurant we were in. It started with me asking her, "Why the hell didn't you go home with John Astin that night?"

"'Cause he was an old man!"

"But Iris . . . he was Gomez Addams!"

"So what?" she yelled back. "You didn't fuck Evel Kneivel when you had the chance!"

Alice Miller, Iris, and I also tended bar at the Zero Zero. The brainchild of John Pochna and Brainiacs front man Wayzata Camerone, the Zero was an illegal after-hours speakeasy masquerading as an art gallery; it reopened at a new spot every time it got raided. Van Halen's David Lee Roth was an investor, presiding over the back-room VIP area; the board of directors consisted of Tito Larriva of The Plugz, John Doe and Exene, and Phil and Dave Alvin. Bartending at the Zero meant opening beer cans and doing the drugs left as tips. There were always people to party with, and because we barmaids weren't above flashing our bras to solicit better tips, we got all the action.

When the place closed at 7:00 A.M. there was always an after-party; sometimes they'd go on into the next night. David Jove of cable tv show *New Wave Theater* held cocaine-infused gatherings in the Fairfax District, and Beverly Hills socialite Electra played hostess in her living room. Nothing like seeing members of FEAR puking into a priceless antique chafing dish! Around noon I'd usually tire of the party and call a cab, paying for it with my Zero bartending tips: a Solo cup full of quarters, haphazardly stuffed into my purse.

After several busts and location changes, the Zero could no longer sustain itself. Eventually John Pochna transformed it into a legit art gallery.

If it weren't for Jeffrey Pierce, I'd never have been in bands. He practically *forced* Texacala of Tex and the Horseheads and me to be singers—in fact, he put together our bands for us. Tex's band lasted, but mine with Jeffrey didn't. We were The Cyclones. I wrote the lyrics, he wrote the music, and we rehearsed in Jeff's mom's living room. Jeff and Johnny Nation played guitar, Jon Oliphant was on bass, and Brad Dunning— also the original drummer for The Gun Club—played with us. Our first and only show was September 18, 1978, at Gazzarri's, opening for

The Go-Go's and The Last. We were all completely stinko—our set ended in an onstage fist fight that Jeff started. I ran off the stage when the audience joined in and equipment started getting thrown around. It was so "punk rock" that Black Flag asked us to open for them, but we never played again.

In 1982 I formed The Screaming Sirens. The concept for the band—the sound, look, and feel—came to me in a dream. After years of writing lyrics and The Cyclones debacle, I was *ready*. It had to be all girls, not only 'cause of my close association with The Runaways and The Go-Go's but also because I heard Andrews Sisters–like harmonies in my head. I envisioned a gang of female outlaws, equal parts Old West saloon girl and honky-tonk angel meets Hell's Angels, with a touch of Tura Satana thrown in.

The hardest member to find would be a female drummer—they were practically unheard of. I figured once I got that under control, finding other chicks would be easy. Bypassing the usual route of placing an ad in the *Recycler* (a newsprint equivalent of Craig's List) I preferred to find one on my own. But the only chick I could think of was Boom Boom Dixon, who played with rockabilly singer Keith Joe Dick. She was hella talented. The only problem was that I *detested* her . . . and the feeling was mutual. I'd seen her numerous times dead drunk getting thrown out of a club, struggling violently with a bouncer, cussing and screaming bloody murder—and she'd seen me in the same condition on several occasions too.

So I decided to ask her to join my band.

After circling around each other suspiciously, we realized we had much more in common than bar fights; soon we were inseparable. A couple of years, an album, an English single, some film soundtracks, and a few tours later, I asked her why she accepted my suggestion to meet about forming the band. She told me she thought it was so twisted that I had even called her, she just had to take me up on it.

The original lineup was Genny Body (of Backstage Pass) on guitar, Boom Boom, and her sister-in-law Fur Dixon, who left after a few months to join The Cramps. We rehearsed regularly, but we hadn't played out yet when my husband, Levi, gave me an ultimatum: it was him or the band.

Instantly I chose The Sirens and, to prove my point, ran off to San Francisco for a tryst with skater Steve Olson. Soon after, Enigma/Bemisbrain Records signed us. By this time Rosie Flores was playing guitar, Miiko Watanabe replaced Fur, and I'd stolen fiddler/rhythm guitarist Marsky Reins from The Radio Ranch Straight Shooters. We had a couple of tracks on the *Hell Comes to Your House II* compilation before recording our first album, *Fiesta!*, released in 1983.

The Sirens were known for being completely out of control on and off stage. The wild, hard-drinking female outlaw fantasy was now a reality: we played country music at punk speed on malfunctioning musical equipment amidst broken glass and home-wrecking, love-'em-and-leave-'em affairs. Band members changed constantly. For a while we borrowed Kathy Valentine from The Go-Go's, then Annette Zilinskas from The Bangs, and another time we had Jimmy and Marshall from Jimmy and the Mustangs play with us . . . in full drag. During shows we'd pull guys up from the audience and make out with them during our song "Love Slave." One of my specialties was biting all the buttons off their shirts with my teeth and spitting them out of my mouth like a machine gun. The Germs' drummer Don Bolles summed up our infamous reputation by dubbing us *The Semen Siphons*. During an evening of misbehavior at Cathay de Grande, Boom Boom and I were downing full bottles of beer in one gulp and smashing the empties against the wall. Michael caught us in the act, and even his louche sensibilities were offended—he banned both of us on the spot.

"You can't kick me out," I yelled. "I *work* here!"

He shot back, "You can come in during the day to book the bands, but you're 86'd after 7 P.M. for the next month!"

We were bad enough in L.A., but on the tour we were full-on *Spinal Tap*-style road pigs. We played every night and—if we were lucky—crashed at local punk houses. Though we couldn't afford motel rooms, people gave us copious amounts of drugs. The rules were that there had to be enough of the same substance for the entire band so we'd play as a cohesive unit. We traveled in an old Winnebago conversion van that lacked heat and air conditioning, so no matter the season, it was always uncomfortable. The ceiling was festooned with fishnet stockings, band stickers, Halloween decorations, and our own lipstick graffiti. The floor was awash with fast food wrappers, bondage belts, broken guitar strings, piles of cowboy boots, and empty bottles of Everclear, illegal in California but abundant (and super cheap) in the South. The windows were plastered with torn-apart Tampax boxes to block out the sun.

We toured constantly across North America, playing with everyone from The Ramones to Roseanne Cash; Social Distortion, T.S.O.L., The Sea Hags, and X to Nicolette Larson, Jason and the Scorchers, and Tammy Wynette. All of us had "a man in every port," and we toured often with our boyfriends' bands, mostly Texans. A couple of our favorites were Poison 13, a swamp blues/sludge rock band; The Reverend Horton Heat; and The Hickoids—so we played in Houston, Dallas, Austin, and San Antonio frequently. To the amazement of our roadie Jon Lee, we'd all start fixing our hair and applying our Wet N Wild lipstick as the van sped toward the city that every member of our band had taken to referring to as "Ahhhh-Ahhhh-Austin." After a particularly insane gig with The Hickoids and Daniel Johnston at a club called the Beach, we stayed to party until dawn. Hours later in New Mexico we made a pit stop. Our roadie arose from his makeshift bed atop our amps—to our surprise, he was joined by a sleepy blonde . . . who looked like she was about twelve. As she hopped out of the van in her bandanna-print square-dance dress, I had visions of being jailed for the Mann Act. When I discovered she was sixteen, I marched her to the phone booth, making her call her mom collect, informing her that we were delivering her daughter straight to the door.

On the first day of a 1986 US tour we'd pulled into the parking lot of the Mason Jar in Phoenix when a guy ran up to our van saying he was a huge fan. He'd found a credit card in the parking lot at the mall that afternoon and said he'd host an after-party for us. We adjourned to our van for a band meeting. Laura, who was an accountant by day, said that if the card was stolen, the cardholder would only be liable for $50, so we told the guy we'd love an after-party.

Later we found out that Gene Loves Jezebel were playing at a nearby college and staying at the Kon Tiki, the same motel we were at—all the bands stayed there. They were cute, and we wanted to meet them. The Hot Credit Card Guy had taken the room next to us and ordered

$194.25 worth of liquor and beer, a ton of money back then. We got lit and loud, so, naturally, the Gene Loves Jezebel guys came over. They looked enviously at the spread and asked what record company we were with, telling us their label never sprang for parties. When we told them it was a hot credit card from a stranger, they looked at us like, "American women are crazy," but we all got smashed. The next day the Hot Credit Card Guy filled up our van's tank, and we were off to the next adventure.

In 1986 I met TV director Max Tash. He was writing a film about an all-girl band and interviewing The Go-Go's, The Bangles, and The Sirens for details that would make the story ring true. After I took him to our gigs, suddenly we were cowriting the screenplay, The Runnin' Kind, named after one of our songs. Our office was in the Taft Building on Hollywood Boulevard, around the corner from the Zero. It took the better part of a year to finish the script; he raised money, and the shoot started. He was directing, The Sirens played The She-Devils, and all had speaking roles; the locations and extras were all culled from the local scene. A few of the principals were professional actors—it was Juliette Lewis's first film role—but many were local scenesters. Much of it was shot at Disgraceland, Raji's, Club Lingerie, and the Zero, featuring Fishbone, T.S.O.L., and Tex and the Horseheads playing live. Amazingly, The Runnin' Kind was picked up by MGM and was released theatrically and on VHS in 1988.

By 1987 I'd noticed a trend reminiscent of the last days of the Hollywood punk scene: once again our insular scene was being invaded, this time by hair metal. Sirens' Enigma/Bemisbrain label-mates Poison were at the forefront of this movement, along with Mötley Crüe and Guns N' Roses—all of whom were informed by The New York Dolls. We played lots of shows with Poison; they were fun and great in performance. Many bands who came after were derivative bar bands that came to Hollywood hoping that lipstick and teased hair would be their "big break." Nope! As a result, once again many women pulled out of the scene, this time not from violence but from the rampant sexism and misogyny.

Since 1985 Iris and I had already been devoting time to our literary side, and the Hair Metal invasion made us lean farther in that direction.

We'd formed a writing group made up of local lead singers that we called The Ringling Sisters, 'cause we all hated clowns. Texacala Jones, Debbie Patino of Raszebrae, Debbie Dexter of The Devil Squares, and Johnette Napolitano of Concrete Blonde were members. We also raised money for Hollygrove Orphanage by holding all-acoustic Holiday Fundraisers that started at Raji's, quickly moving to the thousand-seat Palace on Vine, and continued for over a decade. We had fabu artists like Babes in Toyland, Jim Carroll, Screamin' Jay Hawkins, and many more, including, sadly, The Gun Club's last show. Eventually The Ringling Sisters turned into a band, with Dave Catching (now of The Eagles of Death Metal), Larry Mullen, and Gary Dixon playing with us. We published chapbooks of our prose and poetry and performed shows with spoken word integrated. At the same time as The Screaming Sirens had a new album coming out, Lou Adler signed the Ringling Sisters to Ode Records, distributed by A&M. The Ringling Sisters played what we called "surf lounge" and was a balance to the hair metal stupidity taking over.

This time, watching my beloved eighties scene start to disintegrate, I wasn't distressed the way I was when the seventies punk scene splintered. Instead, I felt empowered and invincible, looking forward to creating all kinds of new music, art, and mayhem in the future.

LOS LOBOS:
LOS ROCKSTARS ACCIDENTALES

by Louie Pérez

I could feel the rush of air hit the stage from a thousand middle fingers shooting up at the same time. We hadn't even got to the middle of the first song when the entire audience went nuts and started throwing everything they could get their hands on. I don't recall exactly how long we played before stuff bigger than a breadbox started to fly and we got the hell out of there. I'll bet that Conrad still has about a buck fifty in change that flew into the sound hole of his guitarron.

It was May 4, 1980, and Los Lobos were booked at the Olympic Auditorium to open for Public Image Ltd., John Lydon's newly formed band, and we had just been unceremoniously fed to the lions.

It's probable that any other East Los Angeles Chicano band with the tiniest bit of dignity or any common sense would have retreated back to their safe bubble and resumed their routine of weekend gigs playing weddings and backyard *pachangas*. But this band—maybe out of pride or the pursuit of another adrenaline buzz—came back for more.

There is a need for clarification. Los Lobos were not the first band to cross the L.A. River to mix it up with the punk rockers and the swift-haired new wavers. There were The Undertakers, The Brat, Los Illegals, and at least a half dozen more. We just so happen to be the only ones who kept our old-school name.

Los Lobos formed in 1973 not from classified ads or from one guy's rock 'n' roll vision—even though Cesar and Frank Gonzalez did come up with the idea—but from the natural progression that transforms five high school buddies who happen to be musicians into a band. As the saying goes, if you hang around at a barber shop long enough, you'll eventually get a haircut. Cesar Rosas had an impressive R&B band, replete with a horn section and all of the rest of the necessary accoutrements. Conrad Lozano had a three-piece power trio that insisted on being louder than everything else, and David Hidalgo and I were content jamming with borrowed gear in the living room of his little house that was about the size of a box that cowboy boots come in. We'd been out of high school for a short while, living at home with nothing much to worry about, when Cesar began spending time at Frank's house playing guitars. He invited the rest of us over to join in. But what was different about what we were doing was that instead of learning and rehearsing the popular songs of the day, we made the decision to play the music that was not of our time, the traditional music of our mothers and fathers—a radical move for young kids in their late teens to make. In fact, kinda punk rock when you think of it.

We stashed the Fender guitars and Twin Reverb amps in the garage and went off in search of the instruments we saw on the covers of old Mexican records that we found in the back bins at local record stores and in our folks' collections. We found some in pawn shops, and for the ones we couldn't find, we repurposed stuff we had. It was when we set upon the task to learn the songs that we discovered it wasn't that easy. Here were a bunch of kids who thought they knew everything and sincerely believed that the entire world revolved around rock 'n' roll, sweating to make it to the end of a Son Jarocho. I think that was what attracted us: the challenge, the adventure, the excuse to hang in the backyard playing music with a cold six and a pound of string cheese from the Armenian deli down the street. Life was darn all right.

It was a typical warm sunny Los Angeles afternoon when we arrived at a local park for one of our first gigs. Moms and dads, grandmas and *tias* laid out blankets and set up lawn chairs picnic style on the grass that fine day. There were vendors rolling carts along the perimeter walkways, selling tamales and corn. There were two men, one carrying a stick tower of cotton candy and another with a pole covered with caramel apples, facing off as if they were about to have a wacky medieval joust. Little kids were running everywhere.

We unloaded the van and went about the business of setting up. Even with our *guayaberas* shirts and straw hats, we still looked like a rock band to most. When we broke into our premier tune, a Mexican *huapango* called "Mil Amores," we confused the shit out of everyone.

Some had been readying themselves to leave. They had already heard a couple of mariachi bands and maybe even an accordion or two, but now it was time to turn it over to the *chavalos* and their rock. They certainly didn't expect to hear traditional tunes being played by a group of long-haired hippie dudes, and those who were our age couldn't make heads or tails of it either. And so began a pattern of doing things slightly off center. Not for shock value or to get attention but simply because it felt like the right thing to do at the time. And it sure as heck wasn't a career move.

By 1978 we were known on the eastside as Los Lobos del Este de Los Angeles, a nod to our northern Mexican musical ancestors who chose to name their bands after wild animals and tropical storms. By 1980 we had shortened it to Los Lobos so it could easily roll off the tongue and fit on a marquee. We had already burned through a half-dozen years and developed a solid reputation on the eastside as a good band that could play anything, anywhere, and anytime. But as time passed and the complexities of life set in, we found ourselves stuck playing in a Mexican restaurant out of the need for a steady income to support our new families. Out of boredom, we began to sneak electric guitars and amps into our set and eventually got canned for playing "Wild Thing" way too loud.

Not long after that infamously messy night at the Olympic, Los Lobos crossed the L.A. River once again, this time to check out The Blasters live at the Whisky a Go Go. We had admired their first record, hearing something in it that resonated with us. Within the scene of mohawks and studded leather emerged a splinter group of bands who embraced the roots of American rock 'n' roll. Rockabilly, jump blues, and even country were being injected with the energy and rebel spirit that was the trademark of what was going on in the basement clubs in Hollywood. We thought there might be a place for our brand of roots in there somewhere.

After The Blasters' absolutely blistering set, we boldly made our way up the steps leading to the dressing room above the club, intent on introducing ourselves to the boys. "We're Los Lobos from East L.A." one of us announced. Phil Alvin, sweat still glistening on his face, stuck out his hand and said, "We're The Blasters, and we're from East L.A. too!" That sealed the deal. We talked until the club gorillas pushed us out at closing time and followed Phil and Dave back to their house in Downey, carrying on the conversation while listening to old 45s on one of those two-tone mono-record players and drinking cheap beer all night long.

The big coming-out day for Los Lobos was when The Blasters invited us to open for them at the Whisky a Go Go. The place was packed to the rafters. We were freaked out but dug in and let the adrenaline carry us through our thirty-minute set of Tex-Mex accordion tunes and bluesy rock 'n' roll played nervously faster than the legal speed limit. This time we weren't treated like spittoons, and there were no projectiles speeding in our direction. But I do remember a moment of hesitation, as if it took a second for the audience to digest what was happening. Then the applause came, which signaled our welcome into their scene.

That's when we really dug in. Hollywood became the new home for our crazy mix of Mexican Norteño, blues, vintage rock 'n' roll, and original songs modeled after all of the above. Again we found ourselves doing the irrational, passing on a good-paying wedding on the east side for a gig in a rogue basement club on Sunset Boulevard for fifty bucks, most of the time having to chase the promoter around the block to get paid.

We did it because there was something that felt good about it. There we were, part of a music community whose purpose was to free music from the kidnapping by mainstream rock. It was unabashed, liberating, and obnoxious. It was more about spirit than how good you played. I bet that some bands were formed in the van on the way to the show.

Above all, there was a camaraderie. I may be romancing it a bit, but there was a sense of union that went beyond the friendships we formed. We were all surviving, and the music we created, no matter how dissimilar, was like nutrition, the fuel that kept us all going and showing up at those dingy spaces that served as makeshift venues. There was absolutely nothing sexy about them, with their sticky floors, poor circulation, and bad lighting. The Cathay de Grande on the corner of Argyle and Selma Avenue in Hollywood was a popular one. Chinese restaurant by day and punk rock showroom by night, it was considered one of the craziest joints around. I remember one particular night when the place was so jammed that the audience had to pass the band's gear over their heads to the stage.

It seemed like we were playing almost every night of the week somewhere, and before long we had built a solid reputation and following. Whatever was so intriguing about this mixed-up band from East L.A., we were completely oblivious to. We were just riding the wave like any other band in that scene, playing just to play with no big rock 'n' roll dream.

I'd be lying if I said there wasn't a tiny bit of ambition, that somewhere stashed away was a glimmer of that rock dream. But at the moment we weren't investing too much into it. We were plain and simple, just having a great time with our new friends. Before long the local music critics started showing up at gigs, and cool things were written about us in the papers the next day, which led to interest from a few record company scouts. Most of them took a pass because they couldn't figure out into what niche to put these four brown dudes whose music was all over the place.

Bob Biggs, the chief at Slash Records, was one of them. I really don't think that any of the company reps hated us. In fact, they probably liked us but couldn't see us on their roster. Bob was the one who finally decided to take a chance. Of course, it didn't hurt that two of his bands, X and The Blasters, threatened him with bodily harm if he didn't.

We went into the studio in the fall of 1982 with T Bone Burnett to record a seven-song EP because the label didn't want to put up the full record budget for a band who had low odds of anyone paying attention. When *A Time to Dance* was released in the fall of 1983, we hit the road for the first time in an old fifteen-passenger van that caught fire during our initial swing through the Pacific Northwest. We finished the tour in a 1968 Pontiac Bonneville station wagon that we hired from Rent-a-Wreck. We got the van fixed, and off we went to tour the rest of the United States. We covered a lot of ground in the following few months and came to realize that it's unwise to put out a record in the fall because it's likely that you'll find yourself driving through frozen Iowa cornfields or playing Oslo, Norway, in January—unnatural for four kids from the West Coast. Like Cesar Rosas says even to this day: "In Southern California we keep our snow in the mountains."

We discovered a lot during those first trips out. The vast American landscape, the distinct seasons, the deep history that clearly make the West Coast the new kids on the block. But most of all we found that there is a lot more that makes us the same than makes us different. We never felt that we had to censor ourselves. We'd go up on stage in places like Burlington, Vermont, or Chapel Hill, North Carolina, and play exactly the same set that we would play in our neighborhoods. Music was the connective tissue that held us all together, despite geography or ethnicity.

The record began to percolate in the press. It was voted best EP of the year in *Village Voice*'s year-end poll. Influential music critic Robert Christgau gave it an A rating. *Rolling Stone* magazine, *Trouser Press*, and even *Melody Maker* and *New Music Express* in the UK raved about it. But the real kicker came when "Anselma," one of the Tex-Mex tracks, won the GRAMMY for Best Mexican American performance. Huh?! This little record was expected to maybe put a couple of smiles on faces and that was about it.

Once we got done touring our butts off, the pressure was on to make a new record. Slash Records had made a deal with Warner Bros. Records to distribute, the first time an indie punk label got mixed up with the big time. As a result of that deal, Warner brought us over to the new Slash/Warner Bros. Record Company, which was essentially Warner Bros. with a small Slash logo on the record label. We now had their attention, so they gave us the money to make a real record—no more fooling around. We went into the studio in early 1984 to cut our first full-length album, once again with T Bone Burnett and our newly minted band member, Steve Berlin, producing. *How Will the Wolf Survive?* was released later that year to great reviews, and by the end of 1984 we became *Rolling Stone*'s Band of the Year, tied with Bruce Springsteen's E Street Band.

All right, so what's going on here? We weren't exactly the savvy biz types who were determined to make it to the top, banging our fists on executives' desks or carrying on like we believed our own press. We were a band for eleven years before any of this happened. So in a way we had made the decision to become rock stars as adults and really didn't take anything that seriously.

We would attend meetings with the company's A&R staff and sales reps, listening quietly and respectfully as they presented their strategies and ideas about direction, and then we'd go off to do whatever the hell we wanted. It didn't hurt to have Lenny Waronker, veteran producer and company president, on our side. I think he recognized, like many others we encountered in the business, that we weren't a bunch of bull, that we really meant what we were doing and had the work ethic and commitment to make the music we wanted to make.

After "La Bamba" became a worldwide hit in 1987, Los Lobos, the accidental rock stars, walked into Lenny's office to discuss our next move. We presented him with a recording of us from the early years. He popped it into his machine and listened to us playing the music of our grandmothers and grandfathers, the music we still held close to our hearts. He looked up and said, "This is beautiful," and our response was, "We're glad you liked it. We want this to be our next record." I know it crossed his mind to say we were crazy to follow a triple-platinum-selling record with an album of Mexican songs, but what came out was, "You really want to do this, huh? Okay, go make your record, and I'll figure out the rest," which meant that he had to walk through the connecting door into Mo Ostin's office and tell the chairman of Warner Bros. Records that Los Lobos wanted to commit commercial suicide.

La Pistola y el Corazon came out in September 1988 to good reviews. (It took a bit for most reviewers to catch on.) The record went on to win a GRAMMY at the 1989 awards presentation and has become a favorite among fans and critics all over the world. We had taken the spotlight that we had from our huge commercial hit and refocused it on the regional Mexican music that intrigued us as young rock 'n' roll kids.

I have fond memories of those years in Hollywood. There were so many factors that it qualifies as one of those things that can never be repeated. The years 1980 to '87 served as an incubation period for a lot of bands. For us it was a new chapter.

Whenever I'm doing an interview or if I'm in front of a roomful of students I'm frequently asked what advice I would have for an aspiring musician. I tell them that I really don't know if there is a formula besides working hard at learning your instrument. But that there is one thing I do know, and that's to do it because you love it and for no other reason. And I add that if you want to play music because you want to be a rich rock star, you'll probably be disappointed, but if you do it because you love it, it will never let you down.

CHAPTER 13

TOP JIMMY: IN THE MUD AND THE BLOOD AND THE BEER

by John Doe

The best storytellers, the mythic characters, the ones who choose lifestyle over life always attract the dangerous, outlandish, and absurd adventures. Somehow events or drama seem to follow and find them on a weekly basis. And when that doesn't happen, they turn the mundane into something from a well-written short story.

You'd often hear Top Jimmy before you'd see him. His slight southern drawl cut through the cigarette smoke and whisky air like a fog horn. When you'd tell him to quiet down, he'd hunch up his shoulders with a kid-like grin and say *sshhh* with his finger to his lips. He'd go unshaven for weeks, then shave and look like a teenager. He told Ex-ene that his mom let him stay home from school the day a new Sam Cooke record came out. He said they went out and bought it and then listened to it all day. Jimmy's sister later told us that was totally untrue, but it was a great story. He'd hang around someone's house for days but always make a beautiful pot of chili or get up early to make bacon and eggs for everyone.

When a new story would happen he would tell it at least three times during the course of an evening. To the point of someone yell-ing, *Jimmy! You already told us!!* On one Greyhound bus ride from Las Vegas a woman asked Jimmy to hold her baby as she went to the bath-room. Almost immediately the baby began to cry, and everyone on the bus glared at Jimmy so he would quiet the kid. Of course he couldn't, and he would end the story with "What am I supposed to do? Throw the baby out the window?"

He married a gorgeous woman named Luci who looked like she could be a movie star. Somehow this didn't shock anyone because Jimmy had a way about him like a younger, handsomer Charles Bu-kowski. They were married in Tijuana, and all was well for a while. They both drank like their lives depended on it, and maybe they did. But one night it went very bad, and in an argument Luci threw a drink at Jimmy. It hit him square in the face, slicing a long piece of skin off the bridge of his nose. After a weirdly quiet but desperate call from Jimmy, Gil T raced over to find Luci crying hysterically, blood all over Jimmy and the wall where the glass had smashed. Luci and Jimmy split up soon after. Jimmy carried the scar for the rest of his life, and some-how this didn't surprise us that much either.

One day in Mount Washington, as I added to one of Jimmy's single-needle, stick & poke tattoos, he drank most of a fifth of I. W. Harper whiskey. It was a tedious process, over three hours, making a chain, an eight ball, and a cross. At one point he grabbed the toothbrush han-dle I'd inserted the needle into, proclaimed, "YOU WANNA KNOW WHAT THAT FEELS LIKE? IT FEELS LIKE THIS!" and he poked my forearm with it five times. It's probably my favorite tattoo.

CHAPTER 14

OUR WOLF

by Chris Morris

I have had my fun, if I never get well no more.

—"Goin' Down Slow," St. Louis Jimmy Oden,
recorded by Howlin' Wolf in 1961

It doesn't seem to matter what town you live in—there will always be a musical legend or two whose reputation will not travel outside the city limits. I will tell you the story of one such musician and his band, who played a big part in my life and the lives of many Los Angeles punk rockers. I figure that if I don't tell it, no one will hear it, and time will claim them all.

Of necessity I must speak here of the blues, how I came to know them, and where I found them in L.A. I first met them face to face as a Chicago teenager during the summer of 1968.

I was doing apprentice work in the publicity department of WTTW, the Windy City's public television station, via the good and nepotistic graces of my father, who was the program director. In that capacity he had created and produced *Our People*, the first weekly talk/variety show created expressly for the city's large black population.

One afternoon I was running an errand near the station's basement studios when I encountered an apparition. Down at the other end of the hall, near the canteen, stood a towering, coal-black man clad in crisp blue overalls and a brakeman's cap with upturned brim cocked atop his head. In my eyes he was nothing less than colossal. Though I had no idea who he was or what he did, he emanated power and authority. "What a spectacular-looking individual," I said to myself as I went back up to the press office.

An hour or two later I happened to be downstairs again. Passing by the larger studio, I heard an incredible syncopated racket that was loud enough to seep through thick soundproof doors. I quietly went into the control room, and peering past the board where the director sat, I saw the gigantic man I'd seen earlier hurling himself around behind a microphone, declaiming a raucous blues while blowing a gale through a harmonica he cupped like a toy in his huge paw as a band stomped and wailed behind him.

This, I would shortly learn from one of the crew on *Our People*, was the legendary Howlin' Wolf, the week's musical guest. I was agog.

I grew to love the blues, first via white practitioners like the Paul Butterfield Blues Band and the Siegel-Schwall Band and then through the original black musicians they covered and emulated. During my years as a late-night FM DJ in Madison, Wisconsin, I did a weekly Monday night blues show. Jim Schwall of the Siegel-Schwall band, who had relocated to Madison, became a drinking buddy.

During my radio tenure I became powerfully alienated from the standard rock gristle of the day—Fleetwood Mac, The Eagles, et al.— and began cocking an ear to the first recorded fruits of the New York punk scene. I relocated to Los Angeles on Good Friday of 1977, just as the local punk scene was beginning to go nuclear.

I soon discovered that some of the nascent punk types shared my bluesy orientation. My first friends in town were the editors and writers at *Back Door Man*, the proto-punk mag that had been founded two years before *Slash* hit the streets. This hip posse of knowledgeable musicians and record collectors—Phast Phreddie Patterson, Don Waller, Tom Gardner, and D. D. Faye—understood that The New York Dolls was at heart a mutant R&B band and that Iggy Pop had wanted to start a blues band before he ramped up The Stooges. They were my kind of people.

By 1980 Valley boy Jeffrey Lee Pierce had begun spinning his Delta blues fantasias in The Gun Club; the band's debut album *Fire of Love* would sport covers of Robert Johnson and Tommy Johnson songs. Then Pleasant Gehman and Anna Statman, who both worked part time at the film exhibition company that employed me, started raving about a new band from Downey that had just released a great album on the local rockabilly imprint Rollin' Rock Records.

That band was The Blasters, and from the first their sound extended well beyond ducktail bop into the blues of Junior Parker, Billy Boy Arnold, and my boyhood idol Magic Sam. Having learned at the feet of T-Bone Walker and Big Joe Turner, they were drinking deeply from the blues tributary, and their gutsy roots sound became part of the punk firmament.

I encountered the hero of my tale in 1979 or 1980, right around the time he was filmed by Penelope Spheeris as John Doe gave him a homemade skull-and-crossbones-and-ball-and-chain tattoo for her documentary *The Decline of Western Civilization*.

I don't clearly remember the first time I ran into James Paul Koncek, better known as Top Jimmy, but the earliest encounter I can recall involved his near arrest. I was walking up to the Starwood, local gangster Eddie Nash's big rock club at the corner of Santa Monica Boulevard and Crescent Heights, when I spotted some of the venue's staff in a heated colloquy with a couple of club patrons. Shortly an LAPD squad car disgorged a couple of uniformed cops, who tried to sort out the situation.

The miscreants were Top Jimmy and X's guitarist Billy Zoom, who had been escorted to the pavement after some kind of beef with security. A set-to with the hammerheads who worked at the Starwood was nothing out of the ordinary, but X happened to be *headlining the club* that night.

By the time of this street hassle Jimmy and Billy had known each other for nearly a decade. The pair had met not long after fifteen-year-old Jimmy had arrived in L.A. in November 1970 (on Friday the 13th, he would later recall) after serving a short jolt in juvenile hall for joyriding without a license in Tacoma, Washington, where his family had moved from Kentucky some years earlier. His mother had since relocated down the coast to L.A.

In X's early days Jimmy served as one of the band's roadies. It was not a full-time gig, and for some time he eked out a living slinging burritos at the Top Taco stand near Sunset and La Brea, across the street from what was then A&M Records' offices. There many a hungry punk rocker enjoyed Jimmy's under-the-counter largesse, and thus he acquired his enduring punk rock handle.

Unlike other pals and hangers-on who schlepped gear for the O.G. punk bands of the day, Jimmy possessed genuine talent of his own. His grandmother had operated a roadhouse in Kentucky, and he had been reared on the funky blues and R&B records stocked in her jukebox. He sported a singing voice of formidable power and could shout the blues with an authentic soulfulness rivaled only in the vocalizing of The Blasters' front man Phil Alvin.

The instant I heard it I recognized it as a voice I had heard before. Big, deep, raw, and thoroughly unmannered, it emanated from somewhere deep within him. I would always think of Top Jimmy as Los Angeles punk's equivalent of Howlin' Wolf. Our Wolf, if you will.

He started playing out in 1979. His first bands were makeshift affairs. Often billed as the All Drunk All Stars, the groups sometimes enlisted the members of X, but many other punk communards passed through his lineups as well.

In 1980 he was backed by the surviving members of The Doors—including X's producer, Ray Manzarek—singing "Roadhouse Blues" at the publication party for Danny Sugerman and Jerry Hopkins's Jim Morrison biography *No One Here Gets Out Alive* at the Whisky a Go Go. The song would become a cornerstone of his own sets and something like a personal credo:

Well, I woke up this morning, I got myself a beer.
I woke up this morning, I got myself a beer.
The future's uncertain and the end is always near.

The cat clearly had skills, and he possessed an outsized personal sweetness that ingratiated him to all within the L.A. punk community. But Top Jimmy might have become merely a dim footnote in punk rock history had he not acquired a full-time group potent enough to put across his sound and a regular gig that pushed that sound right up in L.A. punkdom's faces for most of the eighties. I came to think of Top Jimmy and the Rhythm Pigs as L.A. punk's house band.

The group began coming together in 1980 after Jimmy was introduced to a guitar player from Cypress Park named Carlos Ayala one night at the Hong Kong Café. Spinning dense Freddy King–inspired lines on a Stratocaster with heavy-gauge strings that resembled telephone cable, Carlos—soon notorious under the professional sobriquet Carlos Guitarlos—became the key component of Jimmy's new and permanent unit.

These two imposing, loud, heavy-drinking, and talented musicians were joined by a third impressive figure: the forceful bassist and East L.A. native Gil T, who was recruited after a Christmas Eve gig at the Hong Kong. Even bigger in girth than Jimmy and Carlos and just as inclined to a work-time-as-party-time ethic, Gil (né Isais) would serve as The Rhythm Pigs' good-humored peacekeeper for the duration of the band's longest-lived lineup.

The outfit was filled out by ex-Accelerators guitarist Dick Aeilts, aka Dig the Pig, on rhythm; drummer (and sometime harp player) Joey Morales; and saxophonist Steve Berlin, a peripatetic Philadelphia transplant whose long punk L.A. résumé at that point encompassed work with Beachy and the Beachnuts, Phast Phreddie & Thee Precisions, The Flesh Eaters, and The Plugz.

In 1981 Top Jimmy and the Rhythm Pigs completed the album that became the only recorded evidence of their long, demonic career, and it was only released six years after the fact.

The record, which became known as *Pigus Drunkus Maximus*, was produced by Steve Berlin. It was cut during four days of sessions, nearly all of which took place at a studio facility at Melrose and Heliotrope owned by Austrian director Rene Daalder, who was then in the final stages of plotting The Screamers' catastrophic July 1981 Whisky a Go Go multimedia extravaganza "Palace of Variety." In return for Berlin's musical services, Daalder gave The Rhythm Pigs comp studio time.

Recorded with DJ Bonebrake on drums (and Morales playing harp) and Gene Taylor of The Blasters guesting on piano, the majority of the material on the record would serve as the bedrock of The Rhythm Pigs' nearly immutable live sets deep into the decade. Carlos contributed the only original songs, the upbeat "Dance with Your Baby" (which name-checked John and Exene) and the slow blues "Hole in My Pocket"; his instrumental "Backroom Blues" was later supplanted on stage by his durable theme "Pigfoot Shuffle."

The remainder of the tunes were in a mélange of styles, but everything came out sounding like pure blues: Howlin' Wolf's "Do the Do" (a Willie Dixon composition) and Otis Rush's obscure single "Homework" were complemented by Bob Dylan's "Obviously Five Believers" and "Ballad of a Thin Man," Merle Haggard's "Workingman's Blues," Johnny Paycheck's "Eleven Months and Twenty-Nine Days," The Robins' "Framed," and, lo and behold, Jimi Hendrix's "Spanish Castle Magic."

Those and a handful of others were the tunes—songs of partying, poverty, alienation, incarceration, and busted romance—that Top Jimmy and the Rhythm Pigs would perform, week in and week out, after they secured a weekly gig on Blue Mondays at the Cathay de Grande circa August of 1981. It was a residency that stretched on for several years and proved unique in the annals of Hollywood punk.

Located at the northeast corner of Argyle and Selma in the grimy heart of yet-ungentrified eighties Hollywood, the Cathay was nearly the last of L.A. punk's storied holes-in-the-ground. Like the Hong

Kong Café and Madame Wong's downtown, it was a former Chinese restaurant that moved into its old-age catering to the punk trade.

The dive had two levels. The top floor sported a bar and dining area where people drank and kibitzed. Down a narrow flight of stairs, the basement was where the musical action happened. You would walk past a couple of aromatic bathrooms with perpetually overflowing toilets—some of the stoppage no doubt hastened by patrons who deposited their used syringes there—into a low, wide room with a small bar in the corner.

The stage, such as it was, rose maybe nine inches off the floor, which led at times to interesting interactions between the performers and members of the audience. The room was unmistakable in the many photographs shot there. The musicians' heads hovered inches below the room's derelict ceiling panels, which always appeared ready to crash down with the detonation of a power chord.

The joint was owned by an attorney named Michael Brennan. Tall, surly, and unhealthy looking, the saturnine Brennan bore a facial resemblance to the demented character actor Timothy Carey. There was never much love lost between Brennan and his unruly charges, but The Rhythm Pigs and their faithful fans adored the club's manager, Dobbs. Born Danny Wilson, Dobbs was funny, generous, and enthusiastic, where Brennan was angry, tight fisted, and morose. He called his friends and regulars "Bubba" and could be relied upon to pony up a free drink if you were tapped. Short, wide, stubbled, and balding, he was the soul of the Cathay's revels.

Though they continued to take jobs all over town, The Rhythm Pigs came to consider the Cathay de Grande their home, to an extent that proved surprising. One evening down at the club I asked Jimmy, who was always seemingly indigent, where he was living. "Oh, I live here, man," he said. I gaped at him in disbelief, and in response he withdrew his driver's license from his wallet. On it appeared the Cathay's address, 1600 Argyle Street.

By 1982 Jimmy and the Pigs were well installed on Mondays at the Cathay, and I became a regular, mingling with the band's mismatched audiences of old-school Hollywood punks, hardcore beach-punk invaders, weekend warriors extending their days off, curious straight people, the occasional celebrity, and a large contingent of drug dealers.

It was an infernal scene straight out of *Ulysses*'s Nighttown, and it quickly attracted the antipathy of neighborhood merchants and residents and the scrutiny of the *polizei*, who were called in to break up scrums between the Cathay patrons and the homeless who prowled the area. I learned with a measure of relief that The Pigs' wry, fierce roadie Tommy Pacheco packed a loaded shotgun at their gigs. (A Gary Leonard photo of a mirthful Tommy brandishing his firearm graced one of the monthly band flyers designed and hand-lettered by Carlos.)

Inside the club's walls things could get self-policing. Jimmy was a laid-back host, but he would bark and sometimes step right off the low stage into the crowd if someone got up in his face. Carlos—who was truculent, physically strong, and frequently deranged—would sometimes take matters into his own hands, and on more than one occasion I saw him drop somebody with a single punch. (Steve Berlin told me that during a showcase gig at the Roxy on the Strip Carlos flew into an uncontrollable rage and chased him out of the dressing room brandishing *a coffee table.*)

Though things could get aberrant, the action was mainly easy on Blue Mondays. Top Jimmy and the Rhythm Pigs were at heart a dance band, and people came out to shake off the early-week blues. The group drew a hard-drinking crowd, and they matched their audience beer for beer and shot for shot. This sometimes had an impact on Jimmy's ability to perform, when he would sit down drunkenly on the edge of the stage, and I, in my capacity as mascot, would be beckoned to sing Elmore James's "Something Inside Me" or fill in on "Who Do You Love."

During The Pigs' Cathay residence, guests far more famous than myself would front the group for a song or two. Jimmy's best-known fan was, of course, David Lee Roth of Van Halen. The antic vocalist of the hugely successful metal band had gotten to know Jimmy and Carlos in their respective roles of bartender (pushing white-label generic beer) and bouncer at the Zero Zero Club, the weekend punk after-hours joint that held sway in a big dim space on Cahuenga in the early eighties. He later famously celebrated The Rhythm Pigs on "Top Jimmy," a number from Van Halen's *1984*, which shifted ten million copies during its titular year of release. The song proved to be the band's greatest claim to fame.

Roth may have proclaimed Top Jimmy "the King" in his tune, but by 1985 he was minus a throne. Under siege by the police and enraged neighbors, Michael Brennan decided to shutter the Cathay de Grande. He bluntly told the *Los Angeles Times*, "I decided the hassles weren't worth it anymore. The place is a goner."

However, Brennan's aide, Dobbs, moved in to fill the need for a rock 'n' roll toilet in central Hollywood by securing a silent partner's backing and opening Raji's a few blocks up the street. Located on the site of the earlier hangout King's Palace in the ancient Hastings Hotel, it was the final home for the city's first-generation punk gypsies; it ultimately gave up its ground to the Metro Rail's Hollywood and Vine subway station. The club became infamous enough to be featured in Elmore Leonard's novel *Get Shorty*.

For a time, under Dobbs's auspices, The Rhythm Pigs continued to percolate on Mondays at Raji's, and occasionally word of the band inexplicably clambered up out of the underground. In 1986 their name became the punchline of a gag in an episode of Lucille Ball's short-lived network comedy series *Life with Lucy*.

Then, in 1987, *Pigus Drunkus Maximus* finally surfaced, via the good graces of Steve Wynn, the lead singer and guitarist of The Dream Syndicate and a major Rhythm Pigs fan, who secured the rights to release the long-shelved LP and issued it on his Down There imprint, which was distributed by the prolific L.A. indie label Enigma Records. The album was a suitably smoking document of one of L.A. punk's most formidable live bands. But by the time it was released, the group heard in its grooves was essentially history.

By the late eighties Top Jimmy was a beloved institution among club warriors, but his band was inevitably destined for local-hero status. The Pigs sported none of the necessities for longevity in the music world: they never rehearsed, they had no personal discipline, they wrote no new material, and they were all boozers and carousers. They didn't give a damn.

The first to depart the fold had been Steve Berlin, who was long gone by the time the record he produced finally reached the street. After splitting his time between The Blasters and Los Lobos, he became a full-time member of the East L.A. group in 1983, coproducing their early records with T Bone Burnett.

Gil T's involvement—which was discontinuous between 1982 and 1984, owing to a serious motorcycle accident—ultimately ended in 1986 when, with some exasperation, he left The Rhythm Pigs to join The Allnighters, the band Dave Alvin formed after leaving The Blasters. Gil, who today resides in Austin, Texas, says of The Rhythm Pigs, "We were the most famous band that never did nothin'."

The final nail in The Pigs' coffin was the exit of Carlos Guitarlos. In 1988 the increasingly erratic guitarist bolted the band to follow his estranged wife and young daughter to San Francisco. His problems, exacerbated by an undiagnosed case of diabetes, deepened in the Bay Area, and he ultimately wound up homeless in the city's Mission District, playing for change on the streets.

Carlos returned to town in 2003, somewhat mellowed by adversity, and released his first solo album. Many of his old friends and adversaries were astonished when the *Los Angeles Times* ran a page-one story about his travails and his uneasy rehabilitation.

Some in The Rhythm Pigs' orbit were not as fortunate as Carlos, and their lives played out like blues songs.

The band's first manager acquired AIDS from a dirty needle and died in the mid-eighties. After years of clean living in Florida, Jimmy's ex-wife Luci succumbed to a drug overdose in 2014. Perhaps saddest of all was the demise of Dobbs: following the closure of Raji's and a sports bar he operated, he, like Carlos, became homeless. I would see him regularly in Hollywood, usually not far from the sites of the clubs he had run, and I would always give him a handout and some smokes. He died in 2010.

Before his own fortunes went south, Dobbs attempted to help out his best-known former charge. In 1997 he put together the money to start a humble indie label, T.O.N. Records, and released "The Good Times Are Killing Me," the aptly titled final recording by Top Jimmy.

Jimmy had abandoned L.A. in 1993, moving to Las Vegas to care for an ailing sister. He never disappeared from the L.A. scene; during the nineties he commuted from Nevada to play gigs in Long Beach. By most reports he was crashing around, couch surfing in Huntington Beach.

He was going down slow. He had been a heavy drinker for years, and his drug habits contributed to a case of hepatitis. (At a screening of a 2011 documentary about Thelonious Monster's lead singer Bob Forrest, I was startled by a clay-animation sequence that depicted Jimmy giving Forrest his introductory shot of heroin.) The last time I spoke to Jimmy on the phone he said his doctor had told him that if he didn't stop drinking, he wasn't going to live long.

In May 2001 his liver gave out, and he died in Vegas at the age of forty-six.

Please write my mother, tell her the shape I'm in.
Tell her to pray for me, forgive me for my sin.

CHAPTER 15

GRAND THEFT PAPER: A CONVERSATION WITH BILLY ZOOM

by John Doe

While on tour with X, Billy Zoom and I sat down to talk about his influence, insanity, and how lucky we were to cross paths with the one and only Top Jimmy: the leader of the notorious Rhythm Pigs, and the man who brought authentic and psychotic rhythm and blues into punk rock like no one before or since.

ZOOM: In 1968 in Tacoma, which was where he was from, fourteen-year-old Top Jimmy decided to take his friend for a ride in his grandmother's Chrysler. They started cruising around the Tacoma/Seattle area and the cops tried to pull them over, so they decided to outrun the cops. As Jimmy always said, you can outrun the cop but you can't outrun his radio. It turned into a big police chase, during which three police cars were wrecked and two were totaled. At his trial they made a big deal about the cost to the community, and so, at fourteen, he was sent to juvenile hall. While he was in juvie his mother and his two sisters moved to Hollywood. When Jimmy got out he flew down to Hollywood and went to Hollywood High, where he started dealing pot. He was fifteen then. When I met him he had just gotten to L.A. and was living in an apartment a couple of blocks from Top Taco with his mother and two sisters and niece and nephew. He was kind of lonesome. He was this red-faced fat kid. Having been a fat kid myself, I kind of had empathy for him. Jimmy would come by after school and hang out because he didn't have any friends and didn't know anybody. At some point I got invited to Jimmy's house for dinner, and the first thing I noticed was that in his bedroom the only records he had were like the James Gang and other crap like that.

DOE: Like Lynyrd Skynyrd?

ZOOM: No, it wasn't even that cool. [Laughs] I felt sorry for him. So I told him he couldn't listen to that music anymore and I was going to get him some good music to listen to. I started playing him a little bit of everything. Ray Charles, Gene Vincent, Chuck Berry. Country, R&B, rockabilly, rock 'n' roll—stuff I listened to.

DOE: What was his reaction to it?

ZOOM: He seemed to take to it, although I think he secretly still listened to Lynyrd Skynyrd.

DOE: When did you first realize he could sing? Or did you?

ZOOM: He used to tag along with us. When I was in that band The Alligators, in '71–73, he was our roadie. He's the only guy I've ever seen fall *up* a flight of stairs carrying a PA cabinet. But he landed on his back, holding it up above him and smiling because he didn't drop the cabinet. He used to get up and sing with us. He'd usually sing "Leopard Skin Pillbox Hat" at every show. I don't know why he picked that one. I told him he could sit in anytime he wanted. You have to remember we were playing five-hour gigs.

DOE: You also told me a story about him on his motor scooter.

ZOOM: Jimmy had a Honda 50. Jimmy was a big kid, and he was on this little tiny Honda step-through. He was working at the Top Taco stand by then. He hung out so much that the owner eventually gave him a job. That's how he became Top Jimmy. He was Top Taco Jimmy. They had this Orange Bang machine, which was like Orange Julius with orange frothy stuff swirling around. We used to make screwdrivers with it; it was a regular thing. One day he was working there, and he had a bottle of vodka. He was going to save it for later, but then he decided to have a drink while he was there. He was finishing up at work, and he had this almost full but open bottle of vodka. He was coming over to my house right after work, which was about four blocks away. I talked to him on the phone, and he said, "I'll be right over." So he decided rather than riding with an open container of vodka, because he was underage, he would drink it all there, and then if he drove straight to my house, he would be at my house before it really hit him.

DOE: And this was a fifth of vodka?

ZOOM: Yeah. But you gotta remember the way Jimmy explains these things it makes sense. It seemed so logical. So he chugged the bottle of vodka and locked up, but this guy Kim came by and started talking to him about his new motorcycle and they hung out for a while and BSed for about twenty minutes. Then Kim left, and Jimmy had to ride his Honda 50 to my house. Of course by that point he was pretty inebriated. My house was on the second floor, and I had a balcony. There's a traffic light that I could see from the balcony. I was sitting on the balcony waiting for Jimmy, and I saw him pull up to the red light. I could see him sitting there on his Honda 50. There was a cop car right behind him at the light. Jimmy was trying to stay as upright as possible and look really straight, and the light turned green and he gave it some gas and lifted his foot up off the ground, and it was in neutral. In sort of slow motion Jimmy and the bike fell over to the left, and he landed on the ground but he was too drunk to get the bike back up. He tried to play it off, but he couldn't stand up, so they took him to jail for that. That was just one of many times. He beat a lot of DUIs by refusing to take a breathalyzer test because he didn't trust them, saying he wanted a proper blood test, so they took him to the jail. Then the nurse in jail couldn't find a vein, so he made a big fuss and they ended up taking him to the emergency room and he had to sit there for an hour and a half. By the time they took the blood he had sobered up enough to just barely pass it.

DOE: I was talking to Gil T about Jimmy because he stayed in Gil's garage quite a bit. Of course Gil's mom was a big softy, and she took to Jimmy because he always wanted to be mothered. Gil said Jimmy was just like a big house cat.

ZOOM: I was like his dad. I was always telling him to get off his ass and do this and do that. Trying to give him advice to keep him sort of on the right road. I guess I didn't do very well.

DOE: Well, you did the best you could. You got him to be in a band.

ZOOM: Yeah, I did.

DOE: You remember the time he took the elephant tranquilizers and fell asleep on his arm so his arm didn't work for about two months?

ZOOM: Yeah, I remember that. He got those from a guy who later got killed in a drug deal. Jimmy was one of the funniest people I've ever met in my life. He was really smart. He was a lot of fun to be with, but there was that sad thing that he was trying to destroy himself all the time.

DOE: Was it the way he could tell a story?

ZOOM: He was just so good at it. He would tell you the most ridiculous thing and make it sound like it made sense. It was hilarious, and you kind of wanted to do it too.

DOE: What do you think it was that attracted all the bizarre occurrences to him? Crazy shit would happen, and it always seemed to happen to him.

ZOOM: He was walking down Fountain about two blocks from my house one afternoon, and cop cars came from all directions and surrounded him and got him on the ground. They were looking for some bad guy, and the only description they had was it was a white guy wearing blue jeans and a red shirt. And he just happened to be walking down the street wearing blue jeans and a red shirt. They were really mean to him. Turns out he had a bag of whites in his pocket, so they found that. So then he went to jail. I watched that from my balcony too.

DOE: He had this ability to just attract insane stuff. There was a part of him that was pretty fearless. He would just kind of go off and do things. He had a big mouth. I remember that time that he got stabbed.

ZOOM: Yeah, behind the rehearsal studio. I think it was at Mars Rehearsal Studios. He walked in the alley out in back and got into some kind of altercation, and he got stabbed.

DOE: The way I remember it was classic Jimmy. Someone had said there were a couple guys in the alley with some pills or something. Jimmy said he'd go out and check it out. Then in ten minutes or so he came back in looking a little pale but otherwise normal and said, "I think I just got stabbed." He lifted his shirt and sure enough on the side [of] his gut there was a two-inch knife wound. Everyone freaked out—everyone except Jimmy. So after a bunch of arm waving Exene & I drive him to the emergency room to find out it had missed his spleen or liver by a quarter of an inch. Boy, did he tell and retell that story. But Jimmy would mouth off to anybody and everybody. Telling them what to do, what not to do, and how fucked up they were, but he didn't really get into that many fights.

ZOOM: Well, he got stabbed and got arrested a lot.

DOE: What else did he get arrested for?

ZOOM: There was some article in the *L.A. Times* about me, pre-X. They used to have those vending machines on the sidewalk in front of Denny's where you could put in a quarter, lift the cover up, and then take a paper. He did that because he wanted to get the article. It stole his quarter and wouldn't open, so he got mad and hit it really hard, and it popped open. He decided he may as well take five papers so he could bring me a couple. A cop saw him do that, and they arrested him for Grand Theft Paper.

DOE: I'm sure that's what he called it. [Laughs] Grand theft has to be over like $500 or something.

ZOOM: Yeah, well, they made a big deal out of it.

DOE: That's so Jimmy, to find a title for it.

ZOOM: "They got me for Grand Theft Paper!"

CHAPTER 16

PREP SCHOOL CONFIDENTIAL: FINDING MY VOICE

by Shepard Fairey

Punk rock and skateboarding saved my life. Maybe not literally, but growing up in conservative Charleston, South Carolina, in the 1980s, attending a private prep school, I was miserable, mean, desperate, and about to blow. Then I discovered skateboarding and its partner in visceral rebellion, punk rock. Contrary to the common belief that punk amplifies angry feelings and leads to aggressive and antisocial behavior, it actually diffused those feelings in me, or at least channeled them in more constructive ways. I felt unhappy, isolated, a lone secret dissenter in my prep school until I found my muse in punk and my tribe in its devotees. With punk in my life, the preps, jocks, nerds, etc. seemed like mere cretins in the rearview rather than my torturers or captors. Punk rock liberated me mentally and helped me find my voice and confidence. I liked art as a kid, but until I got into punk, art was simply a tame and traditional technical exercise. Punk had a very democratic, unintimidating, visual language and opened my eyes to the do-it-your-self empowerment potential of art. I wasn't intentionally seeking out L.A.-area punk—in fact, I was open to ANY punk I could get my hands on—but I think largely because the L.A. punk scene and skateboard scene were so intertwined, I ended up loving a lot of the L.A.-area bands, and they had a tremendous influence on the development of my art, ideas, and methodology. There is no question that I wouldn't be the same person without punk, and bits of inspiration from L.A. punk can be found in my art and design from throughout my career.

I'm from South Carolina and born in 1970, so I completely missed the NYC and UK punk movements because I was too young and clue-less. Living in the cultural vacuum of Charleston, to access any edgy music you had to be clued in to subculture, which I wasn't! I'm proud to say that my taste wasn't all bad, because even listening only to pop radio, I gravitated to music that crossed over to pop but had roots in L.A. punk. I loved The Go-Go's and Joan Jett and bought their records long before I had any idea that they were part of early L.A. punk. I remember how LOUD Joan Jett's "I Love Rock 'n' Roll" was pressed. We had a pretty low-fi turntable and speakers, so I was thrilled that I could blast that record. My parents complained, but they had no idea of the "abrasive ruckus" that was on the horizon. The first punk mu-sic I consciously understood as genuinely antagonistic and counter to the mainstream was The Alternative Tentacles' compilation *Let Them Eat Jellybeans*, which featured mostly California punk and experimen-tal music like Flipper, The Offs, Dead Kennedys, Black Flag, and The Circle Jerks. It was 1983, and my good friend Chris's uncle, who was only eight or nine years older than us, left the *Let Them Eat Jellybeans* cassette sitting around the house. Chris's uncle was kind of a danger-ous mythical figure who was old enough to drink beer and date girls but young enough to let us in on some adult taboo stuff. I wanted to seem cool enough to like the music on *Let Them Eat Jellybeans*, but I wasn't ready for it other than as a novelty that served as parental Kryptonite. Chris and I would gleefully blast that album, knowing the noise would irritate everyone within earshot, so our enjoyment came more from mischief than an appreciation of the songs. Regardless, I liked Flipper's "Ha Ha Ha," Black Flag's "Police Story," and The Dead Kennedys' "Nazi Punks Fuck Off" enough to be tentative but curious. I didn't skateboard yet, so I didn't have a Pavlovian, euphoric association between fast, aggressive skateboarding and fast, aggressive music yet, but that was about to change.

My friend Chris, the same one with the cool uncle, also had a skateboard. At the end of 1983 Chris left his Santa Cruz Duane Peters model at my house, and I started messing around with it in my driveway. I loved the exhilarating solo progression, with no sports team dynamics to worry about. My fourteenth birthday was approaching, so I let my parents know I wanted a skateboard, a request that was met with frowns and wrinkled brows. My dad's coworker had an older skate-punk son who was a weed-smoking dropout. My parents warned me I was going down a dangerous path and insisted I earn half the money to pay for the skateboard, figuring I'd never earn the $60 needed in a month. I mowed lawns etc. and came up with my half of the dough, so they kept their side of the bargain. February 15, 1984, my mom drove me to the surf/skate shop thirty minutes from our house to get my first real skateboard. While I was assembling my first board, in a serendipitous coincidence that now feels like fate, the shop was simultaneously unpacking and putting in the VCR *Skatevisions*, one of the earliest skateboard videos, which was soundtracked entirely by the band Agent Orange. The excitement of setting up my first board coupled with the sounds and sights of *Skatevisions* was a sensory overload and an epiphany: I was not going to be the same person from that moment on. My life before that day was B.S. (before skateboarding), and I was through with that meek, uncool version of myself. Now I just needed to get some music by Agent Orange, which I'd decided would be the soundtrack to my new life. I called a few of Charleston's record stores, but no one had Agent Orange. My parents got curious about this band whose records were elusive, and I said, "Uh, Agent Orange, they're a new wave band." If I had said the word "punk," my folks might have banned Agent Orange, so I side-stepped that debate. Since I couldn't find an actual Agent Orange album anywhere in Charleston, I rented *Skatevisions* and recorded the Agent Orange audio from the skate video. I related to the lyrics of dystopian songs like "Living in Darkness" and "Everything Turns Grey." The energy Agent Orange transmitted infected me, and I was on a mission to find more punk, like an addict needing a fix.

I found another kid at my school who liked punk, and he told me that if I brought him a blank tape, he'd tape me The Circle Jerks' *Golden Shower of Hits* album. I loved the music from the moment I put the album on. The opening track, "In Your Eyes," was a blisteringly fast but catchy screed about lies and alibis. "Coup d'État" had great musical tension and an infectious, insurgent chorus. "Product of My Environment" fueled my disdain for private school. Basically, I felt like the *Golden Shower of Hits* album was written for me.

Another L.A. punk record that ended up in my collection early on was the first Suicidal Tendencies album. I first heard about Suicidal while reading an interview with skateboarder Corey O'Brien. He referenced Suicidal as a "punk" band he liked, along with others like Black Flag, The Dead Kennedys, and Bad Brains. I also noticed that Gator wore a Suicidal hat in the *Skatevisions* video. With Suicidal Tendencies it was a case of "one person's trash is another's treasure," because my friend John Reigart had been given a copy of the first Suicidal record by a BMX'er neighbor who claimed the record was "that punk shit" instead of the heavy metal he'd been promised. When I first heard Suicidal, I was attracted and repelled at the same time. The music was pretty hard and abrasive, with some dirgy metal-influenced moments that I was scared might not suit my "punk" self-image. However, after playing the album a few times, mostly to try to repel some rednecks congregated near a ramp I was riding, I began to love it. The music was heavy and energetic. The lyrics like "I'm not anti-society, society's anti-me" or "Mind control, the easiest way, sponsored by the C.I.A., it's a weapon you cannot see, it's propaganda subliminally" (from the song "Subliminal," which inspired the name of our art gallery, Subliminal

Projects), and "No mom, I'm not on drugs, I'm OK, I was just thinking, why don't you get me a Pepsi" were very provocative to me, as I was just starting to question authority and develop a sense of personal and world politics. In addition to digging the music on the album, I was mesmerized by the artwork on the sleeve. The Suicidal Tendencies' type treatment is iconic and has an aggressive barbed look to fit the music. There was also a disturbing photo of the band hanging upside down from a jungle gym at dusk. My favorite aspect of the sleeve was the many photos of hand-drawn shirts that used variations of the Suicidal type and skull iconography. The anonymous creators of the shirts seemed like a dangerous secret society of outsiders I wanted to be a part of. The closest I could come to joining the Suicidal army was listening to the album obsessively and making my own Suicidal tee on top of a turquoise tee with a wave and palm tree that my parents brought me from Hawaii. In those days hip threads were hard to come by, so I ended up making a lot of my own T-shirts, influenced by the handmade fashions of punk. One day, when I wore my homemade Suicidal tee to school, I was pulled into the guidance counselor's office to discuss my "suicidal tendencies." The guidance counselor saw the shirt as a cry for help, but I explained it was a band and that I was no more maladjusted than any other teenager whose parents just don't understand.

I discovered that the image on the Suicidal cover of the band hanging upside down was by photographer Glen E. Friedman, who also shot The Circle Jerks' *Golden Shower of Hits* cover of gold records in a urinal being pissed on. I did not know this at the time, but Glen also commissioned Suicidal's other iconic tee and sticker graphics from Lance Mountain, who drew the skull with the bill flipped up and the skeleton skating a drained pool. I loved those images, and the punk/skate crossover made me want to one day create art that would become known symbols in those cultures. Suicidal had a very recognizable visual language to their art and graphics, which made me think about the importance of a cohesive style or look.

One of the next L.A. bands I discovered probably made the biggest impact on me in terms of the intensity of their music, lyrics, art, and DIY ethos. Black Flag scared me but also transfixed me. I had decided to revisit the *Let Them Eat Jellybeans* comp, which featured Black Flag's

"Police Story," and the anti-authority hostility in that song electrified every hair on my body. The lyrics "This fuckin' city is run by pigs . . . they take the rights away from all the kids" hit home with me because the cops were already hassling me for skateboarding. I probably owe a big chunk of credit to that song for inspiring me to make my first "art" screen print (a print on paper rather than just on a T-shirt). That print featured a kid holding a skateboard being grabbed by a cop. The version I made for a sticker and a T-shirt included the text in Old English "Prevent police boredom . . . skateboard." My art teacher told me to leave the text off of the print on paper, which I later realized was shitty advice. "Police Story" made me want more music by Black Flag, and a friend loaned me their *Damaged* album. The *Damaged* cover was a dark and menacing Ed Colver photo of vocalist Henry Rollins with his knuckles bleeding after punching a mirror, which has shattered, and the cracks fragment the reflection of Henry's face and shaved head. The bold Black Flag type, staggered bars logo, and "Damaged" text are all in red. Black and red were used in all three of the L.A. punk album covers I had, but the *Damaged* cover and back cover, with its high-contrast shattered glass and red type, stuck with me as a very powerful color combination . . . a color combination I would later employ for the majority of my artwork. To skip around chronologically for a moment, several of my other favorite L.A. punk albums used red, white, and black as their color schemes, including X's *Los Angeles*, FEAR's *The Record*, and Youth Brigade's *Sound and Fury*. Those were all albums I picked up fairly early on and, noticing the prevalence of the black-and-red color combo, started considering not only the visual power of those colors but also the likely economic benefit of printing with only two spot colors. *Slash* magazine also printed early issues featuring Alice Bag, Debbie Harry, and Johnny Rotten on off-white newsprint with just black and red ink. When I later fell in love with Russian propaganda art and realized that Kinko's copy center had machines with a black toner cartridge and a red toner cartridge, the punk cost-saving technique of black and red printing re-entered my consciousness, and I decided to make my extreme financial limitations an asset rather than a liability. Using only red and black became a way for me to keep costs down and make my art cohesive in an intentional and disciplined way.

Back to Black Flag's *Damaged*. The first three songs on the album are probably my favorite opening three-song sequence of all time. The album starts with "Rise Above," which is a musical and lyrical powerhouse! The lyrics of that song, like "Jealous cowards try to control . . . RISE ABOVE we're gonna RISE ABOVE!, they distort what we say, try and stop what we do, because they can't do it themselves . . . RISE ABOVE we're gonna RISE ABOVE!" became the closest thing to a manifesto I had ever embraced. I have frequently used and continue to use RISE ABOVE as text in my art. The next song, "Spray Paint," is a thirty-four-second explosion of feedback and distortion with the lyrics "It feels good to say what I want . . . it feels good to knock things down . . . it feels good to see the disgust in their eyes . . . it feels good I'm gonna go wild . . . SPRAY PAINT THE WALLS." Skateboarding gave me an adrenaline-fueled outlet for my frustrations, but the song "Spray Paint" planted the seed that running around late at night with a spray can be an equally liberating and exhilarating pursuit. Since then I have tested and validated that theory more times than I can count. Track three on *Damaged* is "Six Pack," which starts with an ominous rumbling bass line and builds to a squall of guitar and a vocal that critiques the singer/protagonist's pathetic justification for drinking the pain away while exacerbating his troubles. A lot of Black Flag's *Damaged* is heavy musically and emotionally, but there are moments of levity and satire, like the song "TV Party," which pokes fun at creatively deficient people who can't survive without inane TV programs to occupy them. "TV Party" was used to great effect in Alex Cox's movie *Repo Man*, an important L.A. movie for me as an L.A. scene outsider, which I'll discuss more later.

Damaged was such an intense force that I made an effort to find anything else by Black Flag that I could. I soon realized that almost all the other Black Flag albums, EPs, and singles had art by Raymond Pettibon, the brother of Black Flag founder Greg Ginn. Pettibon's artwork on the Black Flag records and flyers took comic-style illustration in a dark and ominous, anti-authoritarian direction with a subversive sense of humor. I was disturbed but seduced by Pettibon's art, and there was no doubt that his art gave Black Flag a unique and cohesive story with many pages. Pettibon was incredibly prolific with his black ink drawings, which provided a wealth of material easily adapted for Black Flag's photocopied flyers that were needed very frequently due to their heavy touring schedule. Black Flag's imagery was instantly recognizable, provocative, and widely disseminated. I read some of Henry Rollins's stories about Black Flag doing graffiti of their logo and pasting up show flyers many late nights, and their success through diligent self-promotion and a serious work ethic stuck with me. I have taken inspiration from Black Flag in many ways, but their willingness to promote their art and get themselves and their music in front of people by any means necessary played a big role in catalyzing my mission of driving all over the East Coast with a load of posters and stickers, sometimes sleeping in my car. I realized that poverty is not something to be ashamed of when I had uncompromising art output to be proud of. Black Flag set the bar very high with their Spartan work ethic and discipline. Still, to this day I'm in awe of the amount of rigorous effort Rollins puts into everything he does. Reading interviews with Rollins in the Black Flag days made me want to be outspoken, courageous, and articulate, but Henry has only become more politically astute and effective as a communicator in the ensuing years. Black Flag's Greg Ginn also started SST Records, originally putting out Black Flag's music but quickly expanding to release records by local L.A. and national acts who were unlikely to get mainstream distribution. SST put out great records by The Minutemen, Hüsker Dü, Bad Brains, Sonic Youth, and Dinosaur Jr., among others. Even though I now know that SST was accused of underpaying royalties, during its heyday the label came across as an artist-run, artist-friendly incubator that was the perfect example of creating an alternative ecosystem to promote and support nonmainstream artists of merit and integrity. In the mid-nineties I saw many parallels between the SST family and an art collective called the Visual Mafia that I was a loose part of. The Visual Mafia put together many DIY art shows, with the members providing art and various other resources to make things happen. I frequently screen printed flyers, posters, and stickers for events. A crossover I pointed out, even at the time, was that I was printing stickers for Sonic Youth, and their members Kim Gordon and Thurston Moore would often attend Visual Mafia events at the Alleged Gallery and other venues. SST, along with other L.A. independent labels like Slash, Frontier, Posh Boy, B.Y.O., and Dangerhouse, provided a template for how to make things happen with and for like-minded peers! To make an analogy, I saw street art as a means of self-distribution, bypassing the major labels—in the case of my world, the major labels being the galleries. By starting my own printing studio, I built my version of my own record-pressing plant. Not only did I print and disseminate my own art, but I also helped other artists and musicians produce their works too. I even placed my earliest ads for people to send a self-addressed-and-stamped envelope for stickers and my "manifesto" in *Flipside* punk magazine. The model of successful independent punk labels gave me the courage to bypass the usual gatekeepers.

Since I didn't grow up in Los Angeles, my understanding of the L.A. scene was through articles in *Thrasher*, liner notes in albums, and a couple of movies. I turned on HBO in late 1984 or early 1985 and heard The Circle Jerks "Coup d'État" playing as a crowd of punks slam-danced. The movie was Alex Cox's movie *Repo Man*, and it had a sly sense of humor and a great soundtrack. The Circle Jerks had a couple of songs on it, and the *Repo Man* logo was clearly inspired by The Circle Jerks' logo. Other bands featured were Suicidal Tendencies, Black Flag, FEAR, Burning Sensations, and The Plugz. I loved Iggy Pop's "Repo Man Theme," which I only later realized was played by a band including Steve Jones, formerly of The Sex Pistols, and Clem Burke from Blondie. *Repo Man* as a soundtrack celebrates punk, but the movie itself is a bit more ambiguous, making punk look rebel cool in some scenes and then making fun of it in others. One thing I gleaned from the flippant attitude toward punk in *Repo Man* is that subscribing to any subculture-scene orthodoxy is as narrow-minded as not questioning the mainstream. *Repo Man* is punk in a self-deprecating way. What I was most fascinated by in *Repo Man* was the seedy side of L.A., with its desolate industrial areas and seedy downtown and East L.A. dive bars and tow yards. When I did a year of art boarding school outside of L.A. in 1987–1988, we took a trip to downtown L.A. to see a pop art survey at MOCA. As we drove in, I was keenly interested in the downtown landscape because of *Repo Man*. Scrutinizing every street corner, I noticed several black, white, and yellow posters pasted on electrical boxes with an unflattering painted portrait of Ronald Reagan and the text CONTRA above and DICTION below. The posters, critiquing Reagan's nefarious role in Iran-Contragate, I later found out were the art of Robbie Conal. Robbie's posters were a huge inspiration to me as I began to explore using posters for my own street art and political commentary.

Another L.A. punk film that made a huge impression on me was Penelope Spheeris's *The Decline of Western Civilization*. It was tough to get a VHS copy of *Decline* in Charleston, but the only punk record store had a copy and would rent it along with an $80 credit card deposit, which my mom was very reluctant to put down. Because the live footage was so energetic and raw, I had no idea at the time that most of the live shows in *Decline* were recorded at a soundstage but with L.A. punks invited to be the audience. I love the live performances in *Decline*, with the sloppy charm of The Germs shows really standing out as an example to me that feeling is more important than virtuosity. There are so many great candid moments in *Decline* that made an impression on me. The scene with X doing homemade tattoos while talking about religious pamphlets and dark realism stuck with me because John Doe and Exene had a great sense of humor and ease about a life of struggle. A sense of humor is prominent in almost all the different bands' segments in the film. I use humor not only as a personal coping mechanism but also as a tool of disarmament in my art to help my ideas get through my audience's usual defenses. I grew up in a middle-class family, and everyone I knew seemed to aspire to affluence and condescendingly judge those who hadn't made it. The universal comfort with poverty from every band in *Decline* made me far less insecure about my years of financial struggle as I pursued my art. I realized that my ability to live frugally gave me creative freedom, and this was the most important thing to me.

There are so many L.A. bands, albums, songs, labels, graphics, 'zines, etc. that made an impact on my life that there isn't space to cover it all, but I do want to give special mention to a few. Gary Panter's Screamers logo is one of my favorite music graphics ever. The distillation of that illustration to concentrate an essence of anger and exhilaration into a black-and-white portrait is brilliant! I've often used that logo as a source of inspiration when I'm making graphics and portraits that I hope will be arresting and memorable.

Through their lyrics FEAR wanted to provoke and antagonize politically correct sensibilities. I have no idea what Lee Ving's real political leanings were and are, but my suspicion is that he is a precursor to Stephen Colbert, forcing the audience to look at the pervasive insensitivity and demeaning hostility in the world and decide if they want to process that through nihilism, humor, or activism. For me FEAR posed the question: How do you respond to button-pushing—by whining, or do you have a better plan?

Youth Brigade put out great music with their album *Sound and Fury*, including songs questioning police brutality, war, and factionalism within the scene. I find Youth Brigade especially important, though, because of their DIY ethos with scene activism and the founding of the B.Y.O. (Better Youth Organization) as gig producers and record label.

T.S.O.L. evolved from super-fast political hardcore on songs like "Abolish Government/Silent Majority" to more of a melodic goth sound on "Weathered Statues." I love the "wake up silent majority" lyric from "Abolish Government/Silent Majority," but there is a less polemic, more poetic depth to the lyrics about the cost of war and how quickly the soldiers who sacrificed are forgotten in "Weathered Statues." T.S.O.L. fused different styles without worrying about punk orthodoxy or pandering to their audience.

X made great punk records, but there was always more to the band's sound, with nods to roots, rock 'n' roll, rockabilly, and country from the beginning. I doubt I would have looked into Jerry Lee Lewis, Johnny Cash, Chuck Berry, or Eddie Cochran (maybe I'd have checked out Cochran because of the Sex Pistols) if I hadn't loved X's different sounds. X's lyrics tackled seedy desperation, the "New World" under Reagan, music industry conservatism, death, lies, betrayal, and other classics of human existence with wit, passion, humor, depth, and a dynamic interplay between John Doe and Exene Cervenka. John and Exene being a couple as cowriters and front people of a band had my mind racing with excitement and possibility for my romantic and creative future!

The Minutemen not only made tense, jittery, punk funk but also covered Creedence Clearwater Revival. "History Lesson Part II" basically sums up The Minutemen's philosophy that punk was the next generation's version of Bob Dylan and a vehicle for life on your own terms. Minutemen bassist Mike Watt always emphasized "rolling econo," meaning saving money to keep the band afloat.

L.A. punk of the eighties was far from monolithic or one dimensional. There are many things I learned observing the L.A. punk scene, including lessons in work ethic, fearlessness, self-promotion, media creation, scene building, graphic art, outspokenness, and so on. All of those things are incredibly valuable, but probably the most valuable thing I learned is that true punk is the freedom to fulfill your own vision without worrying about stylistic orthodoxy or commercial appeal. L.A. punk looked and sounded a lot of different ways, but they were all about freedom—the freedom to forge your own path, make your own sound, and say what you want to say. L.A. punk lit a fire in me, a desire for creative freedom that takes shape in every aspect of my life. Some people dismiss punk as an art form that burned bright and short, but I see the fires sparked by L.A. punk carried on the wind and burning bright in countless manifestations. Live fast—die never!

CHAPTER 17

YOU SAY YOU WANT
AN EVOLUTION

by Tom DeSavia

I tried to be a skateboarder, but I wasn't terribly good at it. I soldiered on, nonetheless, proud of every wound and scrape I earned trying to ride.

I tried to be a hardcore kid, but I wasn't any good at it. Not that I didn't dig hardcore bands—I did. It's just that I was just 135 pounds soaking wet and always felt like a bit of a potential victim at gigs. The few times I ventured into mosh pits in my youth would find me thrust around like a rag doll and emerging bruised, both physically and to my ego.

I don't remember how I first heard about Rank and File, but I remember vividly the day I brought their record home.

It was on Slash Records and was the new band from some guys who were in some punk band called The Dils. (I was fifteen and knew little of L.A. scene history yet.) The LP's artwork spoke to me the way punk album covers were supposed to: its illustration of barbed wire with a shock of red-and-yellow sunset behind it beckoned attention from the bins.

It felt like I was buying a punk record. I purchased it with that same sense of pride that I would buy a punk record, cherishing the "atta boy" nod I would get from one of the cooler-than-I-could-ever-be clerks in the shop. But this was allegedly supposed to be sort of a country record? I wouldn't call it that around my friends, probably. It was on Slash. That alone validated its worth in my young eyes.

Sundown was the name of this new Rank and File album, and I remember like it was yesterday dropping the needle on side one of the record. An instantly memorable and hooky yet punkishly aggressive country-rock guitar riff filled the room as the album's opening track, "Amanda Ruth," took hold. Suddenly, an unconventional, almost jarring harmony quickly pierced the proceedings and confirmed that this record was going to take the listener on a whole different trip. Chip Kinman's tenor wrapped itself around brother Tony's riveting baritone and soared as an unconventional sibling vocal conspiracy. It was love at first listen with this one. "Amanda Ruth" was an incredible slap in the ears and one that would help alter and define my musical taste for a lifetime.

Los Angeles punk rock—steeped in the genealogy of rock 'n' roll, country, folk, rockabilly, rhythm and blues, and Latin music—was naturally sprouting roots of its own. The Kinman brothers were among the first to reach me in a meaningful way as a kid, much in the same way X and The Blasters had recently done. Around this time the local press had started to enthusiastically report on the emergence of The Knitters, a side project/punk supergroup made up of members of X, The Blasters, and The Red Devils, who were equal parts golden-state country outlaws and a supercharged 1950s folk quintet.

As the first wave of L.A. punks were hitting the road, splitting town in vans headed for all points U.S.A.—some garnering major-label deals along the way, some dissolving, some shuffling off this mortal coil—a next wave of regional new music was taking hold. The diversity of the graduating class was paving the way for splintered-off genres: the country/roots side, exemplified by Rank and File and The Knitters, would be labeled cowpunk, and the Three O'Clock and The Bangs would be among those dubbed leaders of a movement known as the Paisley Underground. Albums by the aforementioned, plus The Long Ryders, Dream Syndicate, Green on Red, Blood on the Saddle, Rain Parade, The Beat Farmers, The Screaming Sirens, and Tex and the Horseheads, were suddenly dominating the club circuit and our turntables.

Unlike some of the coming-of-age punk environments where I sheepishly dipped my toe in the water, this rootsier and janglier place was where I instinctively felt comfortable, like I belonged. I distinctly remember my first time hearing the Three O'Clock's punky power-pop classic "Jet Fighter" or The Long Ryders' country-rock rave-up "Final Wild Son"—I knew then that I was hearing songs that would become some of my best friends for life, aurally speaking.

My tastes and the makings of what would become my own personal musical history were getting more and more defined, with The Knitters exposing me to the music of The Delmore Brothers and Merle Haggard, The Long Ryders leading me deeper into albums by the Buffalo Springfield and Gram Parsons, The Blasters shining a bright path to Little Willie John and the King Records catalog, The Bangles opening up my ears to Big Star, while Green on Red grooved like deep tracks on early Stones records.

The punks were not only about revolution; they were part of music's evolution, consciously or otherwise—American music that honored its past, while blazing a trail for its future. For myself and countless others this era served not only as a true musical history lesson but also as an example of the enduring influence of art throughout generations. And when it had a good beat, you could dance to it.

TOWER RECORDS

WELCOME

LONE

SUN

5

MAY

4

PM

SUNSET, Hollywood

CHAPTER 18

THIS WORLD IS NOT MY HOME, I'M JUST PASSING THROUGH

by Maria McKee and Tom DeSavia

My lineage is decidedly Californian. My ancestors' roots trace back to all over Europe, but on my dad's side we go back generations in California, to pre-California Mexico, actually. My great grandfather—who was Sicilian—was literally a homesteader in a covered wagon who landed in Reche Canyon, which is San Bernardino, California; my great grandmother gave birth to seventeen kids, with eleven surviving to adulthood.

My mother, Elizabeth, married George MacLean, an unsung brilliant L.A. architect, when she was really young, about seventeen, and they had my brother Bryan. After George and my mother divorced, she married my dad, Jack, when Bryan was five years old. Bryan was a true child musical prodigy who eventually went on to become a founding member of the influential sixties rock group Love. He wrote a bunch of songs for the band, including one of their most notable tunes, "Alone Again Or." I quite literally grew up among the whole Laurel Canyon scene, in a really baroque atmosphere, because my brother was at the center of it . . . the Whisky a Go Go culture.

I was two or three years old and pretty regularly around folks like Frank Zappa and The Doors and David Crosby and everybody else from that world. There was an eighteen-year age difference between Bryan and me, and he was my big brother/hero from as far back as I have memories. My mom would tell this story of how we were in a car accident when I was about three years old, and my sole reaction was screaming, "Is Bryan okay? Is Bryan okay?" All I cared about was Bryan.

As a child Bryan was obsessed with musical theater, but once he became a teenager he really took up guitar and was completely swept up in rock 'n' roll. He was a true Hollywood kid and quickly became friends with all these musicians from the early Sunset Strip scene and basically became the Boy Friday for a lot of band guys. Bryan had started out being the roadie for The Byrds, and he was on a Rolling Stones tour when he was really young. He met up with Arthur Lee and joined Love in the mid-sixties for a couple of years and then bailed and moved to New York. While on the East Coast he got a deal to develop some of his own material for Elektra Records—he recorded some demos, but it never evolved into anything real. In what I suppose was some despair over his struggling music career, combined with then-undiagnosed mental illness, he fell into a world of drugs that started a cycle of disappearing for long stretches of time. After months and months of not hearing a word from him, he showed up on our doorstep one day with a Bible under his arm, explaining that he had found Jesus while wandering Manhattan. This charismatic Christianity that he used to carry himself with would become a constant in my surroundings growing up; that culture actually really informed a lot of my performance as I started out.

Bryan continued to come and go unpredictably. He'd go back to New York, ultimately winding up back home and God knows where else in between. Finally, when I was around eight years old, he parked—he was home in L.A. and that was it. When people say, "Oh, Bryan MacLean was your half-brother?" I always tell them no, from age eight he was *my brother*. When I was a child he was more present than my dad, who worked all day long and would come home late. My brother was always there.

Bryan never stopped playing and writing, and my growing up is filled with memories of listening to music with him and singing with him. I became absorbed in musical theater; I was this kid who was equally as transfixed with the *Little Rascals* and Shirley Temple and Judy Garland and *Guys and Dolls* and *Mame*—that was all Bryan's influence. By the time I was in school it just felt destined that I was going to end up on Broadway or at least be headed in that direction. It felt obvious. By the time I was thirteen or fourteen I was *that* kid—the kid who was the lead in all the school musicals, the theater obsessive.

Beverly Hills High School had a really important theater department—they were sort of like New York's High School of Performing Arts on the West Coast—and I was in theater classes with people like Nicolas Cage and Crispin Glover. I was going to go to New York, I would go to Juilliard, I had an agent, I was going to be an actor—it was fait accompli. One day Bryan heard me singing along to a record—a Bonnie Raitt record or something—and he told me in no uncertain terms that I wasn't going anywhere. "I'm putting a band together for you," he said. "You and I are going to make a million dollars." That's how it started. I used to hang on his every word, and I would do whatever he told me to do. Because I was raised in this Christian cultish environment, I had come to believe that anybody who had any sort of charismatic presence was seen as a prophet, including my own family members—*especially* my mother and *especially* Bryan. So when he said, "You. Are. Going. To. Be. A. Singer," there was nothing I could do. I couldn't fight it—the Oracle had spoken. I remember crying my eyes out because I knew I had no choice in the matter.

Together we would drive around and listen to the radio a lot, and he got me into a whole bunch of classic soul and Harry Nillson and Van Morrison. He would tell me stories about Phil Spector and Janis Joplin, both of whom he encountered in his years with Love. Soon enough he and I made our first real demo, and we started playing gigs—performing both at the church and regular "secular" gigs.

When I was fourteen and started discovering "new" music, the first person who really spoke to me musically was Rachel Sweet. I hadn't really gotten into punk rock yet, and new wave for me was more about fashion and style than it was about the music. I just loved new-wave glamour. Musically I was liking things like Blondie and The Clash, but when I heard Rachel, it just shook me to my core. She was around my age, she was so cute, and she was a powerhouse singer and doing punky country and punky pop. I just fell in love with her. I was listening to a lot of country rock, like Linda Ronstadt and all that stuff, but Rachel Sweet was really my biggest influence for Lone Justice: she was a postpunk girl who did country and folk and soul and new wave and punk all at the same time. I would spend endless hours upstairs in my parents' bedroom singing along with those records.

Around that time my friend MJ was turning me onto the edgier side of the arts—stuff like The Velvet Underground and films by Goddard—and we started going to gigs together. We really got into the whole mod scene and wound up becoming friends with bands like The Untouchables and started to dress like mods and ride around on scooters—the whole thing. There was a club in Hollywood we were hearing about named the Cathay de Grande, and soon enough we were on our way to becoming regulars there, going whenever we could.

Every Monday night was Blue Monday at the Cathay, and all we knew was that it was a blues night. We had to go. That night was the first time I was introduced to the music of Top Jimmy and the Rhythm Pigs, who anchored every Blue Monday night for years. I was completely flipped out—it was like seeing The Doors at the Whisky in their heyday. I instantly knew that this was my place, these were my people, this was my world.

Bryan's band and I played a gig somewhere in the San Fernando Valley where Top Jimmy was playing the very next night. I wrote him a note—I can't remember if I left it in the dressing room or if I wrote it on the wall. It basically read, "I'm your biggest fan. I'm a singer. Please come see the band I sing with . . . the Bryan MacLean band." And it worked. He ended up at our next show.

I used to close the set every night with "I Never Loved a Man (the Way I Love You)" by Aretha Franklin, and I remember watching Top Jimmy singing along. It was amazing. He came up after the show and asked if we would open for him at the Cathay and then suggested I should join The Rhythm Pigs for a few songs.

Top Jimmy asking me to sing with him was a major turning point in my life—barely sixteen years old, and my dreams felt like they were coming true. It's all such a blur, but we sang some twelve-bar blues, and I think he had me sing the Aretha song—it was all so surreal. Ray Manzarek was there, Dave Alvin was there, John Doe was there—all three of them regular guests at Jimmy's gigs. Ray actually wanted to produce me at that point—he and Bryan were old friends—and he had produced X, so I was really excited. But when he told me he saw me as the next Ronstadt or Bonnie Raitt, I lost interest. "No!" I thought, "You produce X! You were in The Doors!" Those records had become part of my DNA, and I wanted to make raw rock 'n' roll. I completely rebelled against the idea of doing anything else, much less country-pop records. I dug my heels in deeper and basically started living at the Cathay, my home away from home.

On the far west Sunset Strip there was a Licorice Pizza record store across from the Whisky, and I used to hang out there a lot. There was a flyer up on the bulletin board there that read: *Girls needed to form all-girl band. Influences: Love, the Velvet Underground, the Last, Beau Brummels. Call Sue.* I couldn't get to a phone fast enough. "Hey Sue, my brother was in Love, and I saw your ad, and I want to put a band together too!" She's said, "Okay cool, where do you live? I'll come right over!" And that was how I met Susanna Hoffs, who was putting together the band that would become The Bangles. I told her how I idolized Janis Joplin and X, The Cramps, as well as Creedence Clearwater Revival. She's talking about The Beatles and I'm talking about The Stones, and she tells me that she wants to do an all-girl Beatles, which sounded cool to me. Then she explains that she wants to be the John Lennon in the group—and I'm like, wait, what? *I* want to be the John Lennon. So that was that. My friend Annette Zilinskas had answered another ad Sue had posted and wound up joining her in The Bangles (then known as The Bangs) shortly thereafter.

Through some friends I heard about these guys in Orange County who wanted to put together a rockabilly band—these two brothers named Johnny Ray and David Lee Bartel—and they were looking for a singer. The Bartel brothers would hang out in Downey with The Blasters, and they were all friends. It was too perfect. This was going to be my band—this was it, I knew it. Unfortunately for me, it turned out that David Lee had this girlfriend named Emmy Lee, and she played a Charlie Christian guitar. She was a gorgeous Puerto Rican girl dressed in perfect 1950s clothes, and it seems they had already put this band together called The Red Devils. My heart was broken. Emmy Lee was being compared to Patsy Cline, and they were opening for X and opening for The Blasters—opening for all my heroes. So instead of joining my dream band, I became a big Red Devils groupie and eventually ended up dating Johnny and became a part of their whole rockabilly crew. People knew I could sing, but I wasn't really doing anything about it.

We all used to hang out at this place called Angelo's down in Anaheim, which was a 1950s drive-in, and often they would have vintage car nights. I drove a '55 Crown Victoria, pink and white. One night there was a rockabilly jam session, and Ryan Hedgcock was there. That's the night we met. Ryan had a band at the time, and when he heard me sing at the jam, he got my number and called me the next day, suggesting we put a group together. "I have this band right now and I'm done," he said. "You and me, let's do it!" I agreed, and our musical partnership began. He would regularly drive up from Torrance, and we would just sit in my room and listen to records nonstop.

I had already started to research my growing interest in blues music, reading books and learning about Jimmie Rodgers, the Carter Family, The Blue Sky Boys—stuff like that. Ryan turned me on to George Jones and Merle Haggard, not to mention a ton of local punk rock stuff. We both loved blues and soul music and were obsessed with Motown and Stax.

We were both really young purists. I would go into my local bookstore and just pore over books by Depression-era photographer Dorothea Lange, obsessing over her pictures of the Dust Bowl. I was captivated by movies like *Paper Moon* and *Coal Miner's Daughter*, watching them over and over again. I'd go into vintage clothing stores and head directly to the 1930s section and find these old gingham dresses, building this whole cinematic image in my head. Ryan was doing the same thing—wearing fedoras and vintage clothes. We knew we were brewing something.

The Cathay had an upstairs bar where they'd have performers or DJs, and Ryan and I would do acoustic duo sets, really just doing covers. We'd do songs by Rose Maddox, Jimmie Rodgers, Merle Haggard, and some rockabilly. I was dressing up in my Depression-era outfits and experimenting with silent film–style makeup. Hillel Slovak used to come see us and bring Alain Johannes; Kim Fowley was always hanging around too. One night this guy named Marvin Etzioni, who was in this local band called The Model, showed up. Marvin was kind of a new-wave singer-songwriter in the Elvis Costello vein—he worked at Aron's Records on Melrose Avenue and went to Fairfax High. He saw Ryan and me and stuck to us like glue immediately. That was it. He was telling us how he really wanted to produce us; he was really the first "showbiz" guy we ever met, even though he wasn't really a showbiz guy. But, unlike the vibe of a lot of people from our world, he had this drive, and he definitely saw and explained the pathway to success he envisioned.

Marvin, Ryan, and I started hanging out, and he would come over to our places with stacks of his own records. It was Marvin who turned me on to bands like The New York Dolls and Television; he played us deep cuts from Patti Smith LPs and reintroduced me to The Velvet Underground and Lou Reed, and played me Bowie records that I didn't know. My life was quite literally changed when I heard Television's *Marquee Moon*, and I owe that to him. That was Marvin. It was ON— we decided to put a real band together, and Marvin would manage and produce us.

Ryan knew some guys we would recruit: a bass player called Fluffy and a drummer named Don Willens. The five of us would go down to

Torrance to a furniture warehouse that Ryan's dad owned, and we'd just play and play, refining our vibe. We were really into Rank and File because they were the only other band who was kind of taking their sound past rockabilly and moving it into something that was decidedly more country—they were so courageous. What they were doing wasn't new wavy or postpunk; it was country. They were starting a scene, our scene. Shortly after our getting together, Fluffy had left the band, so it was decided then that Marvin would join the group and pick up bass duties. The newly formed, newly named Lone Justice recorded our first demos shortly after that, and I was determined to get them to Rank and File's Chip Kinman. I managed to meet him at a show and give him our demo, and that led to one of our first breaks: their manager, Carlyne Majer, took us on as clients.

It was actually Linda Ronstadt who got everything started for us on the industry side. Lone Justice was doing this gig in a tiny San Fernando Valley club, and hardly anybody was there. I remember going into the ladies room and Linda was in there, and I wondered to myself if she was there to see us. I have no idea how she heard about us or how she wound up in this shitty little Valley dive bar. So we do the gig, and the next day David Geffen calls because Linda told him he had to sign us. After a bit of a lengthy courtship—and a competing offer from Warner Bros. in Nashville, who wanted us to be a straight-up country-pop act—we would sign with Geffen Records.

Lone Justice was starting to play a good number of shows around town. We'd played the Cathay and different rooms around Orange County, leading up to fairly regular gigs at the legendary East San Fernando Valley honky-tonk bar, the Palomino. Ryan and I had previously played some talent-night slots at the Palomino, which was finding a renewed life as younger audiences were flocking to the club to see the growing number of local roots-oriented acts that were causing a stir on the local scene.

I remember John Doe showing up at one of the Palomino gigs, and he brought Jeffrey Lee Pierce from The Gun Club. I announced from the stage that my favorite country singer of all time was in the audience tonight, John Doe. Suddenly Jeffrey Lee freaked out and started shouting "fuck you!" and he came right up to the stage and was flipping me off, just inches from my face. John would drag him off the dance floor and bring him back to the bar, but Jeffrey kept wiggling away and returning to his stance in front of the stage, middle finger at alert. He was intoxicated and just thought I was a little shit, and my verbal praise of Doe as a country idol obviously triggered him.

My dad would always be at the Palomino gigs, buying drinks for everybody all night long. Country Dick Montana from The Beat Farmers, Doe, Top Jimmy—everyone knew my dad. Our shows started to attract some luminaries like Dolly Parton, David Byrne, and Emmylou Harris. Benmont Tench, who was starting to play with us a bit, brought Stevie Nicks one night, and I was terrified. Everything was happening so fast. I couldn't describe it as anything other than Fellini-surreal.

Geffen wanted us to get on the road, and when Rank and File asked us to tour California with them, we jumped at the chance. The reviews from our live show started to come in, and they were insanely positive. Mikal Gilmore—the American journalist and music critic—wrote one of our first reviews, comparing us to all sorts of country and rock and punk legends—it was nuts. Soon after that, Chris Morris came and wrote about us for the *Los Angeles Reader* and became a huge champion of us in the press and around the local scene.

We headed into the studio to record some more demos, this time with producer David Vaught at the helm. Those recordings—raw and energetic and unapologetically hillbilly—were the best representation of that band that everyone was flipping out over. The band on those recordings was the real Lone Justice. The long-bootlegged demos would eventually get a proper release in 2014 as *This Is Lone Justice: The Vaught Tapes 1983*.

When we signed with Geffen Records I was nineteen. I remember running into John Doe at a gig one night, and he looked me straight in the eyes and said, "People are telling you a lot of shit right now, and you've got to be careful that you don't believe it"—basically saying "stay grounded and don't turn into an asshole." I remember having sort of a "relax, man, it's cool" cavalier attitude about the whole thing, but I'll always remember him caring enough to look out for me. John was one of my heroes. He and Exene. I was one of those little girls who would go to their gigs dressed like Exene and would draw the

X logo on my arm like a fake tattoo. I would hover around her like a weirdo stalker. I was obsessed with them. We all were.

So now Lone Justice is gonna actually make a record, and we have to decide who's going to produce it. We're told we need a big name, and we have the corporate muscle behind us to land one. We made a list: Todd Rundgren was on there, along with Steve Lillywhite, Robbie Robertson, and maybe John Cale? I think at the bottom of the list was Jimmy Iovine. Not that we didn't love him; Patti Smith's *Easter* was huge for me, and I've been a massive Bruce Springsteen fan as long as I can remember.

We had set up base in a rehearsal studio, where we were meeting all our producer suitors. Jimmy Iovine came in, and we played for him, and we were just going to do what we did with all the others—which was meet the guy and then discuss it amongst ourselves and try to figure it out. As he was leaving the studio that night he turned and said, "This is going to be fun. I can't wait to start recording!" Boom. That was it. He hired himself. I remember so clearly Ryan turning around to me and saying, "I guess Jimmy Iovine is producing the record?" We were adopted by Iovine, and that relationship was one of the most significant creative relationships of my entire life, across the board. I love Jimmy. It was terribly hard because he was a *star maker*—I knew that from the outset, and deep down inside I always knew I couldn't be that person for him.

We parted ways with our drummer, and we had the great pleasure of welcoming Don Heffington, legend, to the band. Don really took us to a place where we were playing in time. We sounded like a *band*, finally. Our previous drummer, the late Don Willens, struggled with intense drug addiction, and as such, he was the definition of a slow-down/speed-up player. He did give us that crazy sound in the beginning; his playing was so out there that it was almost metaphysical; it was like jazz in a way. He gave those early demos a real wildness. But when Don joined the band, it was "okay, we're a real rock band now." It was transformative.

The record took a long time to record. During that time we started writing a lot more and gigging a lot more, and our local reputation was growing and growing. The press adulation continued: punk rock had received great national press, edging into the mainstream with bands like X and Rank and File becoming real critics' darlings, opening the door for acts like us. Suddenly, *People* fucking magazine and the *L.A. Times* are doing features on Lone Justice. We were being set up to be The Next Big Thing, and the pressure was mounting, personally and professionally.

I existed in a world of adulation and, really, kind of a charmed life. I had that intense combo of panic and fear, always haunted by the feeling that I wasn't good enough and everything was destined to fall apart. Having this exaggerated sense of yourself is just a breed of narcissism, and it can be destructive for yourself and everybody around you. So, out of panic and insecurity, I would succumb to temper tantrums and spoiled-brat behavior—diva behavior. I would find myself quite literally in a sort of "terror paralysis" at times—going to meetings at Geffen and putting my head down on the table and not being able to lift it, with everyone asking if I was okay but very few actually caring if I was okay. The questions and implications were mounting: Did I look as good as I did a year ago? Maybe I put on a few pounds? I'm going to have my photograph taken, and we're going to film some videos. Then that tension begets an eating disorder, and you know, it's a classic fucking shit. Yes, a textbook bullshit cliché, but less spoken about and less discussed back then. Members of the band were looking out for me, but we were *all* young, all babes in the woods, all dealing with this pressure. Our dreams were supposed to be coming true, but we weren't prepared for what was happening to us.

My brother Bryan was struggling with our newfound success and his own demons. He and I were supposed to conquer the world together, but it hadn't worked out that way. Bryan became my shadow, my bodyguard, for better or worse. We had covered one of his songs, "Don't Toss Us Away," which had become a staple of our live set and one of the better-known tracks from our album. The combination of drugs and mental illness were taking a toll on him. I was raised with homeopathic medicine, and I will always practice that stuff, but I believe in integrative medicine, and if you fucking need psych meds, you take psych meds. If he had, I believe my brother might still be alive. He died in 1998 at the young age of fifty-three. His heart gave out from years of abuse.

I would meet and work with some people who were really kind, like Benmont Tench and Steven Van Zandt. Steven was one of the first professionals I met to treat me like a grown-up artist—you know, somebody with a brain and ideas and so on. Jimmy Iovine wanted so bad for me to be the female Bruce Springsteen, so he hooked me up with Steven—he, Benmont, and I wrote "Sweet, Sweet Baby (I'm Falling)" for the first record, which was a very intentional single for us. Jimmy humored the hillbilly side of Lone Justice because he knew our fans liked it, but it drove him nuts. Recording the album had been a struggle, to say the least—dividing the band and playing to all our insecurities.

Our A&R person at Geffen was Carol Childs, who also happened to be Bob Dylan's girlfriend. One day she comes up to us and tells us that she's going to get Bob to write a song for the album. Jimmy's lips were smacking at the possibility—so were Marvin's. I'm not as impressed—you know, he was my mom's favorite, but I hadn't really gone through my Bob phase yet . . . I was nineteen years old. Bob Schmob, whatever. Now, if she had said Paul Westerberg is writing a song for you, I would have been over the moon. So Bob comes to meet us at the studio with a song he's written for us called "Go Away Little Boy," and he's got Ron Wood in tow. Ron and Bob started drinking Jack Daniels while fiddling around with the song for hours, and I'm just in fucking hell. After what seemed like an eternity with the band just sitting on the sidelines, Bob starts to teach me the tune—but every time I go in to do a take, he would just start screaming "No! No no no no!" He'd play the song and sing it, but every single take was "No! Try it again!" At this point I was at my breaking point, wanting to shriek, "Fuck you, Bob Dylan!" Iovine senses this and takes me aside, saying, "It's Dylan! Show some respect!" All I'm thinking is that Dylan made his first record already, he had his time, this is *my* turn, this is *my* band! So finally I just went "fuck it" and went and just sang the most over-the-top Bob Dylan impression I could muster, just to piss everybody off. I walk out of the vocal booth, and Bob exclaims, "I knew you could do it!" Touché, motherfucker. Touché. The song wound up not making the album; it was a B-side.

I did not want to record what became our first single, an unreleased Heartbreakers song written by Tom Petty and Mike Campbell called "Ways to Be Wicked." I was still very involved in the Christian community at the time, and when I first heard the demo the lyric "You ain't afraid to let me have it, you ain't afraid to stick it in"—which was repeated throughout—felt bluntly sexually explicit to me. I was very much sort of a golden child in the Christian community, with a very, very overprotective brother and mother. Look, I recognized at a young age that because I had this sort of chaste image on top of being a sexy young girl on stage that it had this intense power play over a lot of folks—I knew that. Even though I played that power a little bit, I didn't really want to be objectified sexually because it made me very uncomfortable. Women are speaking about this stuff now—there are many, many ways to say time is up—but it was very different then. It's not just about assault but about that feeling of powerlessness as a woman in a man's world and your sexuality being somehow a power player in all of this, whether it's out in the open or discussed in hushed tones. Whether it was my virginity or my sexual charisma being used to further the band's career, all it did was leave me with a sense of powerlessness and, at certain times, crippling insecurity. So, for really the first time, I put my foot down: I did not want to sing that line, and I made it very clear that if we were going to do the song, Jimmy would have to talk to Tom about rewriting it. Jimmy kept trying to assure me that nobody was going to think the line was sexual, that he's talking about a knife in the back, he would explain: it's a metaphor, it's a metaphor. All hell broke loose. That *was* going to be the first single; it was predestined. "You don't understand. Tom Petty gave you a song that he's never recorded for your album. You have to record it as is." I felt powerless. I felt there was nothing I could do. At home I was under a tremendous amount of pressure *not* to record the song. Finally the delivery was "You're singing this fucking song or it's the end of everything." So I just compartmentalized it and gave in and sang it. I recorded it, and I stopped thinking about it . . . we eventually filmed the video, and I still didn't think about it. Sure enough, we go on our first tour of Europe, and our first London gig ever is full of teenage boys waving skateboards over their heads—because I was riding a skateboard in the video—and chanting, "Stick it in! Stick it in! Stick it in!" Every interview with the British press—who famously love to torture people when they can—is asking out of the gate: "So, 'stick it in'?" It was the topic of every conversation, and I was embarrassed and angry at myself for capitulating. I *knew* this would happen. I just remember holing up in a hotel room, just wanting to go home, aggressively staving off a lurking nervous breakdown.

When I look back at that first Lone Justice album—which was half punk-hillbilly and half heartland rock—for me Marvin Etzioni's song "East of Eden" was the tune on that record that was by far the truest to the band we started. We were playing with different stakes: the playing field wasn't set up for us to have a sweet, fun little development record and grow from there. This was ride or die, and we knew it. But "East of Eden" sounded how a good indie-rock band should sound.

The album came out, and we were thrust into the whirlwind we thought we were prepped for. No longer in local clubs surrounded by our family and friends, we were suddenly playing arenas, opening massive tours for U2 and Tom Petty and the Heartbreakers, and doing a ton of TV appearances and massive amounts of press while everyone watching waited for those predictions of world domination to come true. The band continued to dissolve; we were so far away from those kids sitting in an apartment in Los Angeles listening to The New York Dolls and dreaming big. We all became increasingly isolated from one another. I was obviously set up for a solo career, and I willingly began to venture on that path, trying to find my voice along the way and becoming more confident in my songwriting. There's a bond we all share—especially Ryan and me—that won't ever fade. We all found each other and learned from one another and left our little mark. I know there are a lot of people out there who would like us to get together again and "finish" what we started. I don't know if that's the answer. Not every film needs a sequel, you know. I don't believe in that kind of thing usually, meaning doing anything differently to alter the past or resculpt history or its memories. The only thing I believe in doing differently is trying to make amends if I treated people poorly or if I'd hurt anyone's feelings or was abusive when I was drunk or anything like that. I believe in taking moral responsibility for stuff and apologizing if I've hurt people. But as far as protecting yourself from whatever path fate led you down as a human being, artistically or personally, you've got to accept it and keep moving. And keep creating.

CHAPTER 19

THE PAISLEY UNDERGROUND, AMERICANA & ME

by Sid Griffin

It is sunny, and I am walking down the street. Shops, restaurants, and taverns are heaving with people. I've been here long enough that an occasional voice cries out a greeting, even though this big city is supposed to be so impersonal.

Yet this is not Los Angeles. It is London. I pause by a bookstore that has discounted overstocked paperbacks on sagging wooden shelves outside their front door. Twice I have seen one of my books humiliatingly displayed on these public discount shelves, where passersby can glance over and notice how neither your name, your research, nor your literary point of view was enough to sell the fifty thousand heartfelt words you poured onto that particular book's untouched pages.

A garish black, white, and pink book cover catches my eye. It is a history of the Masque, the punk rock club I literally stumbled into when I slipped on something slimy in its doorway forty years earlier. I had moved to L.A. from my Kentucky home, arriving October 11, 1977, and I was green as suburban grass. It was only two months since the late great Brendan Mullen, a wise Scotsman I was proud to call my friend, opened the joint when I entered its filthy portals.

Picking this book up, I found it had more black-and-white photographs than it did text, and to my astonishment many of the photos were not of the bands who performed at the Masque's original location—the Mau Mau's, F-Word, The Alley Cats, The Dils, The Zeros, The Eyes . . . I saw 'em all there—but of the fans, posers, and punters who made the place swing as much as the music did. I hurriedly flipped through its pages, looking for old friends, hoping to see a young Phast Phreddie or Rik L. Rik, perhaps spotting the late Don Waller wonderfully alive again or maybe Belinda Carlisle not long after she was sacked as drummer of The Germs or—dare I think it—a photo of a barely twenty-two-year easy mark whose Stiv Bators razor-cut hair could not hide the fact he was a dumb kid, a rube, a hoe-dad, a wanna-be, and a tinhorn immediately out of his depth the moment he drove west across the Kentucky state line.

Flipping the pages excitedly, I recognize faces, but none are close friends. Out of nowhere and after four decades I begin to grow skittish and full of anxiety. These faces are the SoCal kids who never quite accepted me and who were angry I wasn't angry at life and at Los Angeles as a whole. And I wasn't. I thought Los Angeles terrific after the stifling Southern Baptist existence I had known in suburban Kentucky.

The more I turned the pages searching for old friends appearing so magically young, the more I remembered that this person in this photo laughed when I said I liked The Everly Brothers, the more I remembered that the guy in the next photo wanted to fight me over God knows what social error I committed, and this punk on page whatever had grinningly offered me a beer that I knew the moment I touched the warm can that there was something in it I did not want to swallow.

Those days were a painful cultural childbirth for me. They were not the beginning and be-all of my Los Angeles musical journey, but they were one helluva blastoff. I experienced the possibility that anything was possible, and I thank Brendan Mullen for this to this day. My own personal and quite real sociocultural Ground Zero was a few years away, in the same town with some of the same faces. It was a rather accidental colliding of comet into planet, and I had no idea that my tin-horn naiveté would lead my own band to a musical sea change that represented so much to so many.

God, I was lucky.

My first L.A. band was Death Wish in early 1978. You never heard of them. We did gigs at the Club 88 with the *Newsweek* cover of Gary Gilmore behind us, Gilmore being the first person in ten years to be executed in the United States, a convict who gained great notoriety for *demanding* to be executed. (A very punk rock thing to do.) It was tasteless of us to present ourselves this way, and a few short years later I learned that Mikal Gilmore, the fine music writer, was Gary's younger brother. Let me apologize to Mikal and his family once again right now.

In April 1979 I started The Unclaimed with a singer whose single-mindedness created the band's dark motif while simultaneously destroying several friendships. We were the first West Coast 1960s garage band revivalists, thrilled by Lenny Kaye's *Nuggets* compilation, preceded only by the dysfunctional Droogs from the Valley and The Chesterfield Kings in New York state. We were postpunk before punk needed to be post-anything. To be fair, our singer had tried starting the band before me. In late 1976 he met a newcomer to L.A. at Clancy Muldoon's Ice Cream Parlour on La Brea. They found each other through the *Recycler*, the free newspaper whose classified ads helped create many a local rock band. The musician he met was from Illinois and said he was going to be a conceptual artist and a poet, and in a twist on Johnny Rotten or Sid Vicious he would be called John Doe, the

> SINGER AND guitarist wanted for 60's influenced group; folk-rock, Tex-Mex, soul, surf, psychedelic. Two ex-Unclaimed members want the Byrds, Standells and Seeds to ride again. Sid: 836-7262, after 6 p.m.

generic name used on credit card adverts. At rehearsal three years later The Unclaimed lead singer told us he left this meeting thinking he would never hear of that nutty Illinois guy again.

Eager for fame, we dropped our four-song EP off at Marshall Berle's Hollywood office in the hopes that Uncle Miltie's nephew would book us some gigs. A day or so later Dan Stuart of The Serfers, soon to become Green on Red, visited the office and mentioned our EP to secretary/receptionist Belinda Carlisle. She wrinkled her nose and said to Danny, "Have you heard it? It's *terrible!*" Friends, when you enter the house of mirrors there is no safe place to turn, and after one snafu after another, bassist Barry Shank and I decided to start a new band.

Our Unclaimed drummer Matt Roberts rehearsed with us a bit but then decided his regular drum stool with the Unclaimed was a safer bet, as they had a small name on the scene and could get mentions in the *LA Weekly's* hilarious and influential *L.A. Dee Da* column. Steve Wynn came by, and we rehearsed several times, but he wanted my guitar to feedback on most of his songs, and this blew out my Vox Super Beatle's high-end cones each time I did it, which was fifty bucks a cone to fix. Had I been using a more durable amp, I might have been a founding member of The Dream Syndicate.

In early 1982 we chose ex-Boxboys Greg Sowders as our drummer because we liked him so much. A completely outgoing, positive, up-tempo person then, Greg remains exactly the same to this very day. Greg always dressed in dark clothes and had dyed his hair India ink black, which struck me as curious because his outlook was so bright and sunny. I wasn't overly impressed with his musical audition and expressed my doubts as Barry and I walked down the hall of some filthy rehearsal studio in east Hollywood. "He'll do," replied Barry with a shrug of his shoulders.

For ages Barry and I debated a name. I remember at one point driving north on Fairfax with Canter's coming up on our left and just having passed CBS Studios on our right. Barry was saying The Rainhearts or perhaps The Rain Hearts was a good band name, but I said Joan Jett's crew were the Blackhearts, so no. Barry agreed to The Long Ryders, an idea I got from the movie. After getting an address from the Screen Actors Guild on Wilshire Blvd., we wrote to Stacey Keach, and to my great delight, he wrote back. I lost the letter, but I can remember its first part word for word.

Dear Mr. Griffin,

*   I am touched by your note. My brother and I would be honored if you named your band after our movie. You may wish to consider a different spelling, as this will help you if the studio complains . . .*

The rest of his note I cannot remember, but the above is why it is Long Ryders and not Long Riders. The Byrds did not create this spelling. Stacey Keach did.

Barry, Greg, and I rehearsed as a trio, knowing we had a missing link and our sound was thin. We were a more skinny tie pop–rock band at this point, more likely to be a Bomp! Records act beloved by Greg Shaw than one on SST or Slash and approved by Greg Ginn or Bob Biggs. There was a musical component obviously and painfully missing, but no one knew what it was. Again the *Recycler* newspaper came to the rescue after we placed an advert.

In March 1982 Stephen McCarthy turned up at rehearsal, nine months after leaving his native Richmond, Virginia. We showed him our songs. He told me later he thought we would be "hotshot L.A. players" and was surprised to find regular guys his own age. To be fair, Barry Shank *was* a fine bass player. Greg and I were both more, ahh, musically enthusiastic than musically gifted. Stephen would soon solve both our two outstanding problems. The first was filling in our sound perfectly and quite creatively, and the second was giving our act focus and direction. I had given us a general game plan—Buffalo Springfield with a punk rhythm section, The Clash crossed with Creedence, bowl haircuts giving us a band look—but we needed to hone in on a specific target and hammer away at it.

This early Long Ryders material shows no sign of country music at all. None. Not a speck. Yet I hear Magazine (!), Television, Barry's beloved Power Pop, Wire, a tad of Public Image Ltd., a bit of L.A. folk-rock peeking through, some Velvet Underground (Barry sang "Run, Run, Run" live), and nothing—or almost nothing—that would make you think of The Long Ryders today as we ended up, the founders of alt-country and Americana and all that. Because, when we started the band, there was no such genre as alt-country, Americana, or cowpunk. No radio formats in those names. No rock writer ever used those terms in reviews.

I give Chip and Tony Kinman great kudos for Rank and File getting off the mat with their top-notch June 1982 debut LP on Slash. Jason and the Nashville Scorchers were up and running back east but were yet to shorten their name. So we were not alone when we stumbled onto alt-country/cowpunk/Americana, but we certainly weren't in any crowd. I think of it as akin to the invention of radio: people say Marconi invented radio, but geniuses such as Adolf Slaby, Georg von Arco, Reginald Fessenden, and others were all racing toward this discovery in their own laboratories. Marconi gets the credit today, but in a fairer world no one person gets *all* the credit, as these guys all learned from each other's research. As did The Long Ryders back then.

In musical terms the above translates into a band not yet focused. The Long Ryders were more a case of opening up the coloring box and painting with whatever color you choose, whether or not it made sense to the overall canvas. We did not have the direction Rank and File already had at this time. We'd bought first-class tickets on a train to nowhere, yet we all stuck with it, as the vibe of the band was so strong. Our hilarious male bonding at rehearsal was easily worth whatever musical stops and starts we were collectively suffering through.

The band continued on this serpentine path at our twice-weekly rehearsals until late April or early May, when Stephen McCarthy injected some of his own musical taste into the embryonic Long Ryder group proceedings. At rehearsal in the Miracle Mile garage we converted into a band room, he got us to play some Merle Haggard songs to warm up with. I was surprised that they sounded as spritely as they did, because Barry was not a C&W fan, Greg didn't appear to be, and I had not played or sung a country song since a cover band let me sing The Osborne Brothers' classic "Rocky Top" in Kentucky some eight years before. Yet Barry's fine bass playing nailed the low end, Greg took a few minutes to learn how to shift to a shuffle from a straight beat on the verse (and then back again at the end of Stephen's Clarence White-esque solo), and I played low-end arpeggios like a bluegrass guitarist or strummed simple chords like a folkie, always hitting the root note hard on the downbeat, the chord softly on the offbeat. Stephen sang and played brilliantly as ever, and we all looked at each other. "Whooooo-eee . . . that was *fun*, brother," I can still hear Greg say even now, grinning from beneath his then India ink black hair.

The guys and I had stumbled on to a formula, although we were slow to recognize it: playing country or any roots music with the chip-on-the-shoulder attitude of a punk rocker. Not the musical punch, guitar distortion, or anger of a punk, no, but with the raw, confident *attitude* of one. Not of a stadium rock star but of a punk rocker . . . there is a difference, dude. So thank you, Joey Ramone. Thank you, John Doe. And thank you, Merle, Jean Ritchie, Carl Perkins, The Staple Singers, and everyone else who organized the party, 'cause we were about to tap the keg. Oh, we had not played C&W at a gig yet, but a big show was coming up. August 11, 1982, The Long Ryders played the Central at 8852 W Sunset Blvd. on the Sunset Strip, across and down a bit from the Whisky. The Central was later famously rebranded as the Viper Room, but in the 1940s it was the Melody Bar, where mobster Bugsy Siegel held court with his henchmen.

Our set that night was:

01 Down to the Wire (Buffalo Springfield)
02 Romantic Education (Barry Shank)
03 instrumental (?)
04 Ivory Tower (Barry Shank)
05 Run Run Run (Velvet Underground)
06 Second to None (Sid Griffin)
07 Brand New Heartache (Everly Bros.)
08 Masters of War (Bob Dylan)
09 Holy Holy Holy (Sid Griffin)
10 The Trouble with Cinderella (Sid Griffin)
11 Join My Gang (Sid Griffin)
12 10-5-60 (Sid Griffin–Greg Sowders)
13 You Don't Love Me (Magic Sam version)

True, the above doesn't look unique today, but it was that evening in that year in that town. In any town, probably. A song by Neil Young's

first successful band, a Velvets' cover—commonplace now, not then—
an electric drone version of a Dylan acoustic song, a West Side Chicago blues classic, and our own punk-meets-John Fogerty music. As
Nashville's Jim Lauderdale says today, *"That's* Americana!" Barry's intro to song seven was, "Just so we can be all things to all people, we're
gonna explore the roots of a couple of the guys in the band . . . we're
gonna do it traditionally as possible," and then a wall of loud, sardonic
"hee-HAHs!" start, complete with a cheerfully intoxicated Michael St.
Pierre yelling, "Ride 'em, Sid!"

"Brand New Heartache" ends with applause, no heckles, and a
sense of relief on the part of the band. So we thought we'd try it again.
This was a decision pushed forward both by the successful experiment
we'd now had with the song and with the forthcoming departure of
Barry Shank on bass. He was a power-pop guy, a fan of melody, musical dynamics, and the clever chord change, not of songs about high
lonesome heartache, dear sweet mama's cooking, the old hometown,
or empty whiskey bottles. One gig down, a thousand to go.

The Long Ryders were beginning to get a name for ourselves. Favorable mentions would appear in the *LA Weekly* gig listings, Chris
Morris would give us a sentence or two in the *L.A. Reader*, other musicians started bigging us up, and you somehow could feel the wind filling our sails. August 16 was part of this—the Music Machine was about
three-quarters full, a good turnout for a weeknight, and our set was:

01 intro
02 Romantic Education (Barry Shank)
03 Touch and Go (Sid Griffin)
04 Down to the Wire (Buffalo Springfield)
05 Run Run Run (Velvet Underground)
06 Brand New Heartache (Everly Bros.)
07 Wise Man (Barry Shank)
08 Masters of War (Bob Dylan)
09 Holy Holy Holy (Sid Griffin)
10 The Trouble with Cinderella (Sid Griffin)
11 Join My Gang (Sid Griffin)
12 10-5-60 (Sid Griffin–Greg Sowders)

13 Do You Believe in Magic? (Lovin' Spoonful)
14 Green River (Creedence Clearwater Revival)

You can see roots rock growing deeper into the ground already. There is a tape of this show, recorded as it was Barry's Last Stand (the show was even billed that way in the *LA Weekly*). Track six is pure C&W, a duet where I take the low vocal part and Stephen takes the high harmony, and at the guitar solo Greg smoothly shifts to a shuffle, coming back out at the end of the guitar's twanging. It is our second public attempt at straight C&W, and we are audibly more confident.

As we played it, I looked at the audience, and many were staring at the stage with a "WTF?" look. This could go either way, I thought. We come to a smooth halt, our Phil and Don duet over. The crowd applauds enthusiastically, and I comment, "It's nice to be back at the Palomino." For Stephen this might have been a musical step *down*; for the other three of us it was a step up into an exciting new world . . . punk was about doing anything, right? And for the audience it was, as many have told me since, the first time they had ever heard a straight country-and-western song played live by young, hip musicians. Some even said it was the first time they heard C&W performed live. Period. If this sounds implausible, remember there was no Americana radio format then, and no one used the term alt-country. Contrast this to today, when Robert Plant, Ray Davies of The Kinks, Robyn Hitchcock, Chris Difford of Squeeze, and John Oates of Hall & Oates are all considered Americana artistes. I have no problem with this, but such folks certainly were not playing C&W duets and country shuffles in August 1982.

This Everlys' song performance on August 16, 1982, was the beginning of Stephen publicly adding his own flavors to our homegrown brew, and it changed *everything*. It was The Long Ryders' own Big Bang. We now had a focus. We could play America's music back at a young American audience, as Los Lobos or The Pogues performed music of their particular cultural heritage to a young, hip audience. Each time we walked onstage we knew many of our L.A. audience were hearing it live for the first time, and all of those audiences were hearing such music played with a powerful punk attitude for the first time. Yes, in some aspects Stephen's musical coming out was powered by the absence of

Barry Shank, but our loss was academia's gain. (Barry is now a full professor at Ohio State.) Had Barry stayed, I have often wondered how his power-pop would have meshed with Stephen's C&W, but with him leaving us, it was a sure sign the Roots Rock Revival was on.

At the same time we were thrown into another scene. Guitar bands who based their music on various underground 1960s bands were appearing in town. Bands who had heard and loved punk but didn't play it, bands who did not like the keyboards-dominated synth-pop of the day, bands who you could scratch the surface of and see the deeper inspiration underneath. Check out who made roll call:

The Dream Syndicate
The Bangles
The Salvation Army
Rain Parade

I have said the following many times to Europeans who are half my age and have never set foot in North America but they refuse to believe me: the above four were the originators of the Paisley Underground. No one else. Not your favorite band from San Francisco, Denver, or upstate New York. Just the above four. Soon we were lumped in with the above four, as were Green on Red, but really these four were the primary lineup of the P.U., and, deep breath, it was a social thing as much as a musical one.

Everyone above soon knew everybody else. I would hear or read about another band playing 1960s-styled-guitar rock but with a 1980s postpunk vibe, and I would go and check them out. I saw The Bangles when they were The Colours and when they were The Fans, as I liked the look of them on a flyer. Soon they were The Bangs, not The Bangles. (At the time I suggested they become The Shebangs. Oops, my bad.) Sue, Vicki, and Debbi brought their "Getting Out of Hand" homemade indie single to me at JEM Records in the Valley, where I worked as a salesperson, in the hopes we'd help distribute it. The Rain Parade allegedly liked the Buffalo Springfield, and so I went to see them, with their guitarist Matt Pucci later coming to see us, as he had heard we did a version of the Springfield's "Down to the Wire."

Steve Wynn I already knew, of course, and he introduced me to an intoxicated Dan Stuart, who was spouting idea after idea all evening, even though I could hardly understand a word he was saying. Anna Statman told me to check out The Salvation Army and I trooped on down to the Club 88 on Pico to see them. They were terrific live, with Michael Quercio playing bass and singing in a beige mock turtleneck sweater in an already hot club. Quercio gave an interview to the *LA Weekly* in autumn 1982 in which he described an upcoming gig where his Salvation Army would play with The Bangles and Rain Parade as something from "the Paisley Underground," and the name stuck. All these years later, and we are still talking about the Paisley Underground.

My home from summer 1981 to spring 1989 was the legendary Norton House at 7621 West Norton. Now completely done over by a developer in a rapidly regentrifying West Hollywood neighborhood, the building looks very different, with a second story having been added. Back then a friend of ours in construction assured me you could "knock over this whole structure with a Volkswagen Beetle hitting an outside corner at fifteen miles an hour." This was an image that always stayed with me, particularly during an earthquake, when the house shook like jelly on a dinner plate.

In those eight years the following desperadoes and refugees from law and order lived there for at least a few months. Yes, months. Recognize anyone below?

Me

Debbi Peterson, Bangles drummer

Joey Stella, soundman and roadie to nearly everyone worth a damn

Eric Burdon (lead singer of The Animals)

Billy Bremner (lead guitarist, Rockpile)

Happy Dave Thompson (don't ask . . .)

Bob Carlson (known as the Shakespearean Carpenter, as his construction skills were in demand, his acting not so much)

It gets weirder. John Silva and I found the house. John was then John Nobody, soon to manage the Three O'Clock (formerly The Salvation Army). About 1990 he started managing a young band whose indie album, *Bleach*, made waves but sold little. Today John is credited for breaking Nirvana, helping Sonic Youth hit gold, and getting The Foo Fighters going as well as several other fine acts. He has not answered an email or phone call from me in over twenty years, but I understand. It's Hollywood, Jack.

Silva and I found the house in 1982. We moved in. I went to get groceries. I walked west on West Norton and turned left, going south on Genesee. The sidewalk was blocked by an old smoldering chair, damp with water but oozing smoke in places, right in front of what I knew was the home of John Doe and Exene Cervenka, as I had seen them come and go. The chair stayed put for a few days, no one seeming to mind. It smelled awful, even though it was outside.

And then Life happened. Slowly disintegrating like a proud marriage where the happy lovers fail to notice the mistrust creeping into their daily routine, The Long Ryders began to fray at the edges. It was as if we entered a tunnel at speed and simply could not get out of the tunnel until the light at the end. I was always doing a lot of promotion with movers and shakers on the scene and friends in the media in order to keep the band's name out there during down time, and my activities sometimes led these same folks to think of The Long Ryders as my band. The other three did not appreciate any reference of this kind, and I can't say I blame them.

We probably signed to a major label too soon. Another LP with a hip indie label would have cemented our cool outsider status, but we were young, with visions of sugarplum glory dancing in our heads. Island Records started out an enthusiastic fit, yet in six months the gentleman who signed us was gone, as were his staff. Our A&R man was a hero who had raised Cain about our first single, "Looking for Lewis and Clark," getting a big enough budget to press up enough copies for a proper hit single. He got his way in the Island staff meeting but ruffled feathers doing so.

The single came out and was number sixty-two in the UK charts in the midweek report on Monday, quite good for a new band. Industry people were telling us it would go Top Forty for sure. Sad to say that the Island fellow in charge of the single's budget had actually *not* approved the money for more singles, even though it had been agreed upon at the staff meeting. He could not see "Looking for Lewis and

Clark" being a hit in an era when guitars were seemingly out of fashion. After all, it was an out-and-out loud, poundin' guitar rock 'n' roll song played by guys in denim and plaid shirts in an era of soft-synth pop in which acts dressed in clothes from the twenty-third century.

So the next week "Looking for Lewis and Clark" climbed all the way to . . . number fifty-eight, where it died. Nationwide there were no more singles left, they were all sold out, and this prick—whose name I damn well know—had to admit his gross misjudgment in the next Island staff meeting. By the time more singles could be pressed up, our proud record was dead. Christmas was coming, and the record plants had their huge orders for holiday music already. It would take two to three weeks to get more singles in the shops. It might as well have been two to three months. And so an Island employee killed our (almost) hit single right there and then and put a further knife in us by lobbying to get our A&R man fired. In early December our A&R hero, Nick Stewart, was let go and so were his staff.

Their replacements at Island resented us. To them we had been signed by someone else, and they saw little reason to help us. As our live show was our greatest strength, we hit the road yet again, doing enough touring to break us personally but not enough to break us nationally. Returning home to L.A., we saw the scene we were part of start to splinter. For some reason several of the Paisley Underground musicians completely rejected the moniker. I thought it was a terrific way to get everyone more ink as a musical/social scene, and it gave rock writers, always hungry for a different angle, a cool slant for an article on any of the bands involved. But some of my musician friends didn't want to be associated with it. Me? I am a United We Stand, Divided We Fall kinda guy. Those words are written on the Kentucky state flag, and as any union member knows, those are words to live by.

By early 1988 The Long Ryders were no more, but the seeds we helped plant were deep in the ground. It took a few years, but after a while the fresh green shoots of Americana and alt-country began to push out of the soil. I had no idea back then that The Long Ryders would have any influence on our collective cultural future, yet it is apparent today that we did. Back then L.A.'s musical scene had shifted to hair bands and arena rockers, but we got 'em in the end.

I remember drummer Greg Sowders explaining to a curious journalist, "The Long Ryders broke up 'Beatles style' with money problems, personal problems, girlfriend problems and 'hey fellas, what about my songs?' problems." That sums up my time in the big leagues quite well.

I moved to London in February 1992, never dreaming that Kurt Cobain, in a plaid shirt and jeans just like The Long Ryders wore six years previously, would (almost) singlehandedly destroy the aforementioned hair bands of 1988–1992 Hollywood. Thanks, Kurt. I owe you one. And I never would have dreamed that my old roommate John Silva would oversee this cavalry charge. Thanks, John. The irony of this is not lost on me.

So now I live in European exile. Yet my attitude to life, not just music, was forged by my time in Los Angeles. On the few warm days we have in London I defiantly wear the shorts of a happy American, with a loud, colorful T-shirt declaring allegiance to the Dodgers, the Lakers, or maybe The Blasters as I wistfully stroll down streets once trod by Dickens, Disraeli, Edmund Burke, and Virginia Woolf. Okay, that list isn't as hip as McGuinn, Mullen, Darby Crash, and Big Joe Turner, but hey, it will do.

CHAPTER 20

TEN SHORT YEARS ON THE SUNSET STRIP

by Peter Case

When the Whisky refused to book us, The Nerves decided to put on our own shows with the little bit of money we had, and we began to search for bands to perform with. Since 1975 we'd had short hair, played fast two-minute songs, wore suits on stage, and played music that was relentlessly minimal—no solos, no bullshit, and against the grain of everything that was going on at the time. It was one of the reasons we left San Francisco for L.A.—the people just weren't ready for us.

We'd had crowds at gigs chanting, "Kill the band," over our refusal to bend. We had begun to think our only chance with the music world might be with the coming of punk rock.

We ran into Tomata du Plenty and Tommy Gear from The Screamers at an art show on Gower and Sunset, and they looked and seemed amazing, with intensely spiked hair and super-bad attitudes, so we asked them if they wanted to play, but they insisted they weren't ready.

None of the bands were quite ready. Punk hadn't really happened in L.A. yet—it was like the hour before dawn.

We'd met a band called Zolar X, who weren't really punk but were very strange, as they lived their image, which could be described as "space-voyaging transgressives from another galaxy," and we had to admit, they were committed. Over at their house Zolar X relaxed in matching *Star Trek*–type casuals and fatigues, but when it was time to go to the liquor store for more beverages, they went into the "space-suit locker" and donned full protective gear, including fishbowl space helmets.

I guessed Zorrie and Ronnie and the gang had heard a few David Bowie records on their trips through the starry realms. They sounded like a far-out version of a glitter band, and we booked them for the first show at Gower Studios, the theater we'd rented for the show. We had to settle, since punk bands hadn't surfaced yet. Anyway, Kim showed up on time and emceed, and that was cool, but the fire department arrived too, and the gig was soon shut down—again.

The following week we were down in the labyrinths of the Columbia lot. In one of those rooms where we went to rehearse, the group booked in front of us was running down some incredible material. Through the door we could hear them wailing about a "Life of Crime" and being "Teenage," while another song just repeated the phrase "Do the Dance" a thousand times at high speed. We immediately barged in and asked them to perform with us, and they wanted to but didn't have a drummer. They called themselves The Weirdos.

We argued with Cliff Roman and the rest, telling them that "you'll find a drummer at the gig!" They sounded rocking without drums, and anyway, they had a very driving and exciting ramshackle sound.

They said okay, they'd do it.

Meanwhile a politically radical group from Carlsbad, California, The Dils, led by brothers Chip and Tony Kinman, got ahold of us somehow. They were a four-piece then and seemed right, sort of like a fast, angry, communist version of The Who. We liked them and added them to the bill.

Another band called Atomic Kid heard we were looking for bands, contacted us, changed their name to The Zippers, and were in. The Zippers were part of the *Back Door Man* magazine gang. They had a great sound and were super tight and rocking, with Danielle Faye and Bob Willingham trading off vocals. All the stylistic differences between bands hadn't been codified yet; the definitions of "punk" and "new wave" and "power pop" were still up in the air, unspoken. The scene was just being born.

The show with these bands and a few others we billed as the "Punk Rock Invasion." It was held in a large rehearsal room at SIR on Sunset, on Dave Mason's gear, which just happened to be there. We advertised on posters and KROQ and got a great crowd for that one, with everyone entering through a side door so the studio management wouldn't get wise. Phast Phreddie handled the introductions for the bands, The Weirdos electrified the crowd and found their drummer in Nicky Beat, Billy Zoom (pre-X) showed up with his pal Steve Allen (pre-20/20), and the gig was a blast. The studio managers were furiously angry at me when they discovered what had happened. They had no idea of our intentions when I rented the room for the night. A mic was busted when The Dils lead singer Jeff Scott spiked it, and on Monday SIR told me I'd never work in Los Angeles again. Oh well.

The Nerves arranged for the next two of our punk shows to be at the Orpheum Theater. We played the first one and then left town to tour the country coast to coast, the first national tour—at least that I know of—by an independent band.

We put twenty-eight thousand miles on a 1969 Ford wagon and played shows in San Francisco, Denver, Chicago, Cleveland, Toronto, Boston, New York, Washington, DC, and East Saint Louis. It was super exciting, and we met everyone everywhere—an incredible experience. We played and hung out with The Nuns, Pere Ubu, Devo, DMZ, The B-Girls, The Diodes, and a lot of other groups in their hometowns.

Jello Biafra, still wearing long hair and later to be front man of The Dead Kennedys, attended the show in Denver at Wax Trax.

The second leg started in Cincinnati, Ohio, opening for The Ramones on their Rocket to Russia tour. We played with them in Ohio, Wisconsin, Illinois, and Texas, including a show at the infamous Randy's Rodeo in San Antonio several months before The Sex Pistols show when Sid got attacked on stage. We got attacked too: the club owner had left the janitor's closet open and "fans" were taking swings at us with brooms. Later in the tour we played with Mink DeVille in Chicago, then drove home to play the Whisky a Go Go on Bomp Night.

Years later, when I was opening a show for fIREHOSE out in the Inland Empire, playing solo, I spoke with their bassist and leader Mike Watt, who told me, "Hey man, I loved The Nerves. I saw you guys at the Whisky a Go Go's Bomp Night. Me and my buddies from Pedro were right up by the stage, in front on the left. It blew our minds. Your guitar player was so jacked up, at the end of the set he ran up the stairs at the side of the stage, so manic and in such a hurry to get off stage he forgot to unplug his guitar. He dragged the amp halfway up the stairs after him. It was one of the greatest, wildest things I've ever seen!"

So The Nerves made it back to Los Angeles, played at the newly opened punk club the Masque, finally got a shot at the Whisky, then fought a lot and broke up. We never put out an album during the life of the band. The Nerves had imploded. Maybe we went crazy on the road. We had strong ability in songwriting and could have gone far with that when Blondie cut our song "Hanging on the Telephone." I wrote punk rock story songs like "One Way Ticket," and Jack created a psycho-pop monster, "Paper Dolls," that was covered by punk bands all over the world. What we didn't have was the ability to get along.

The first intimation I had of the growing Nerves fandom was a phone call from the leader of San Diego postpunk band Rocket from the Crypt, John Reis, who had just toured Japan and picked up a Nerves live bootleg that he was raving about. "The Nerves are like the missing link of rock 'n' roll!"

Years later a Nerves following grew among young rock 'n' roll fans beyond anything we saw during the band's initial run. Billy Joe

Armstrong of Green Day was performing The Nerves' "Walking Out on Love" in the *American Idiot* show on Broadway.

Paul and I did a tour in 2012 across the USA, performing songs of The Nerves through a series of packed clubs, culminating in a riotous gig at South by Southwest, introduced by Bill Murray, playing for a huge crowd of moshing, stage-diving teens and twenty-somethings who weren't born in '77. We were amazed that the whole crowd knew the words and sang along to "When You Find Out," "Working Too Hard," and the rest of The Nerves' material.

I call the next period, from 1978 until 1983, the rock 'n' roll juggernaut, the high tide of the scene taking off from its original elements.

Phast Phreddie began throwing a series of "Drink to the Death" parties, so I got invited and went. "Drink to the Death of Charlie Parker" and "Drink to the Death of Brian Jones" were two I remember. These were insane parties, held in Phred's apartment on Sunset Boulevard, to recognize the person's death anniversary. Their music would be played while everyone would just drink and get wasted. I met Jeffrey Lee Pierce at the "Drink to the Death of Charlie Parker," and we hit it off. He was in Phred's room, sitting on the bed, wearing a suit, quietly playing a Gibson 335 guitar. We started talking about music, and I gave him a copy of The Nerves' EP, and that's what led to Blondie recording "Hanging on the Telephone," as Jeffrey, unbeknownst to me, was their fan club president and gave the band a tape when they were flying to Australia. By the time Blondie arrived in Tokyo, they were hooked on the song, and when the cab driver at the Tokyo Airport heard the chorus on Debbie and Chris's boom box and began to sing along, that sealed the deal. I don't think "Hanging" songwriter Jack Lee even knows that story.

A little bit after The Nerves disbanded, Paul Collins and I tried a new group but soon parted ways as well, and I spent 1978 writing songs, painting houses, going to gigs at the Masque and other joints, and trying to get a new band together in Hollywood, one that would feature great songs like The Nerves but more rock 'n' roll and soul oriented. We also had to be able to really blow the roof off some clubs.

The Plimsouls were Louie Ramirez, Eddie Munoz, David Pahoa, and myself. That's two Mexican Americans, a Hawaiian, and me, an

English/Irish knucklehead from Buffalo. We formed on the first day of 1979 to play a five-sets-a night, three-nights-a-week gig at a country and western bar in El Monte, backing up a blind guitar player called Doc. Louie was the keystone; his drumming really drove the excitement in our shows. David was a natural musician—could play anything he picked up—and with us it was bass. Louie and Dave were best friends and grew up together in Paramount, California, next to Compton and south of Los Angeles. Eddie Munoz grew up in San Antonio; was schooled on the Austin, Texas blues/rock 'n' roll scene; and brought what we termed the "big note" guitar style to the band. We all saw eye to eye on the desire to include the influence of soul, blues, and R&B in our sound. After several months of the El Monte covers grind, I got fired for "being on acid," the group quit, and we started playing in Hollywood at places like Club 88, Blackies, the Troubadour, Madame Wong's, and the Hong Kong Cafe, doing original tunes.

My motto was "We never call for gigs, but we'll do every gig that calls us." That meant we also played a lot of parties all over the area.

We made a record right off for Steven Zepeda's Long Beach label, Beat Records, the *Zero Hour* EP, produced in Hermosa Beach by Danny Holloway. The record sounded good and immediately got on the radio, and the following we'd already built up at the clubs in Hollywood doubled, then quadrupled. The shows began to be packed everywhere we went.

The secret to outfits like The Plimsouls and the only way we could achieve "critical mass" was playing nonstop, gaining momentum over a number of gigs, and finally getting to the point where we would be "playing over our heads." I had to be sure the songs were great in the first place—inspired and put together right—because we weren't virtuosos and nothing about us was outrageous enough to get attention on its own. What got people's attention was, as Steve Hufsteter commented later, "The Plimsouls did something most bands couldn't pull off: they could project rock 'n' roll, and it was 100 percent believable." Summoning the spirits. The best bands were all about levitation. With The Blasters, X, The Plimsouls, you could feel the whole room take off and start flying during the set. Everybody felt it; it was undeniable. We transcended the style of music. The 'Souls had punk rockers and rockabillies, rock fans and new-wave people—we reached a wide cross-section of the music-digging public.

What we didn't have was common sense, a drink-proof work ethic, management that could wring respect from the vibe killers at the record companies, or a viable plan of touring and recording that paced us well and allowed us to do our best work.

So it was high times and low times. Things were great, but a struggle.

We got our first major label record deal at this point, when Michael Barackman signed us to Richard Perry's Planet Records, which was part of the Elektra/Atlantic family of labels. They'd been watching us build up the club following and dug the songs. Perry asked me, "Can you keep writing the songs?" and I actually replied, "I've got a million of them!" So they signed us and gave me an Elektra catalogue to look through. I immediately ordered a free copy of the Leadbelly box set!

We could go hear great music every night of the week in Los Angeles. It was unbelievable. The Alleycats were so intense, driving, tight, wailing; "Too Much Junk" was like a primal scream. The Last had classic sixties instrumentation with a combo organ and twelve-string, and the songs were insanely romantic but exploded with a punk rock vengeance. The Direct Hits were Paula Pierce's maximum-pop outfit years before her hard-garage Pandoras. The Falcons never got enough love, playing Steve Hufsteter's great songs, original soulful R&B.

Phast Phreddie & Thee Precisions was like a hole in the universe. I know for a fact they were one of Bob Dylan's favorites from that time. They played Jump R&B as well as jazz classics like "In Walked Bud," "Lester Leaps In," and "Compared to What?" plus Phreddie's heartbreaking original songs. Phred danced like a maniac. Steve Berlin led the horns, Chris Bailey was an incredible drummer, and they were super entertaining—one of the great lineups in L.A. history.

Carol Childs, my A&R person over at Geffen—and, at the time, Bob Dylan's girlfriend—told me that when she asked Bob who she should sign, he always said, "Sign Phast Phreddie." I was sitting in with the band at the Music Machine in 1984, and Bob came to the show and watched. Phreddie and I were the only two people in the club who didn't meet Bob that night—we shied off, too nervous.

One night The Plimsouls were headlining the Starwood, with Thee Precisions opening the show. The place was jammed with people, wall-to-wall kids. I saw Phreddie go onstage clear-eyed sober but holding a full bottle of gin by his side. By the time he came off, everyone in the club was cheering, the bottle was empty, and he was slurring and weaving. He'd gotten drunk in front of the whole place while he sang. I was oblivious to that an hour later, when I invited him onstage to sing with The Plimsouls. He came out and got a big ovation, and we launched into the Wilson Pickett number, "In the Midnight Hour." On the instrumental break in the middle of the song Phreddie did one of those lead-singer moves where you throw the mic out on the cord, then snap it back in, but Phreddie's aim was a little off, and instead of throwing it up into the air over the audience's heads, he threw the mic down, right into the mobbed pit, and it disappeared into the crowd. He began reeling it back in, but by the time he'd pulled the cord all the way back, the mic was gone. We kept playing the vamp while he stood there staring at the empty end of the cable where the microphone should have been. Some kid in the crowd had taken the opportunity and unscrewed the mic, and the bouncers caught him trying to get out the door with it.

Most of the bands drank together, knew each other, hung out together too. I remember one late night very early on, riding around town in a car with Phil Alvin after the clubs had closed, drinking quarts of beer. We sat on a fence by the Whisky, passing his guitar back and forth and playing for each other. Phil was surprised I knew how to fingerpick Mississippi John Hurt and Mance Lipscomb tunes. "The Plimsouls have roots!" "Yeah, man, I played that music on the street for years, up north." That evening included a last stop at the all-night speakeasy known as the Zero Zero. Driving home a few hours later I got confused and thought I was still in Buffalo.

The scene in Los Angeles was beginning to mutate, reconfigure itself a bit. Jeffrey Lee Pierce's band The Gun Club began to take shape. I actually played drums at an early rehearsal over at Fortress Studios, with Thee Precisions' Don Snowden on bass, but Jeffrey quickly replaced me with someone who actually knew how to play. The Gun Club did for blues what The Cramps had done for rockabilly—that is, completely hotwired it with punk rock energy.

I had written a new song, "A Million Miles Away," with my pals Chris Fradkin and Joey Alkes, and we wanted The Plimsouls to record it but didn't want to throw it away by putting it out on Planet. So on returning to Los Angeles after a long tour I went in and asked Richard Perry to let us out of our deal. He said, "Are you sure?" I said, "Yeah," and that was it.

We snuck into a studio after hours and cut "A Million Miles Away" for free, then put it out on our own Shaky City Records in alliance with Greg Shaw's Bomp! It went huge, getting heavy rotation on all the radio stations in L.A., one of the big summer records of 1982.

One night, as I was driving down to the Roxy to headline a three-night stand with The Plimsouls, I turned on the radio, and "A Million Miles Away" was on all four of the stations I had my push-buttons set to—KROQ, KLOS, KNAC, and KXLU.

The gigs grew bigger, the fans got more fanatical, and the money got better, though we had to pour most of it back into our label, and everything was growing, including the pressure. But the rise was big fun and exciting for a while and felt great, like a validation. You could make up a song at home, and the next thing you knew, thousands of kids would be digging it at a show.

One night I was over at Jeffrey's house, writing songs and drinking, and we decided to go get some more of everything up at Turner's on the strip. We stumbled out to my car and headed to Sunset, where the light was red, so we made a right on the light, legal in California. There must have been something about us, because a sheriff's car came up behind with the siren and lights on.

"Oh, fuck, the car's not registered! I have tickets out, and I'm not even sure my license is current! Fuck!" I'd just come in from the road, and these aspects of unfinished business flashed through my mind. I could really get screwed here. Besides, we were both drunk, and who knew what my buddy Jeff was holding. There was no telling.

I began to pull the car over to the side. "Not there!" came the irritated and extremely stressed-out voice of the cop over his crackling loudspeaker. I continued on, nervous as hell, pulled over a hundred feet down, shut off the car, and rolled down the window. Here comes the cop, an African American man with a severe buzzcut, which almost made him look like a skinhead. His voice was shaking with anger. "What were you doing back there! Let's see your license and registration," he barked.

Oh, man. I handed him my ID and started fumbling around, looking for the registration, which I knew was invalid. The car was a mess. I kind of mumbled, "Not quite sure where it is." Jeffrey opened up the glove box, and some old, unpaid traffic tickets came fluttering out and fell to the floor.

The cop looked past me. "What's your name?"

"Jeffrey Pierce."

The cop leaned in to get a better look. "Jeffrey Lee Pierce?"

"Yessir."

"You in The Gun Club?"

"Yessir."

The cop brightened up.

"Hey, you guys are pretty good. I saw you play a couple of weeks ago over at the Music Machine. Look, you gotta watch what you're doing on those right turns. And Jeffrey Lee, tell your friend here to take care of those tickets and registration!"

He walked back to his car, got in, and drove away.

And Jeffrey and I just sat and stared through the windshield.

I did get arrested driving over to see X play at UCLA. I was with my friends Bannister and Judy and had just got back to town after being on the road. I'd forgotten to pay my traffic tickets, and they'd gone to warrant. On Wilshire the cops pulled in behind me and turned on the lights and siren. They made me get out of the car and immediately handcuffed me behind my back. I was pushed into the patrol car and kept there as the officers made some rounds for a while then finally returned to the police station. They handcuffed me to a bench in the hallway. There wasn't much I could do but wait and see if my friends would get it together to bail me out. I was just sitting there, trying not to flip, when a uniformed cop walking by, stopped, bent his face down by mine, and said, "Go ahead, call me a pig now! Let's hear it! Call me a pig!" He seemed really pissed off and tense, like he just needed the slightest reason to beat the crap out of me while I was vulnerable and handcuffed. I said nothing, looked away. A minute later some other cops brought in a girl, and she was crying. "I've never been arrested before," she said between sobs, breaking down. "I've never been in trouble . . . [sob, sniff]." She turned to me, still crying, and between gasps choked out, "Are you in The Plimsouls?"

Several days later I was standing on the corner of Melrose near Aron's Records one Saturday afternoon in early 1983, watching the hundreds of people coming up and down the street shopping in all the boutiques and buzzing with the scene, and it all shocked me. "Where's this all going? What does it mean?" It was starting to seem like the rock 'n' roll–punk–new wave juggernaut was meaningless in the face of the sheer consumerism and materialist waste. A crash had to be coming.

Change was in the air again. It was affecting me and my friends personally.

I'd spent ten-plus years in rock 'n' roll bands, then decided I was going to be a folk singer—a solo singer of songs. My new songs were telling me what to do—so I did it. I've never regretted it. My first solo show was supposed to have been in 1981 at the Cathay de Grande on a bill with Jeffrey Lee, but I was sick nervous, got high school drunk, and had to be carried out before showtime.

I had a breakup and was heartbroken for a while. It wasn't my first experience with romantic disaster, but I felt it intensely. Jeff Eyrich, The Plimsouls' producer, had given me a copy of *Blood on the Tracks*. I'd been a big Dylan fan as a kid, but since my days in The Nerves I hadn't listened to him. I put the record on, and it cut me so deep. It instantly became one of the inspirations for my solo music. It reminded me of something about music I'd known long before The Nerves and 1977: the power of a solo singer with a great song.

It was around this time I wrote "Oldest Story in the World" for The Plimsouls, a song in the acoustic-ballad mode. At the shows I'd pull the harmonica out of my pocket and play the wailing solo in the middle, which took everyone by surprise and always got a reaction.

I played my first solo show at McCabe's in January 1984, cobilling with The Last's Joe Nolte. It scared me to death, feeling so naked without the band and the noise, but I loved it too. You could turn on a dime and take the audience with you. John Hiatt told me, "Playing solo puts you in touch with the real value of what you're doing," and I found that to be true. The solo shows seemed a lot more "dangerous" than doing shows with a band.

In 1984, between gigs, all I did was write songs. I was listening to a world of music I hadn't paid attention to before. Lotte Lenya singing the *Threepenny Opera* songs, Charley Patton's blues, and a lot of other music, including Harry Smith's *Anthology*, which I'd picked up one day at Tower Records, not knowing what it was. I was reading too: "Song of Songs" in the Bible; somehow all the "goats frisking down the slopes of Gilead" helped me understand a key to writing lyrics. And I rented a piano and began to work out the melodies on it.

One of the very first of the folk performers to come out of our scene was Phranc of the band Nervous Gender. Phranc was politically sharp and tuned into the issues of sexual orientation and gender prejudice that continue to roil our society to this day, and she had a lot to say. We played a few gigs together early on in my solo years, including a really memorable one with her and Victoria Williams at the Hollywood Legion Hall. Keith Morris and The Circle Jerks played acoustic that night, and the whole thing was "Wönderful," an affirmation that punk rock is really a form of folk music and belongs to the people.

I'd begun to write songs that told stories. It was a new thing for me, and it just happened. "Walk in the Woods" and "Small Town Spree" are as scary and confrontational as anything that was heard in the bowels of the Masque. These songs were connecting the dots of everything I loved in music and of all that had happened to me in the past, bringing it all up to date with a new twist of the roots.

Funny, a lot of the big transitions in my life have happened on New Year's Day. The Nerves arrived in Los Angeles on January 1, 1977. The Plimsouls began to play our gig in El Monte on January 1, 1979. And we broke up on New Year's Day, 1985, the night of our last show at Fenders Ballroom, Long Beach.

In early 1985 I made a solo record with producer T Bone Burnett, which came out in 1986, and it was seen by some as a big departure from what I'd been doing, but from my point of view it was just another stage in following the songs where they lead. I felt like I was waking up from a deep slumber. Since then many people have told me the record meant a lot to them. It went out to reach a new generation of musicians and fans. On the *Peter Case* album I was lucky to be joined by a stellar cast of special guests, many of whom were heroes of mine for years, including Van Dyke Parks, Roger McGuinn, Jim Keltner, Mike Campbell, John Hiatt, Gurf Morlix, Victoria Williams, Mitchell Froom, Jorge Bermudez, Warren "Tornado" Klein, Rusty Anderson, and Fred Tackett. When my tour went to France, I was in Paris, doing an interview with the magazine *Rock & Folk*, and their first question was, "You had many great musicians . . . how did you get ze Phast Phreddie to play on your album?"

CHAPTER 21

THE KINMAN BROTHERS: AMERICAN MUSIC

by Tom DeSavia

At the top of the 1970s the Kinman family relocated from the southeast corners of the US to a seaside resort city called Carlsbad, located just outside San Diego, California. Caught up with the excitement and inspiration of the dawning punk rock movement, brothers Tony and Chip Kinman formed The Dils, a decidedly politicized power trio who ultimately found a lukewarm welcome in their adopted sleepy beach community. Shortly after forming the band the duo opted to relocate to the then-mean streets of San Francisco in 1977, where they joined other trailblazing bands like The Nuns and The Avengers and helped ignite the Bay Area's burgeoning new music scene, a rock 'n' roll counterculture at war with its own legacy of flower child counterculture.

The Dils became a sensation in the dirty, now-legendary clubs up and down the West Coast and quickly established themselves as young luminaries in Los Angeles's punk rock crowd. In addition to being embraced by the alternative music press, the band gained some national notoriety following a cameo live appearance in the 1978 Cheech & Chong stoner comedy hit flick *Up in Smoke*, which helped spread word of the band across the US and even internationally.

The Dils' run would prove historically brief, with the band releasing their final EP, *Made in Canada*, in 1980. (The record was helmed by the then-unknown Bob Rock, who would go on to massive notoriety as one of the biggest rock producers of the next few decades.) The EP found the brothers exploring somewhat subtler tones leaning toward a growing influence of American roots music, foreshadowing a sound that would affect their creative path going forward. Perhaps feeling constrained by the restrictions of how punk was being defined in this brave new world, reinventing themselves under the influence of such diverse country pioneers as the Louvin Brothers and Waylon Jennings made perfect artistic sense. It became clear that the most punk rock thing they could do was walk away from punk rock.

The disbanding of The Dils led the Kinmans south to Austin, Texas, where—despite industry and peer resistance—the duo formed the unapologetically country-drenched combo Rank and File. The band—along with a small group of like-minded types, such as X side project The Knitters—would help influence the growth and popularity of the as-yet-unnamed L.A. cowpunk movement, opening the door for such prominent California acts as Lone Justice, Blood on the Saddle, The Beat Farmers, The Long Ryders, and a then-unknown urban hillbilly named Dwight Yoakam.

Rank and File soon signed to preeminent West Coast punk label Slash Records, and the notoriety brought by their debut album, *Sundown*, resulted in a move back out west. This time the Kinman boys would settle in Los Angeles and remain important architects of the city's ever-evolving music scene. The brothers would continue with a string of critically acclaimed projects over the years: Blackbird, Cowboy Nation, as well as the Tony-produced/Chip-fronted blues/punk combo Ford Madox Ford.

Illustrating their vast influence, Chip and Tony Kinman saw their songs covered by both D.O.A. (The Dils' "Class War") and the Everly Brothers (Rank and File's "Amanda Ruth"). If you followed them in any way over the years, both tributes made perfect artistic sense.

Shortly after we asked Chip to contribute to this book, his brother and lifelong musical conspirator took suddenly ill. Chip wrote his chapter quite literally at Tony's bedside, conjuring up lost memories and seemingly finally truly acknowledging the power of their artistic journey together. As we were putting the book to bed, Tony left us suddenly . . . his departure from this mortal coil shocked and affected not just the local L.A. community but also the world. A flood of major press, along with testimonials from musicians and fans, revealed what many of us already knew: the Kinman brothers were not only influenced by classic American music. They *are* classic American music.

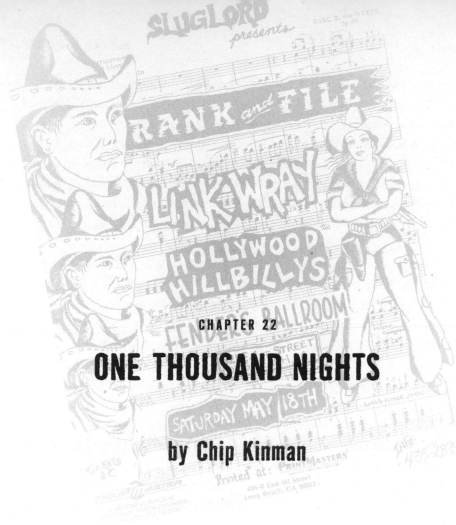

CHAPTER 22

ONE THOUSAND NIGHTS

by Chip Kinman

One thousand nights. That was all we had, and it was all that was needed. One thousand nights divided by three cities: San Diego, Los Angeles, San Francisco. One thousand nights multiplied by one hundred faces.

That was all we had, and it is all that was needed.

It has always been about the faces, never about the things—safety pins, zippers, locks and chains, straps and spikes, crazy colors, rebel flags, sugar skulls, and engineer boots. The flotsam and jetsam of one thousand nights.

To illustrate, imagine a picture of the Golden Gate Bridge. Now imagine a picture of the bridge with Will Shatter in front of it.

It is like the difference between the atom and the atom bomb.

It was Jean Caffeine and Richard Trance, Vale Vale, and Michael Kowalski, Dee Dee and Katherine Kato, Buddy Hate, Zippy Pinhead, Rico and Clancy, Alejandro Escovedo, Javier Escovedo, Rhoda Lopez (who drove me to Bomp! Records one day with no oil in her car), Danny Furious, Grey Ingraham, Penelope Houston and Jimmy Wisley (Avengers always), Baba Chanelle, Hector Penalosa, Jackie Sharp, Jill Von Hoffman and Joe Rees (the unblinking eye), Peter Urban and Beth Ann.

The Pop Tarts members—numbers one, two, and three—practically perfect in every way.

Frankie Fix, Ron the Ripper, Johnny Strike—full stop.

Alan, Alan as Elvis, Alan as Elvis and the B-Dils, Brittley Black, Hobbit and Peter Umpimgo, Vermillian and Heather, as lovely as their names.

Bobbie LeVie—she taught me how to cook and later committed suicide. RIP.

The Whitesides, Jonny and Annie—God bless them.

Craig and DeBisou, ready at a moment's notice. Michael Belfer and Ricky Sleeper. Amy, who made a porno, *The Vibrator Repairman*, Georgia, Debbie Dub, Siobahn, and the indispensable Nico Ordway.

Ted, Turd, Timmy, Tommy, Tina, Tex, and Tipper—now I'm just riffing . . .

Then there was Tony. Tony Kinman or Tony Nineteen, as he called himself because he did not want people to know we were brothers. You may pause to think about that.

Without Tony this story and everything in it would not exist. I would not exist. You may work out the formulation for yourself, but it is essential and true.

With Tony it was all possible. Together we had three things that would serve us throughout the years: a compass, a framework, and a book of tools.

The framework would expand and contract as needed. The bag of tools would be emptied and filled, depending on the situation. The compass was always true.

Tony, Zippy, and I decamped to Barnaby, British Columbia, to record the last Dils singles with producer Bob Rock, "Sound of the Rain," "Not Worth It," and "Red Rockers Rule."

Closer harmonies and midtempo and acoustic guitars, that EP— *Made in Canada*—put an amen to the one thousand nights.

It was simultaneously a stop and a start. Everything starts somewhere . . . somewhere like New York City.

I moved to Manhattan, and Tony moved to Portland. I wanted to start a new band with Alejandro, who was playing with Judy Nylon at the time, along with drummer Kevin Foley.

Not really sure what kind of music we were going to play, I drove across the America in The Dils' "I Hate the Rich Mobile" with Heather Zahl and a few records—Tammy Wynette's *Greatest Hits*, a Columbia Records country compilation, *This Time* by Waylon Jennings, and a run-down standby George Jones LP.

After dropping Heather off in Ohio, I found my way to a residency hotel in midtown Manhattan, set up my record player, and called Alejandro.

He was ready to play and brought along Kevin Foley on drums.

Practicing at an art space owned by Giorgio Gomelsky—our first fan!—it was agreed we would play country music.

I kept in touch with Tony through the USPS, and we began writing songs via correspondence. I would send lyrics and chords, and he would mail them back with ideas and corrections.

Alejandro and I settled on the name Rank and File, and along with Clash DJ Barry "Scratchy" Myers on bass and Kevin on drums, we banged out a set of original country music sure to please all, or so we thought.

We played a few shows around town, attracting the attention of Andy Schwartz, Ira Kaplan, The Gizmos, and a few others who were intrigued by our "high concept" band. Nobody played country music. Nobody.

After a couple of months we decided to take our show on the road. I booked a small tour—six dates—on the strength of the reputations of The Dils and The Nuns. We got in the van and headed west.

When we got to Portland we picked up Tony, who was night clerk-
ing at a motel. He had decided he wanted to play music again, so he
joined the band as a fifth member on acoustic guitar.

After returning to NYC Barry left the band, and Tony moved over
to bass guitar, as he had familiarity with that instrument—a lot of
familiarity!

Being serious about playing country music, we decided NYC might
not be the best place to be. So we pulled out a map to figure out where
we could keep it real.

Nashville? Nope, too closed. Memphis? Great town, but not quite
right. Atlanta? Tulsa? Bakersfield? No, no, and no.

Austin? Yes!

The Dils had played there at Raul's, it was the home of Outlaw
Country, and it was an easy place to live.

Once again we got in the van, and the band—minus Kevin Foley
and plus Bobbi LaVie—moved to Austin, Texas. What could go wrong?

We immediately hit a brick wall. Needing a drummer, we held a
few auditions, and to our chagrin WE didn't pass the auditions! No
one would play with us because we were playing country music.

Finally we hooked up with Slim Evans, the only drummer in Austin who would play with us—bless his heart—and, as it turned out, the
perfect drummer for RAF.

Started rehearsing at a space owned by one of Austin's premier
punk rock bands, and after they heard us we were told that "we were
selling out the punk rock revolution." True story!

I booked a show at Club Foot, Austin's big new-wave venue, opening for Pylon, the other band from Athens.

The club was glad to have us—after all, we were in The Dils and
The Nuns. Following our set we were told in no uncertain terms that
"you are not welcome back." Mind you, this wasn't because we sucked;
it was because we played country music.

We were left with few options. One being four sets a night every
Sunday at the Short Horn—a down-and-out honky-tonk.

Our audience consisted of a couple of drunks, a handful of snuff
queens, and a few college students who wandered in after eating
chicken-fried steak at the joint next door.

We only had one set, so we would play it four times a night to fulfill our obligation.

After a few Sundays the college students started to outnumber the snuff queens. People like Dennis Nowlin, Dickie Lee Erwin, E. A., Dayna, Monte Warden, and Jody Denberg started showing up—understanding and spreading the word.

This was all fine. Austin was easy living, and we were playing country music.

We recorded a couple of songs, "I Went Walking" and "Sundown," at a studio I can't remember and with an engineer who was a big deal in the Austin country circuit who had his larynx removed and couldn't talk.

We took our tape with us to California, where we went often to play shows, and gave it to Jill Hoffman, who gave it to Bob Biggs at Slash. That was the first they had heard of us.

While in San Francisco we played a show opening for The Red Rockers. Will the circle be unbroken, right?

Producer David Kahne came to the show to scout The Red Rockers for a record or producing gig. After we played our set he came backstage and said, "You guys are terrific! Let's start recording"—thinking we were The Red Rockers. We told him we weren't: "We are Rank and File!"

Without missing a beat, he said, "You guys are terrific. Let's start recording."

So he booked time at the Automatt in San Francisco, and since there was little money, we had to sneak into the studio after Jefferson Starship—who had a lock-out on the place—finished recording for the night.

We recorded several songs: "Coyote," "Sundown," "I Went Walking," "Conductor Wore Black," "Glad I'm Not in Love"—a few of which ended up on the first LP; others we rerecorded.

We went back to Austin. Back to playing alternatives to the venues that were alternative to the alternative venues because we still weren't accepted . . . because we were playing country music.

Our David Kahne tape started to get around, and I'm really not sure how Slash Records heard it, but I do know that Dave Alvin was instrumental to getting us signed there.

Back in Austin Jody Denberg—"the man who discovered Rank and File"—convinced Carlyne Majer, who ran an Austin-based management company handling acts like Marcia Ball and Alvin Crow, to come see us play. She did and offered to manage the band. We accepted, and she brought home the deal with Slash Records. We immediately headed back into the studio to finish our first LP, *Sundown*.

After it was released in 1982 everything changed fundamentally and forever, as it had when punk rock exploded in 1977. It was the big bang of Americana. It was the true beginning of "Chip and Tony."

Robert Hilburn gave it a glowing review in the *Los Angeles Times*, as did every other rock critic—this being the glory days of rock criticism and hard-copy print.

John Doe and Dave Alvin really helped spread the word, being label mates and—more importantly—friends. They had a true understanding of what was happening. I will be forever grateful.

We returned to Austin—selling out Club Foot—and prepared to climb back into the van to play country music all across these United States and Canada for another thousand nights.

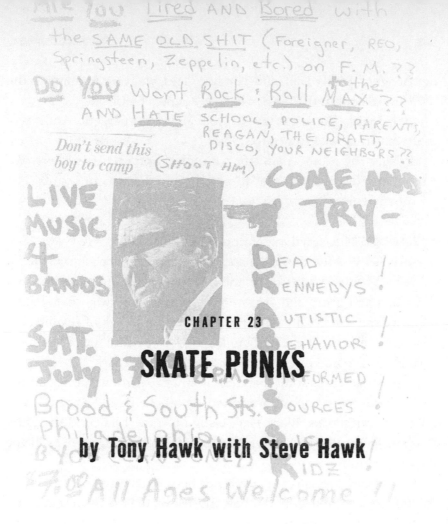

CHAPTER 23

SKATE PUNKS

by Tony Hawk with Steve Hawk

In 1982 or thereabouts, shortly after I realized that skateboarding was the only thing I really wanted to do, I was skating at the Oasis skatepark in San Diego when a promo guy from a local "adult contemporary" radio station, 91X, showed up and began handing out stickers. His plan was to have us sticker our boards or cars or whatever with the 91X logo, I guess to show the world that even edgy skateboarders listened to their station.

What he didn't know was that most of us had already moved beyond his station's lame format to the music that synced with our lives. We were skating to punk. Instead of the smooth, overproduced tracks of Foreigner, Steely Dan, and The Bee Gees, we were listening to the hard atonal sounds of The Sex Pistols, X, and The Clash.

Like skating, punk was raw. It was real. It was energetic. And it was pretty much all we listened to.

So after the promo man left, we took scissors to his stickers. We cut out the "91" and kept the "X" and slapped that on our boards. The promo man never knew.

My first exposure to anything remotely punk had come a few years earlier, when I was ten or eleven and saw a Sex Pistols poster at the local record store. I hadn't heard their music yet, but the poster looked forbidden and gritty and attracted me in the same way that skating attracted me. Eventually punk became the soundtrack of my life.

I don't remember the first punk song I ever heard, but I'm almost certain it was piped through the speakers at a skatepark. What I know for sure is that I was soon spending all my paper-route money on the iconic bands mentioned above and many others: Dead Kennedys, The Damned, Buzzcocks, Black Flag, Gang of Four, T.S.O.L., Devo, Pretenders, Descendents, Adicts, Adolescents, Peter and the Test Tube Babies, and more.

Skating already had created a divide between me and my childhood friends, but my interest in this new music isolated me from them altogether. Once I discovered my ilk in the misfits (and The Misfits) at the skatepark, there was no turning back. Most of the people I hung out with listened to punk and dressed the part. I was lucky that my parents didn't mind if my new skater friends had mohawks or piercings, as long as they were polite. And they were. I remember dudes with nose rings, leather jackets, and spiky pink haircuts giving hugs to my fifty-five-year-old mom at contests. It was both strange and beautiful.

Even though I loved the music—not only the songs themselves but also the way they solidified my sense of identity and individualism—live punk shows intimidated me. The crowds were filled with brawlers, and I was still a skinny preteen who looked like a surfer. At the few shows I went to, I got kicked and slammed and even got an egg in the head.

But I did see some cool bands live.

One summer night in 1980 I was skating the Marina del Rey skate-park when an influx of punks came pouring in. My older brother had driven me there, and I could see that he was concerned but also curious. The bowls began to fill up with bleached hair, leather jackets, and mohawks. A concert was about to happen: Circle Jerks, Venus, and The Stingers. Keith Morris told everyone to get together for a photo in the bowl I'd just been skating. The image that resulted from that gathering became the cover of The Circle Jerks' *Group Sex* album. I had no idea I was watching history in the making; I was just annoyed that I couldn't skate the park anymore. Looking back, I wish I'd been in the middle of it and could point to myself in that photo. My brother says the same thing.

As skating grew in the late eighties, the music came along with it. I got to see Social Distortion play at a skate competition in Seattle, The Chili Peppers on the deck of the vert ramp at the Vision Skate Escape in Irvine, and T.S.O.L. in some kid's backyard in Phoenix because he had a halfpipe. The apex of my live punk experience was seeing Bad Brains open (!) for The Adicts in 1985. GBH was also on the bill but didn't show.

I was seventeen, making a living as a pro skater and able to afford tickets to see the bands I'd grown up listening to. Life was good, and I didn't want the ride to end.

In the early nineties the ride definitely slowed down, though it didn't end completely. When skating migrated from vert ramps to the streets, the skate-punk bond solidified. Skaters found inspiration and redemption in the ugly urban landscape just as punk musicians had. One group danced on it, the other sang about it, but both used the blight to make undying art.

In 1998, when I got the opportunity to work on a skateboarding video game, I knew that music would be an important component, and I was stoked to share the soundtrack of my skatepark days with a new audience. I reached out to the bands I'd idolized as a kid: Dead Kennedys, X, Primus, Rage Against the Machine, Bad Religion, Adolescents, and more. Little did I know that the background music to Tony Hawk's *Pro Skater* would become just as iconic as the gameplay itself. The music turned out to be one of the many silver linings to a life of seeking validation on the outskirts of society.

Partly thanks to that game, I got the chance to meet and become friends with a lot of the musicians who'd inspired me as a kid. I've been backstage at a crazy number of legendary concerts. I've collaborated on a musical with Mark Mothersbaugh of Devo. John Doe and Exene of X recently did me the huge honor of performing at my fiftieth birthday party. It's all so unreal when you think about it.

But maybe it's not so ridiculous after all. When I was a kid people mocked the idea that skateboarding was a real sport, just as they mocked the idea that punk was real music. And even though skating and punk music have found some mainstream legitimacy, they both were created and cultivated by kids who didn't care about being legitimized. Which in the end might be the only thing that matters.

An epilogue: In 1983, about a year after we defiled the stickers that the 91X promo bro passed out at the Oasis skatepark, the station switched formats and began playing alternative/punk music. Thirty-five years later, it still does.

CHAPTER 24

FREE RADICALS:
A CONVERSATION WITH FISHBONE

by John Doe

Uncapped, undeniable, true, free, hybrid, genius . . . FISHBONE!

When we first saw them—back in '82 or '83—we thought they were as original as they come. All five members gave blood, sweat & tears to blend funk/punk rock for us lucky Angelenos, and then for the world. Along with scarce few others, Fishbone blazed a trail that is now a genre unto itself. Here's a conversation I was lucky enough to have wtih those innovators.

ANGELO MOORE: Lay it on me, John.

DOE: So here's you guys—you, Kendall, Fish, and Norwood and everybody—getting your shit together. You're in junior high school and high school, you're not going to clubs, you're not in the scene, but you find out about L.A. music. Punk rock is going on in L.A. So what's your introduction to that? Is it on the radio?

ANGELO: My first introduction was going to see The Dead Kennedys in 1984. Dinner is served at this roller rink out there in Pacoima. I went there, and I still had a Jheri curl and I had my pop-locking outfit on that I bought from Merry-Go-Round at the mall. I went to go see The Dead Kennedys because I thought the name was a crazy name. So I went in there, and I couldn't really understand any of the beats at the time. I just knew that the music was high energy. And it was also rough shit, so I went in there, and I saw this skinhead stage diving and jumping off the stage, right? I was like, man, that shit looks fun as hell, let me go and do it. So I went and did it—I got up on that stage, and I ran across the stage and jumped off, and everybody parted. I landed on my knee. I went to the back of the fucking roller-skating rink, and I watched the show sitting on the floor for the rest of the night.

DOE: Aww. But you guys are rehearsing, you're starting to make a band in, like, '80 right?

ANGELO: In 1979 is when we got together.

DOE: Who all are you listening to?

ANGELO: We were into Funkadelic and Rick James and the Bar Kays and James Brown. That's what I would hear when I would leave the house. But when I was in the house I would hear Richard Pryor and Flip Wilson, all that type of stuff. Duke Ellington. My mom and dad had a real big jazz collection too.

DOE: But there's got to be a lot of stuff that's bubbling up on the south side of L.A. at that point, and you're going "I don't want to do that? I want to play instruments." Why? Because it was more fun? You don't want to just go with what's beginning to happen?

ANGELO: Because it was fun, man. That shit was fun. Everything else we were doing, we were going to Uncle Jamm's Army, and the whole funk scene in Crenshaw, hanging out on Crenshaw Avenue, dancing and pop-locking on Hollywood Boulevard, and then going down and seeing all the low riders and everything—that was the kind of culture that I was putting myself in and out of. I really wanted to be around that 'cuz I was in the Valley, and the Valley was all white people. It was okay, but you know it just wasn't, like . . . once I stepped out of my house it was all white. Once I stepped in the house it was all black. Once I stepped out of the house I'd experience racism here and there—getting called nigger, stepping off the bus, walking home, and all that. I would take the RTD into L.A., into Hollywood, the 420, I'll never forget that man, the 420 RTD.

DOE: So let's jump into when Fishbone is starting to play out. That would be '82, '83? Or a little later?

ANGELO: That would be earlier, like '80, '81, '82. Madame Wong's East and West with The Busboys.

DOE: Was there a moment or a few times when you're getting into that scene that you realize, holy shit, this new music scene is pretty inclusive, and I don't have to worry about racism, or was it like, I'm not sure, I don't know.

ANGELO: Yeah, it was like, I'm not sure, pretty much. It was an "I'm not sure" thing, because, I mean, it was fun. That was the main thing I was looking at, the part that was fun. And I guess because I was playing in a band and people would see us on a stage, we really didn't catch too much of the racism part. We caught some of it, but not as much as I was catching that shit in the Valley. Raji's was the punk rock joint in Hollywood. Yeah, I remember all that shit. It was fun, man. It was fun to me. I wasn't getting none of the racist shit because everybody was onto rebel shit anyway.

DOE: So, talking about rebels, I'm wondering about when you're young and everyone's got some youthful rage. But you guys always seemed like it was a party and it was joyful. Even if there were some dark subjects, it was all about joy. How do you feel like you expressed that rage?

ANGELO: How did we express that rage and joy at the same time, right? It was fucking weird because at the time I was really hating white people. [Laughs] I was really hating white people for some of the shit I had to deal with sometimes in the Valley, you know? Then, when I would get into the punk rock scene, everybody was mad about something, yet they were releasing all of this energy and angst, and at the same time they was having a good time. So that good time part about it, which was the joy part for me, was the part that I enjoyed. So, you know, it was a rebel time in my life. I was dealing with racism here and there. Everything was just kind of backward and upside down. I'd walk out the house, and it'd be all white and wasn't nobody really talking to me. I'd have my friends that I would hang out with, and every once in a while I'd get that nigger shit, and then I'd catch the bus into L.A. because I wanted to be around black people. I was like, I know that black people just don't end in my house. I'd catch that bus, go into L.A. and Hollywood, and I'd jump into that, dancing on the corner, and then I'd go to Raji's and all the rest of the clubs in Hollywood. It was fun, aggressive, and on some rebel-type shit too. It was perfect, man.

DOE: So maybe you and the band getting together was more about being happy and joyful that you got to hang out and do your shit rather than the rage that was going on outside?

ANGELO: We were doing what we wanted. When we started playing in the clubs in L.A., actually before we were called Fishbone, we were called Megatron. So when we'd end up getting booked, we would get booked with these heavy-metal bands because of the name. And then on the stage it was a whole different story.

DOE: [Laughs] Did you hear the screeching of wheels, like "Whaaaat?"

ANGELO: Yeah, it was wheels screeching like a motherfucker. That was our time to convince whoever was looking at us that we were good enough to hang with whoever we were sharing the stage with.

DOE: But you said it was The Busboys that really brought you under their wing?

ANGELO: Yeah, I'd say The Busboys walked us through the door.

DOE: Where do you think it went from there? Was it other punk rock bands saying, "holy moly, these guys are serious, so let's get them on the bill?" Do you remember how that transitioned? Because I remember you guys playing with everybody.

ANGELO: Yeah, we played with everybody. We was taking every gig that came our way. That's when we started playing with X, The

Circle Jerks, FEAR—all that. We didn't see it as something that was really different or abstract or *one of these things doesn't belong here*, because we just saw it as music. Then with our background of funk, soul, jazz, and everything else, that element was in the music already. That's when the horn section came into the picture.

DOE: Right. And you'd say that horns were in there because you had pals that were playing horns?

ANGELO: We started out in band, man. In junior high and high school we had met in band. I don't even know if we made it to marching band—it was just *band*. [Dirty Walt comments in the background.] Yeah, yeah, we got kicked out of marching band, that's right. For some reason or another we got kicked out of marching band. What was the reason?

[DIRTY WALT chimes in.]

DIRTY WALT: Yeah, the band leader said, "You guys go practice," so we go into the men's locker room and start working on our own shit. Then he comes in and says, "You guys are DONE here."

DOE: For working on your own shit?

ANGELO: Yeah, but he didn't really give us a reason. He had the band assistant come tell us. Chicken-shit motherfucker.

DOE: Where does ska come into this? Your first EP, you've definitely got some ska influence.

ANGELO: Really Walt introduced us to all that. Matter of fact, he's sitting right here. You might want to ask him that now. Walt, tell John Doe how we got introduced to ska.

WALT: It came from when I was hanging out with one of my aunt Frankie Hill's friends, like a roommate. A black gay punk rocker. He was listening to The Specials, The Selecter, Elvis Costello—all kind of bands like that. Every time I would go over there I would hear the records, play the records, and then I was so into them that I brung them back to the fellas.

DOE: Right. And you figured, "We got horns, we got energy, boom."

WALT: I just saw it as another avenue of musical ideas we could take other than where we was at. And they ran with it.

DOE: So you guys are making Fishbone a band, I'm talking like '82 to '87, so there's got to be a lot of influence from the early New York rap stuff coming into the south part of L.A. Obviously Ice-T is out there in the clubs. So why didn't you guys say, "Well, this is what's happening down here"?

WALT: We're too weird. If we tried to become a rap group, it would be probably one of the weirdest rap groups and way ahead of its time. So, you know, we couldn't be like P-Funk, because P-Funk already had their stamp on that, so we would just be another imitator. So we had to create our own little niche and groove that we try to hold, which is difficult.

DOE: So maybe your influence with P-Funk and Rick James is, like, "This is too much fun. We all get to play instruments in a band rather than just going with the current trend."

WALT: You know, we get to put all our influences from the different trends that we had joined into one sack.

DOE: Who was the drill sergeant in the band? Like the task master who said, "Okay, rehearsal is at six o'clock, be there."

WALT: Well, I'm usually the guy who tries to keep them in some kind of line. But the guy that calls the plays would be Norwood. And we evaluate the play and try to make it run as efficiently as we can.

ANGELO: And then I'm the one who's gotta go out there and say it.

DOE: [Laughs] Then you get your salesman, Mr. Angelo, to sell it.

WALT: Yeah, exactly.

DOE: Back in that time how did the songs come together?

WALT: Most of our songs would come from jams. We would jam together, and all the sudden somebody'd start singing something, and we'd start adding to it. There's a few songs where individuals may have written it, but then we all get a hold of it and turn it into what we think it should be.

DOE: It's great to hear you, man.

WALT: Good to hear from you too, John. Here's Angelo.

ANGELO: I remember riding on the bus, on the RTD, and Walt had his ghetto blaster sitting on the back of the bus, and I remember he was playing The Selecter. He was playing "Too Much Pressure," and I was, like, "Oh shit, what's that?" After that I knew what ska was, the second generation of ska. Later on I found out the first generation of ska was Jamaican, The Skatalites and all that.

DOE: All right, my friend, I think I got a good picture of what was happening for you all back then. Stay safe, and keep doing what only you can do. And please ask Norwood to gimme a call.

ANGELO: Okay, man. I be talking to you later, peace.

Five days later DOE talks to NORWOOD FISHER.

DOE: You and your brother, when did you guys start playing?

NORWOOD FISHER: I was six and he was four. I asked for an electric guitar for Christmas, my mom got it for me, and he asked for a snare drum. And we went to the business of writing songs.

DOE: At six and four?

NORWOOD: Yep. We didn't get good for a long time, but we were banging at it.

DOE: So when did you switch to bass?

NORWOOD: At age eight.

DOE: So guitar is not your thing.

NORWOOD: When I got the guitar the first thing I did was play bass lines on it. There was nobody around to show me chords, and I just started playing bass lines. I didn't consider myself a bass player, but at age eight I asked for a weight set for Christmas, and on Christmas day my cousin came over. He looked at the weight set, looked at me, and said, "This boy ain't going to lift some weights," and right there he offered to trade me the weight set for his bass. He said he'd throw in his amp, his speaker. The bass was a Fender Lead Bass Two, which I can't find one today. And it was stolen from me—one of my neighbors stole it much later on. The amp was a Peavey Mark 4 amp with a 215 cabinet. He threw in his rock record collection as well because he said he wasn't going to listen to rock anymore; he was going to listen to jazz. That record collection was some pivotal Jimi Hendrix albums, some Jefferson Airplane, Chicago Transit Authority, and a bunch of other stuff—*America Eats Its Young* by Funkadelic. Those probably were the most influential things to my eight-year-old mind. That's '72 going into '73.

DOE: Damn, so by '79 you've got Kendall [Jones] and Angelo [Moore] and all that stuff going on?

NORWOOD: Yeah, around '78 everybody in the band was in school together except for my brother and Angelo. Kendall and Chris [Dowd] would come to our apartment, and we'd jam. Then Chris's uncle would come over, and he'd pick up my amp, pick us all up, put us in his car, and take us to Chris's house because Chris had a piano. We'd bang away and yell into the air, make up songs and whatnot. Then in the ninth grade Angelo came to the school. Then everybody that would be the original members of Fishbone were all together in one school because my brother entered the seventh grade as well. For such a long time rehearsals were in me and Chris's bedroom, which was in an apartment building where the manager of the building lived above us. We disturbed the entire building. Everybody in the building was black. The first time somebody said something positive about what we were doing, the manager of the building came down and said in passing, "Yeah, y'all sounded like y'all got a groove today." And he was talking about the song "Skankin to the Beat." Which I didn't think about until years later, like that is not hood style, and he responded to that. They allowed us to become who we needed to be.

DOE: Wow. So like drum kit, bass amp, the whole nine yards?

NORWOOD: Yep. Loud as hell. [Laughs]

DOE: Oh, God bless your apartment manager. God damn.

NORWOOD: Yeah, they let us be, they let us grow, they took the punishment. [Laughs]

DOE: That's when you all are getting bussed up to the Valley?

NORWOOD: We were all getting bussed in the eighth grade, but Angelo lived in the Valley, so he just came to the school in the ninth grade. From there we just started discovering music together. Funkadelic, Parliament, Rick James, Jimi Hendrix, classic Led Zeppelin, The Who—all of that was a common bond. All of our fathers—me, Kendall, and Chris—our fathers liked hippie music, and our mothers liked soul. So we could all bond over those things.

DOE: Do you think that's why you gravitated toward the punk rock world?

NORWOOD: Absolutely. We were wide open. That was it—we were just open. Funkadelic kind of informed us that anything was possible, musically. They had no boundaries, so why should we, you know? We were just open. In the ninth grade, right as I kind of got into Rush . . .

DOE: Oh no. Well, that's an age that you want to play as many notes as possible.

NORWOOD: Yeah. Some kid at school was, like, "You'll like Rush." And I did. Then right around that same time the noise that was punk rock was getting louder. It was a lot of this stuff in the media like '78 to '79. We were curious about what that was. Kendall's cousin, Ira, happened to be a bouncer at the Vex. He took Kendall to the Vex. Kendall came back scared as shit.

DOE: [Laughs]

NORWOOD: Kendall was afraid of punk rock.

DOE: Aww.

NORWOOD: He was, like, "The devil's in there!"

DOE: [Laughs]

NORWOOD: Kendall wasn't even that religious. It's ironic. Me and my brother went to church with our mother all the time. And Kendall was, like, "The devil's in there!" But we were still curious. Guess it didn't scare us that much.

DOE: Do you remember who he saw?

NORWOOD: He saw Black Flag at the Vex. Which I can understand how that can be scary. [Laughs]

DOE: I think that was one of the things that messed up the Vex. I think Black Flag went in there, and a couple of numbskull fans broke shit.

NORWOOD: Right? [Laughs] Maybe he witnessed that. He saw Black Flag; he went to several shows with his cousin. So whatever he was scared of didn't scare him too much not to go back. When we got to tenth grade Chris went to go live with his dad in Washington state. He'd call me on the phone, and we'd listen to records over the phone. He had Black Sabbath albums and he had Sex Pistols. At some point he came back. Actually, I went to The Who's first farewell tour. I can't remember who came with me. Maybe Kendall and maybe Chris. The Clash opened. So I was excited to see both bands. That was my first time getting into a slam pit. It was just a bunch of jocks. It was not any punk rock there that I could see.

DOE: Would you say your first live exposure to punk rock was The Clash opening for The Who?

NORWOOD: I think so. Then in the eleventh grade there was a punk rock show on my grandmother's block in the hood.

DOE: No kidding.

NORWOOD: In a garage. On the flyer it says Hunt Sales was the drummer. I thought it was hilarious because it was Soupy Sales's son. So me and Fish, we went to our grandmother's house, hung out with grandma, then walked about seven houses down into this garage, and got down with that band. I just moshed around and fucking went, like, "Okay, that was a trip."

DOE: That would be '81 to '82.

NORWOOD: Yep. At our school, Hamilton High School, there was a couple of punk rock kids that were black. At the time the whole thing was influencing us. I was already doing my version of going outside, dressing crazy. A lot of things were happening. We were fans of The Busboys, and so that led us to The Blasters and Oingo Boingo. New wave was happening, right. New Wave got played on black radio in Los Angeles. So from the late seventies, '79ish, you could hear Devo, Blondie, the B-52's, Gary Numan got played on black radio.

DOE: So there's a conventional R&B scene going on the southside of L.A. Was it because you loved Funkadelic so much that you thought the R&B close to home wasn't your thing?

NORWOOD: For us, we didn't think about what we were doing. We just did what came naturally. Because we didn't know any better. [Laughs] People would tell you, "You can't do that," and it was, like, "What the fuck are you talking about?" We did what we wanted to do. It was so not calculated. We did what we felt, what felt natural. I think the reason why was because this Funkadelic thing was so out there, and Funkadelic had no boundaries, so in hindsight I can say that's probably why. But we kept discovering things, because The Busboys were doing it. I remember to this day, the day that Angelo brought in The Bad Brains. We kept discovering these things together. Black radio in L.A. played reggae late at night starting in about '78. You could hear Bob Marley late at night. Then, like, Steel Pulse became a thing. At the same time Peter Tosh was on

Saturday Night Live with The Rolling Stones. I didn't grow up with a great knowledge of reggae—this is how I began to know about it. Then Third World and Black Uhuru came into our consciousness. Because of what we were hearing in the media about punk rock, we took reggae rhythms and just sped them up.

DOE: And kind of got hip to ska at the same time?

NORWOOD: Well, I thought we invented it. Walt had an aunt that was a limo driver, and somebody had given her some cassettes. About three days after I declared, "We invented something new—let's name it!" Walt brought in these cassettes, they were The English Beat and The Selecter. So we dove head first into that. Then before we got really deep, there was *The Decline of Western Civilization*, and *Dance Craze* did a double feature at the Fox Theater in Venice, and the whole band went to see it. That was when we really got shown what the fuck it is. It was that double feature that was, like, "Holy shit," you know, like, "Fuck, dude." That was a pivotal day.

DOE: That's cool. Because you thought, "I can do that, it doesn't look that hard, and we would fit into that."

NORWOOD: Yeah. Yeah, we were already going those directions. We were already toying with it. But at the same time, like I said, black radio was playing the two-tone thing, and it was inclusive. You could look on the TV, and you could see black faces. You could see a black face in The Plasmatics. There was Bad Brains. In our mind punk rock was inclusive. You know? So we were like, "This is what we're doing."

DOE: You mentioned The Busboys. You opened for them?

NORWOOD: Kinda ironically, in '83 I'm a senior in high school, and Walt was going, like, "Yeah, we gotta figure out how to play a club." I didn't know how to go play a club. I tried to go see FEAR at the Whisky sometime in late '82. I didn't know how to get in. Later on, friends of mine talked about how they snuck into that show, right? I was too young to get in. But I didn't know sneaking in to punk rock shows was a thing.

DOE: [Laughs]

NORWOOD: And The Untouchables hit the scene. They had all-ages shows. We actually went to a few shows at their residency at the

Roxy. In '81 we started picking up the *LA Weekly* and reading about the scene. At some point I discovered KXLU. So it was all of those things combined. And Prince, *Dirty Mind* had enough of a punk rock influence in there. That turned the whole hood out. That opened up. L.A. became truly integrated. My generation didn't give a fuck. Then The Time came out, and everybody found out that The Time wore thrift-shop clothes on their album cover for that first record. I thought black L.A. went to Melrose Avenue to Flip and Poseur to buy clothes. There was this moment—it lasted until gangsta rap exploded, until NWA. There was this moment between '82 and probably '86 where black L.A. didn't give a fuck. It was like black girls fell in love with Adam Ant. Everybody watched MV3 and the New Wave Theatre. *Saturday Night Live* has some pivotal shit on it, right? FEAR on *Saturday Night Live*—Devo, The Specials. It was seeing The Specials, seeing *Dance Craze*, *The Decline of Western Civilization*, and P-Funk shows—these are all the greatest shows on earth! We were, like, "We gotta bring it." It was all just natural. You just hit the stage and get it. Angelo especially, he is so authentic to a fucking fault! He is, onstage, a one-hundred-percenter to the max. So having him as a frontman, you just gotta go there. That's all we knew. Honestly, all the bands that we grew up loving were original, you know? People didn't just run around no cookie-cutter sound in the thing.

Then in '83 we all went to go see George Clinton and the P-Funk All Stars at the Beverly Theater. We wanted to meet George Clinton and Bootsy. When we went to the back stage to wait for them, there was Brian O'Neill from The Busboys and Nina Hagen. We had our first club show that week at Madame Wong's Chinatown. We told Brian about it, and he said, "I'll be there." And he showed the fuck up!

DOE: That's a righteous guy.

NORWOOD: Yeah, he saw the band, and he connected us with their first manager, Roger Perry, who happened to manage FEAR at one point too. They're the ones who talked us into changing our name, thank goodness.

DOE: So I'm curious, as gangsta rap is starting to come up, you guys had already devoted enough time, so you didn't want to switch.

NORWOOD: That was not even an option, man. By that point we were living out L.A. punk rock scene shit. Going to shows, figuring out how to sneak in to the shit we couldn't get into. Actually maybe even in the '83 zone, starting to pick up fanzines. Religiously reading the *L.A. Dee Da* section of the *LA Weekly* and Ruben Blue's *Scratch* magazine. We were trying to figure out how we were going to navigate our way into the club scene.

DOE: So was it the level of playing or just the scene that you thought, "This is me, this speaks to me"?

NORWOOD: Okay, so the first time I was in the real slam pit, I was, like, "Oh shit! I wish all my homies from the hood could do this!" I immediately got it. 'Cause we were never gangster. Walt had a brief gangster thing; he did that. But no one else really did. You're friends with these guys before they were gangsters, and all I could think is, "Damn all of that excess teenage testosterone that's being used in gangster activities—this is a positive way to release it!" That's my first thought in the mosh pit.

DOE: Wow.

NORWOOD: I had the same energy—that was an impulse. When my homies talked about gangster activity, I was, like, "Man, I'd kind of like to fight, you know?" [Laughs] That sounds like fun.

DOE: That's really funny because I asked Angelo the same thing about young people. They're just mad. At some point, when you're fifteen to eighteen, you realize things aren't fair—fuck you, guys. You have this rage that's in you just because you're a teenager. But your music was joyful, running around and everyone's going crazy. Angelo said that that was kind of the way that you guys channeled your rage. So would you say that it's similar for you?

NORWOOD: Absolutely. Because, I don't know, there is an optimism to what we do. Wherever that came from, I don't know if that was being born in the middle of the civil rights movement and that legacy kind of following you. I don't know what it was. I didn't know any other way to be, I can tell you that much. Give pause to anger. Like maybe there'd be a better day. So, yeah, ultimately even though we grew up in gangster-related neighborhoods, we weren't gangsters. I understand it. You kind of grow up having a little bit of that energy if you grow up in the hood. But it wasn't us. We were more like nerds! You know what I mean? We were lucky that we grew up in a time where if the gangs saw you were up to something, they gave you a pass. You know? That ended probably a year or two after we got out of high school, like '85. One of my friends who grew up in Compton was, like, "Yeah, they're not giving people a pass no more. If you're in the hood, you gotta put in work." And I'm like, oh man, I grew up running around L.A. with the wrong colors, but I didn't look like I was anybody's enemy. They could look at me, see I was dressed kind of crazy, new wave, punk rock, Prince punk—whatever. They saw it, like, "Yeah, he's not my enemy," and I rolled through unscathed, basically.

DOE: Like you say, you had something that you valued. You valued music, you valued learning how to play an instrument, where other people didn't. You were lucky that something led you to want to play a bass at eight years old. That's pretty great.

NORWOOD: Well, if it wasn't for that moment my cousin was, like, "You're not lifting them weights." If I'd have been the dude that sat in the backyard and lifted weights and got all diesel by the time I was thirteen, I might have looked like a good soldier. [Laughs]

DOE: I hope you thanked your cousin many, many times.

NORWOOD: Yes, about three Thanksgivings ago we had a dinner at his house, my cousin Bud. He looked at me and he went, "You took that bass and you went kind of far with it." And I was, like, "Yeah, thanks for giving me my life, man."

DOE: That's incredible. Think of all the people that you guys have touched, not just you but where it goes from there. Damn.

NORWOOD: Yeah, John, that was, like, that puts me in the "I have lived" zone. If it had to be over, I have thanked the person who gave me my life, you know?

DOE: Part of this book is about the legacy that we all helped make. Have you seen anybody that you can say, "Oh yeah, those guys, they liked Fishbone". Or played with people that came up to you and said, "Man, I saw you guys doing your thing, and it helped me".

NORWOOD: The guys in The Bouncing Souls came up and said, "We used to go see you guys at the Ritz with The Red Hot Chili Peppers and Murphy's Law, and that's why we picked up our guitars." But the first time somebody came up to me and said that and it really tripped me out—it was the guys in Anthrax!

DOE: What!?

NORWOOD: Yeah. They were, like, "You might not be able to tell, but your band was really influential on us." I still am, like, "You guys are too old for that." But there's a ton of bands! You know, No Doubt, guys in Sublime, 311—all those bands—they voiced very clearly that Fishbone is why they do it, is one of the big reasons why, one of many, I'm sure. There's a long list of those bands that, it's actually ultimately humbling beyond words. All I can say is that I know what it feels like to be a fan. And I'm glad that somebody makes me feel like what the music I love makes me feel like. Really, John, when it comes time for me to get into songwriting mode, I'm putting on X. My X record is right next to my Al Green record, you know? It's the music that I love, that I'm a fan of. It was The Clash, it was Funkadelic, it was Sly and the Family Stone. I'm going to put on some Squeeze songs, go listen to some Kate Bush, what the fuck ever, and be inspired.

CHAPTER 25

COME ON, ALL YOU COWBOYS . . . DON'T YOU WANNA GO?

by Annette Zilinskas

I was at the forefront of two separate musical movements that happened sequentially in Los Angeles in the early part of my musical career: the Paisley Underground scene with The Bangs (soon to be The Bangles) and the pioneering cowpunk band Blood on the Saddle.

I played bass in The Bangs, not because I was particularly good at it or had a burning desire to do so but because what I wanted more than anything was to be on stage and perform in a band, no matter what.

The other band that I was in, Blood on the Saddle, was a turn-ing point of personal growth for me, as it enabled me to step out of the shadows, take the microphone, and sing full voiced. Co-fronting a band that was redefining and re-energizing country and bluegrass music turned this shrinking violet inside out. Being able to tour with real support from college radio airplay helped develop my confidence to stand center stage, but really all of this was due to a big push from a tall, dark, exceptionally talented guitar player with intense eyes named Greg Davis. He literally and figuratively pushed me to the front of the stage and said, "Sing!"

Growing up in the San Fernando Valley was a cultural wasteland of just endless waiting and waiting . . . for something—anything! The monotonous days were spent being preoccupied with, say, a cute boy on the block, a new mall, cutting class and hitchhiking to the beach, shoplifting pucca shells from the mall (and maybe getting caught). I was withdrawn and bored, and music was really the one thing that fully engaged me. The only thing I looked forward to was coming home from school, throwing on my PJs, and singing in my closet to Linda Ronstadt's *Heart Like a Wheel* or to Wanda Jackson's "Mean Mean Man." The closet had great acoustics, and I could hear myself really well, plus *no one else could hear me sing*. We were a reserved fam-ily, and stuff like that was not what little girls should do. Any form of taking the spotlight made me feel self-conscious at that age.

At the time my other true love was rockabilly. Songs like Gene Vin-cent's "Race with the Devil," Eddie Cochran's "Twenty Flight Rock," Elvis Presley's "Mystery Train" and "Trying to Get to You," Yardbirds' "Here Tis," and Rachel Sweet's rollicking, punky cover of "Baby, Let's Play House" were the greatest thing to me.

I had problems in junior high, where I transformed from being a shy girl to a popular one in just one summer! I believe music got my mother, Dagmar, through those rough parenting times, as she was under the spell of seventies country music. An immigrant from Ger-many, she loved Don Williams, Merle Haggard, George Jones, Johnny Cash, Willie Nelson, and Waylon Jennings. She would carefully label her compilation cassettes, piled high and stacked up against the radio sitting on top of the refrigerator in our Van Nuys tract home. They were perched like a regal, referential nod to love gone wrong. Songs of cheating or broken promises and D-I-V-O-R-C-E emanating from the fridge like a preacher leading Sunday services. I learned rather young that love WAS just a four-letter word and that it didn't necessarily begin with the letter "L."

But then, during my senior year, something happened, and that something was KROQ-FM's *Rodney on the Roq*, the local and now-legendary radio show that came over the airwaves on the weekends. This is where I heard Rodney Bingenheimer spin The Pretenders and Blondie, right around the time when I started to drive the 101 Freeway south to where life and culture began. I went to the Hong Kong Café and heard The Blasters for the first time while dressed up in a fifties vintage dress and pearly earrings and standing high in pumps. I felt glamorous like the images from the 1950s, which was easily my favorite era then. There were cute boys at these places with slicked-back short hair and biker boots, not the San Fernando Valley stoner look I was accustomed to. These guys were cynical and funny and knew about music and cars and clothing. I began to understand what *cool* was.

I first met Greg Davis at the Whisky when I went with my sister Beatrix and best friend Laurie to see the band X. I don't remember much about anything but the band that night, and I couldn't take my eyes off the stage where X was playing. Exene stood up on stage like a silent-era movie siren from another planet, with teased dark hair and porcelain skin. A punk rock Theda Bara from Venus with blonde-streaked dreadlocks; her vocal wail blended with John Doe's baritone. It was a ferocious musical assault blending punk rock, rockabilly, and blues with country. Their noir-ish lyrics described a nocturnal night life and desperate romance amidst the mean streets of Los Angeles. I was completely drawn in.

Some weeks later, unbeknownst to me, I would meet Greg Davis again, but this time through a *Recycler* ad that he placed. It read something like "Black Flag and Ramones meets Robert Johnson and X at the Crossroads along with Johnny and June Cash." Greg's ad sounded dangerous and mysterious. It was a cool drink of water waiting for me just over the hill, and I was ready to hop in my Volkswagen Rabbit to check it out. Only someone as restless and curious as me from the 818 area code could feel there was some potential lying there for both good and probably some bad too. I didn't care. I was down for it. I called him first, and we talked about my love for Linda Ronstadt, and he said he wanted to pervert country and bluegrass the same way Gun Club did it to the blues and X did to rockabilly. His small apartment on Afton Place in Hollywood was bare and austere. It was furnished with one table, some scattered books, one set of kitchen utensils, one chair, one glass in the cupboard, and, of course, his acoustic guitar that was always within arm's reach. I listened while Greg pontificated on the state of music, his travels to New Orleans, how he learned to play the slide guitar with a Coricidin bottle, learning Robert Johnson songs and playing them on Bourbon Street. He talked about making money as a house painter and having to pawn his Les Paul time and time again when things got lean.

I had some teenage "sass" but nothing to back it up. I had guts and a desire to be in a band and make good music but not much life experience. When he picked up his acoustic guitar the room seemed to change, and I knew there was something special unfolding in front of me. I could sing and he could play guitar, and we had lots of personal chemistry. I didn't know the technical aspects of the guitar, but his playing was so intense that it was actually a little frightening. His personality changed too when he strapped on his guitar: he became more badass, with 'tude.

One of my and Greg's first dates was to see X at the Country Club in Reseda, in my old stomping grounds. It started out fine but didn't end so well. I wound up staying behind. From that point on, my feelings only grew for him. I was in need of some form of excitement, and he seemed to fit that bill. I'd go over to his place regularly, and he'd play and I'd sing because he liked my voice. Boom. Things started to move pretty quickly for us as a couple. He was my first boyfriend, and I was about to start my first year of college. However, there were things happening simultaneously in my life, and that was me playing bass for a band called The Bangs.

Just out of high school I responded to an ad—again!—in the *Recycler* that Susanna Hoffs placed, looking for a bass player. It said her influences were The Monkees, Love, and The Byrds. I responded immediately, even though I never played or even picked up the bass before our conversation. We got on well, and I just wanted to be on stage, in a band, so if that meant learning to play bass, I would do just that. It was a way that I could be on stage even if I wasn't singing. I was a step closer.

Before forming The Bangs, Sue graduated from UC Berkeley as a dance major. She grew up in Brentwood, and the Peterson sisters, Vicki and Debbi, were raised in Pales Verdes but moved to Hollywood to get close to the action. Sue had an outlook on life filled with wonder and curiosity. I was so sheltered and myopic in comparison that it was refreshing and fun to be around her. She introduced me to French new-wave films and filmmakers like Francois Truffaut and Jean Luc Godard and beatnik poet Patti Smith. Vicki was the unspoken leader of the group; she arranged many of the early songs, put them together, took them apart, restructured them until they made more sense. She was a perfectionist.

The Bangs rehearsed at Susanna's Brentwood living space, which was a converted garage. It was not a bad rehearsal space, but we had to play at a low volume and run the mics through our fender amps. The fact that we couldn't turn our amps up very loud made it easier to fine tune the harmonies that The Bangs were becoming known for.

Sue, Vicki, and Debbi had been playing together for a while before I joined the band, and they had already released a 45 on their own label, Down Kitty Records, "I'm in Line," b/w "Call on Me." In my restless and impatient way I couldn't grasp that these girls were responsible and meant business. They were not party girls. They were serious about their music and had discipline. If rehearsal was set at 8:00 p.m., then you were there at 8:00 p.m. sharp! When I joined they began strategizing. Sue took their single to Rodney Bingenheimer, which he loved and started playing immediately. Rodney spinning the single was the push the girls needed to get serious about their plan of attack.

When the band released their single, I decided to cut my long hair into a short Marilyn Monroe 90-degree cut and bleach it platinum. I loved it and never looked back. I said farewell to my "old" self from the San Fernando Valley.

Things started to move fast for The Bangs. I was still seeing Greg and playing music with him, but I could feel the energy that was gaining with The Bangs' career and felt a sense of dread. I just wanted to play in a band and be on stage. The other girls were excited about it, but I was apprehensive. I never joined The Bangs to "make it." It was happening so fast, for so many reasons: talent, timing, and hard work. I felt as if I couldn't tap on the brakes and had no control over it—you were either in or out—there was nothing in the middle. And that's how I felt: in the middle. I was ambivalent. I enjoyed the company of my bandmates and loved the music, but deep down I knew I was a singer more than I was a bass player. I had picked up the bass less than a year before, and suddenly we were poised for fame. I didn't know how to process it. On top of it all, I could sense that Greg was becoming more frustrated as he lived on hopes and dreams of playing in his own band and having to hock his own guitar just to pay rent.

The first show The Bangs played was in a back lot of Laird Studios in Culver City, California. It was fun, and people seemed to enjoy it. I played a VOX hollow body tear-drop 1960s bass. It was a beauty and so easy to learn to play on. I, unfortunately, only realized how rare that bass was after I sold it. The second show was a backyard party in Brentwood at Susanna's boyfriend Ian's house. Again, it went well, a great success. Things were pointed in the right direction. There were no drug habits in the band, no mental issues, no fuck-ups. It was almost spotless except for . . . me. I had an uneasy and unstable personal life concerning my relationship with my boyfriend. When The Bangs played a show at Raji's, Craig Lee, a well-known writer for the *LA Weekly* and former member of The Bags, took me aside and said he would singlehandedly make us "famous." This took me aback. I believed him but didn't really know what to make of it. Generally it was all too much. Much more than I ever expected. On off nights Greg and I were practicing Johnny Cash and June Carter's "Jackson" in his apartment. He had pushed a button in me by increasingly encouraging my singing, which I was still very hesitant about. I didn't sing with The Bangs because, frankly, I couldn't sing three- or four-part harmony, and they already had those bases covered before I stepped foot in the band.

I was living a dual life: one world in which I felt I had absolutely no control over and the other where we were living on rice and beans and singing to old bluegrass records culled from my parents' vinyl collection. We listened to Appalachian singer Roscoe Holcombe, who sang in falsetto in songs like "I Wish I Were a Single Girl Again" and other songs about suffering and plight. In The Bangs—on the eve of becoming "The Bangles"—I was being fitted into custom-made vinyl mod miniskirts for an upcoming video shoot; hair and makeup stylists were hovering over us, while tours and interviews were scheduled. What a study in contrasts.

I felt guilty for the success I received with The Bangles. I felt like a fraud. Still in my teens, it seemed so romantic to lead an artist's life of suffering. Greg convinced me of that philosophy: sacrificing for your art and living in desperation would make us and our art more authentic. He thought The Bangles' music was sort of inconsequential, not relevant to the current climate musically and politically. This was the Reagan era, and Reaganomics was in full effect and gave so many punk bands something to write about.

The Bangles were picking up more momentum. Rodney Bingenheimer asked us to host his radio show one Saturday night while he was out on vacation. Brooke Shields and Debbie Harry both called in! We had fun, and as the night progressed we got sillier and sillier. We played Linda Ronstadt's "Love Is a Rose," then stopped the turntable midsong with the needle scratching and segued into The Ramones. We'd play something off Neil Young's "Tonight's the Night," then went right into Patti Smith's "Gloria."

Through Miles Copeland's management company, LAPD, Mike Gormley became our manager. The first thing on the agenda was to record an EP for their label, Faulty Products through I.R.S. Records. Craig Leon, who had produced The Ramones and was known for a live sound, would helm the sessions as producer. We recorded and mixed the EP in about a week.

Members of Salvation Army—soon to be renamed the Three O'Clock—Dream Syndicate, and The Bangles decided to all go to Catalina Island for a fun-filled weekend. Many friends of the bands were there from the South Bay, some of them straddling the fine line between being punk rock and mod. A handful of these guys shaved their heads on the boat ride there and—*voilà!*—they became insta-punks! We took off on the Catalina Express from Long Beach and landed in Avalon. We brought our sleeping bags to camp out and immediately found a golf course up the side of the island, which we were chased off by some sort of authority figure. By this time many of the kids in the group were frying on acid, so the whole experience seemed even more surreal and absurd. We came upon an abandoned all-girl school and set up camp in the grassy athletic fields. Rows of sleeping bags were lined up around the baseball diamonds. People were coupling up.

It felt like an initiation for the band, like a *Brady Bunch* episode, except on acid. Everyone let their hair down, even Vicki, our responsible, disciplined leader. But I was still the "bad girl" of the bunch. The girl at the prom who would ditch the dance early and ride on the back of a motorcycle to the pier. I was adventurous, spirited, and restless—for better or for worse. By now I was going to a lot of punk shows and seeing bands like Redd Kross, Descendents, and Social Distortion.

As The Bangles were getting bigger, I was leaning into my relationship with Greg and our music. It became my support system and solace when other events were happening so fast. While The Bangles geared up for our first national tour, a new roots punk rock music was making its presence felt in the local L.A. scene: the press dubbed it "cowpunk." Tex and the Horseheads were one of the bands leading the drunken charge, fronted by Jeffrey Lee Pierce discovery Texacala Jones, a possessed, gin-swaggering, desert-prairie vixen adorned in black lace, makeup, and face paint. Tex was a brilliant performer who tempted and baffled the audience as much with her between-song chatter as her singing. While The Bangles were on the road opening for The English Beat, Greg started a trio with Herman Senac on drums and Ron Bothelo on upright bass. They named their band Blood on the Saddle.

On another day off in NYC The Bangles made it to Greenwich Village, where I descended upon the legendary shops Manic Panic and Trash and Vaudeville with a vengeance. These were the only places in the country where I could buy magenta-pink and bright-orange eye shadow. With my bleached-blonde hair, these colors really popped. Sometimes I wore red eyeliner and people would think I was crying. I liked that.

At this point I was really happy and feeling very alive and free. I think the joy just showed in my face. Unfortunately my newfound success was eating away at my relationship with Greg, who was missing "us" as a couple. I was going on the road with a band playing their music, and this was something that *he* wanted to do in his life. I know he was frustrated and down on himself. I understood that.

Soon, though, Greg was getting more and more shows booked with Blood on the Saddle. Their music sounded like a locomotive going 190 mph. I heard a tape taken from the soundboard from one of their shows at Club 88, and now *I* was jealous. I wanted to be a part of *that*, to be a part of a new musical movement coming up from the underground embracing my roots in roots music and punk rock. I could feel the rumblings of a new scene really starting to happen, and I wanted to be there for it. I was becoming more disenchanted with The Bangles, because it was clear that my desire was to sing.

The Bangles lined up a show at the Country Club in the San Fernando Valley, right in my hometown. I was excited about playing there but was distracted too, because Greg and I were working on new material, including a rearrangement of "I Wish I Was a Single Girl Again." The lyrics to some of these songs were based on real life and reflected what was going on between Greg and me. It was clear to anyone paying attention that we were headed for either a make or a break. I know he felt I lived a sheltered and "safe" life and upbringing, and I think that was one of the main underlying reasons for our conflicts.

We had an argument before the Country Club show, but honestly I can't remember what it was about. I was an easy target to get a reaction out of. Things he would say made me feel jealous and insecure, sometimes to the point that I would feel emotionally paralyzed. I would lay down in a fetal position in the hotel room and withdraw. People on the scene started to notice the instability in our relationship. I didn't want the girls in The Bangles to know about some of the tumultuous parts of my life because I was ashamed. I was the punk rock, moody girl, and they were chipper and witty. At times I would shut off when I was around them because I was hiding aspects of my life. I became uncommunicative and sullen. Life was moving way too fast.

There were other consequences of that particular preshow argument that left me dazed and confused. Somehow I muddled through the sold-out performance, but I left quickly afterward. In my haste and disoriented state I left my bass behind at the venue. That was a big no-no to the girls. They saw me forgetting my bass as a statement of disinterest in The Bangles.

Almost immediately following the huge hometown success of that Country Club show, I was no longer in the band. I literally joined Blood on the Saddle the day after exiting The Bangles. I know that to many it was pretty obvious I just wasn't into it any longer, especially as Blood on the Saddle was really ramping up. Greg did not hesitate to let me in. Good or bad career moves never crossed my mind at that age, and I remain so proud of being in both bands. Some might chalk it up to naiveté or just plain stupidity, but I never really looked ahead; I just lived in the moment. The music Greg was playing was literally and figuratively hitting all the right notes for me. I felt like I could express myself more in that band.

We contributed to the now-infamous compilation LP called *Hell Comes to Your House*, released by Enigma Records with a version of the traditional bluegrass song "I Wish I Was a Single Girl Again." This version, different from the one featured on our debut album, showcased Greg playing his chainsaw guitar chords and lightning-speed notes over my high plaintive vocals. The real-life desperation in my performance was what I felt a lot of the time. It got some airplay on college radio, and Rodney played it on his KROQ show too. I felt this track sent the message out to the world that I was no longer a Bangle, and this was why. It did a better job explaining where my heart was at the time than I was able to put into words.

From that record we were able to book more local shows and play on some good bills with bands like The Minutemen. They had a following, and their music was sophisticated, short bursts of political punk rock rants with jazz undertones and an arty free-form song structure played through a trio of guitar, bass, and drums. Honestly, it took me a couple of shows to understand them, but I quickly realized how truly unique, talented, and important they were. As far as I was concerned, D. Boon, the lead singer and guitarist, was a true visionary, a force. In his politics, his lyrics, and his guitar playing, in his way of life and in his artwork, he was a punk rock commie who painted houses by day and played jagged avant-garde guitar jams spouting political and social dogma in a one-minute burst of song. Even though The Minutemen's and Blood on the Saddle's music were quite different from each other, there was a common thread that ran through our bands. At that time D. Boon was playing a lot of Woody Guthrie songs, and he found a kindred spirit in Greg, who knew folk music, history, and politics. We were outsiders who didn't really fit in with other bands, but our two bands gave a sort of nod to the blue-collar working-man ethos in the songs "Born with a Hole in my Pocket" or "Colt 45," played to the beat of The Ramones.

The Meat Puppets were another band whose music was an amalgam of punk rock and country roots but with more classic-rock elements mixed in, and they knew a ridiculous amount of covers. They did the song "Tumbling Tumble Weed" that was played just as fast as anything Black Flag did and was stylistically pretty close to the jacked-up country we were doing. The first venue I saw The Pups play was at a dark club called the Vex in East Los Angeles. We opened for them several times, and our country punk rock scene kept growing and growing.

The Cathay de Grande was in the center of pregentrified Holly-wood and was a place you could see punk bands play for cheap and a spot that Greg and I frequented. Top Jimmy and the Rhythm Pigs played regularly on Blue Mondays, and bands like Social Distortion and The Circle Jerks performed there pretty often. At one point I saw The Replacements play one of their first Los Angeles gigs there to an empty house. After another show we were talking to D. Boon outside the club, and he asked us to be on his label, which was called New Alliance, a subsidiary of SST Records. We sealed the deal with a hand-shake and became label mates with bands like Hüsker Dü, Descendents, and The Minutemen. We were thrilled and, even more, flattered at being label mates with such luminaries.

All the amazing bands and talent on New Alliance and SST almost intimidated me. On these independent record labels it was DIY, with

Black Flag (from L to R): Emil Johnson, Chuck Dukowski, Dez Cadena, Greg Ginn, and Henry Rollins. **Photo by Frank Gargani.**

The Bangs (later The Bangles), English Beat tour, 1982 (from L to R): Debbi Peterson, Annette Zilinskas, Susanna Hoffs, and Vicki Peterson. Photo by Ann Summa.

The Minutemen (from L to R): Mike Watt, George Hurley, D. Boon. Photo by Ann Summa.

Rank and File (from L to R): Jeff Ross, Slim Evans, Tony Kinman, and Chip Kinman. Photo by Ann Summa.

Lone Justice at the Palomino, North Hollywood, 1984 (from L to R): Ryan Hedgecock, Don Heffington, and Maria McKee. Photo by Greg Allen.

Peter Case and Victoria Williams onstage at the L.A. Street Scene, 1985. Photo by Greg Allen.

The Long Ryders, Leed's Studios, North Hollywood, 1986 (from L to R): Stephen McCarthy, Tom Stevens, Greg Sowders, and Sid Griffin. **Photo by Greg Allen.**

Mike Ness of Social Distortion at the Country Club, Reseda, California. **Photo by Greg Allen.**

Carlos Guitarlos as stage security during an X concert at the Whisky a Go Go.
Photo by Gary Leonard.

Top Jimmy and the Rhythm Pigs, Blue Monday at Cathay de Grande, December 1981 (from L to R): Dave Alvin, Gil T, Top Jimmy, Joey Morales, and Maria McKee.
Photo by Gary Leonard.

Los Lobos at Cathay de Grande, November 1982 (from L to R): Conrad Lozano, Cesar Rosas, David Hidalgo, and Louie Pérez. **Photo by Gary Leonard.**

Lone Justice at Tower Records on the Sunset Strip, May 1985 (from L to R): Marvin Etzioni, Don Heffington, Maria McKee, Tony Gilkyson, and Ryan Hedgecock. **Photo by Gary Leonard.**

Cast & crew of *Border Radio* at Echo Park Lake (from L to R): John Doe, Chris D., Devon Anders, Luanna Anders, Dean Lent, Allison Anders, Chris Shearer, and Kurt Voss. **Photo by Allison Anders.**

Movie still from *Border Radio* of Iris Berry in her bedroom at Disgraceland. *Border Radio* filmed by Dean Lent.

Fishbone, University of Southern California, 1985 (from L to R): Angelo Moore, Norwood Fisher, most likely Fish on drums. **Photo by Lisa Johnson.**

L.A. Street Scene riots, 1985. **Photo by Lisa Johnson.**

John Doe and Exene Cervenka, Chinatown, NYC. Photo by Laura Levine.

The Gun Club at Maxwell's, Hoboken, New Jersey (from L to R): Ward Dotson, Jeffrey Lee Pierce, Rob Ritter, and Terry Graham. **Photo by Laura Levine.**

Tony Hawk.
Photo by
J. Grant Britton.

Blood on the Saddle promo shot (from L to R): Ron Botelho, Herman Senac, Annette Zilinskas, and Greg Davis. Photo by Terry Dorn.

The Knitters, 1984 (from L to R): DJ Bonebrake, John Doe, Dave Alvin, Exene Cervenka, and Jonny Ray Bartel. Photo by Michael Hyatt.

Stephen McCarthy and Sid Griffin of The Long Ryders onstage at Club Lingerie, Hollywood, 1985. Photo by Greg Allen.

Shepard Fairey, a self-portrait in his art studio. **Photo by Shepard Fairey/ObeyGiant.com.**

John Doe during an X performance on the riverboat *President*, New Orleans, Louisiana. **Photo by Rick Olivier.**

Exene Cervenka in the crowd and Billy Zoom onstage during an X performance on the riverboat *President*, New Orleans, Louisiana. **Photo by Rick Olivier.**

X at downtown L.A. loft, 1984 (from L to R): Billy Zoom, John Doe, Exene Cervenka, and DJ Bonebrake. **Photo by Ann Summa.**

no interference from the middleman. SST founder Greg Ginn said he was in the business of being a realist: Record, Tour, and Sell Merch was their holy trinity. They were ahead of their time in that regard. Getting college airplay was the catalyst that would get people to your shows and make it possible to tour and push your product. In 1984 college radio was making it possible for bands to survive and receive airplay, regardless of whether they had major-label push or distribution. Perhaps you wouldn't get rich or get commercial radio like The Bangles, who now had scored hits with songs like "Walk Like an Egyptian" and "Manic Monday." But you could still make a living and perhaps tour the world promoting your album while selling your merchandise directly to your fans. I'm proud to say that Blood on the Saddle did just that.

We had a dynamic-looking band. Herman Senac hammered the drums and helped us reinvent the country or bluegrass songs we got ahold of. Ron Botelho would slap the shit out of his upright bass so intensely that he had to bandage up his fingers before a show with silver gaffers tape—those taped-up fingers also gave the bass a more percussive sound. Live, he had his own fan club, a section of kids who stood in front of him during our set.

Live, we packed a wallop, and people loved it. Along with Lone Justice, Rank and File, and Tex and the Horseheads, we were truly starting to make it in Los Angeles. Without conceit, Blood on the Saddle probably fit the term "cowpunk"—especially the "punk" part of it—more than some of the other bands, who were more commercial. We were unpredictable, more rough and tumble and raw.

Even though Los Angeles seemed to like us pretty well, we could really feel the tremendous love and support from other places like Europe or in the rural parts of the USA. Places like Louisiana, where playing in a venue would be like playing in a backwoods roadhouse with an old wooden bar and a stage tucked in the corner. I loved it. Never having traveled the United States as a kid, this was exotic to me. These shanty shacks the band came upon on tour were exactly what I had imagined they would look like when hearing a Leadbelly song through my bedroom walls late at night. Huddie Leadbelly was one of my parents' favorites. Seeing places that still existed that seemed to jump right out of some of these folk/blues songs that we played completely blew me away. These backwater towns had misspelled signs in the store windows and fields of green with insects buzzing around in the hot humid summer. I saw leaves of giant tobacco that lay across branches drying out in the hot and humid North Carolina sun. There were midcentury grocery stores with aluminum ceilings in Missouri. There were ticks covering stray hound dogs in South Carolina. It was all so amazing and foreign to me.

Our music was the perfect backdrop for this. In Shreveport we played in a rural backroad shanty made of dark wood. The show went over great. After our set the band and I went outside to the back of the club to cool off. It was around midnight when a young man came up to me. He looked to be in his early thirties and was attractive and looked intelligent. He turned out to be a local journalist for the Shreveport paper, and he knew I loved Leadbelly. Blood on the Saddle played a version of one of his songs called "In the Pines." The journalist said that Leadbelly's grave was nearby and wanted to show me where it was, and I jumped at the opportunity because his grave was known to be difficult to find unless one knew the area really well.

Another memorable show was in an old Western ghost town some miles outside of the downtown Las Vegas strip. It was in "Old" Las Vegas, and we were opening for Gun Club. The stage was outdoors, with the open desert our backdrop. It couldn't have been more perfect and seemed to invigorate our performance. Gun Club played an inspired set as well. People still talk about that show, which is amazing considering it took place literally "off a beaten path" from the main part of Las Vegas. That gig felt like we were transported to another place in another time.

One day the light that Greg and I had for each other seemed to fade out. We had gotten back from a tour that didn't go well. The audiences didn't respond, and the weather was freezing. The driving was endless and miserable. Greg and I broke up, and I quit the band even though my love for our music and the songs was intact. I will always have the highest regard for his talent, his playing, and what we once had. He believed in my voice, and that always meant so much to me. However, the personal part of our relationship overshadowed our professional life.

The cowpunk scene was winding down, and a new scene was on the horizon. Hair bands like Mötley Crüe, Cinderella, Poison, and Guns N' Roses were taking over the Sunset Strip and the L.A. club scene in general. I found myself looking for other musical projects, propelled by the confidence and bravery I developed from those years of finding my voice in Blood on the Saddle and The Bangles. I founded my own band, Weatherbell, as well as joined an all-female bohemian literary group called the Ringling Sisters, composed of some very talented people, including Pleasant Gehman, Iris Berry, Texacala Jones, Johnette Napolitano, Deborah Patino, Debbie Dexter, Gary Eaton, and Dave Catching. The Sisters put our prose to music and recorded an album on A&M Records, with the legendary Lou Adler producing. I also collaborated with the musical genius of Brad Laner in the early incarnation of shoe-gaze, wall of sound band Medicine. We cowrote a song called "Aruca," which is one of my proudest moments.

I finally had learned how to walk on my own and find my own voice.

CHAPTER 26

AIN'T LOVE GRAND

by John Doe

Never believe your own hype. How did we miss this valuable lesson? I suppose we felt outside the rules. We broke rules. We wrote new rules. It's not as if some rock 'n' roll musicians' guidebook existed and we could turn to page 127 to find out how to proceed after four critically acclaimed but financially underachieving LPs. How did an antiestablishment band like X fall into the most cliché trap?

In only five years, from 1978 to 1983, we had released four records that got so much praise, it almost embarrassed us, a humbling experience that can really spin your head around. We ranked with so many tastemakers like *New York Times*, *Los Angeles Times*, *Village Voice*, *LA*

Weekly in their "Year End Top Ten Best List" for 1980 (*Los Angeles*), '81 (*Wild Gift*), '82 (*Under the Big Black Sun*), and '83 (*More Fun in the New World*). My mother, Gretchen, filled three or four loose-leaf binders per year with our press clippings. They came from all over the US and also several from overseas. As a dutiful son, I would clip them out of newspapers as we grinded out tour after tour from 1980 to 1986. We played two or three times on Dick Clark's *American Bandstand*, *Late Night with David Letterman*, Jerry Lewis's Telethon for MS, *Solid Gold*, *History of Rock 'n' Roll* (with James Brown, Chuck Berry, The Temptations, etc.). We suffered through each one of these appearances with a mixture of anxiety, fear, and hubris. Personally I never felt like I belonged there. I felt like a fraud. Never felt like "This is going to make a mark" or "I deserve this." I felt a deep self-consciousness. I don't remember feeling connected like a band of outlaws the way we did on hundreds of live shows. On those we always pulled together, especially in a foreign territory such as the first tours in the Midwest or the South. On television appearances I never remember a feeling of joy or exuberance, just nerves. Never felt "FUCK YEAH!! THIS IS GONNA FUCKIN' SHOW THEM WHAT WE GOT!" Somehow we managed to get through the three and a half minutes and not embarrass ourselves too badly.

As producer, Ray Manzarek guided us through our first four LPs. He became a mentor to the band and a kind of father figure to both Exene and me. Ray was fucking rock 'n' roll royalty. He had hit songs, gold and platinum records, and, more importantly, records that changed popular culture forever. He was a member of the mutherfuckin DOORS! Dark, mysterious, dangerous, noir, L.A., murderous—not some bullshit hippie band. He believed and told us that X truly added to that legacy in Los Angeles rock music. He said, "You're not The Beach Boys or The fucking Association!" He gave us a deeper confidence that we could step into The Doors' shoes. We could set the record straight that Los Angeles—or "El Lay," as the East Coast snobs referred to it—had every bit as much dark, wild abandon that any leather-jacketed punks from those other scenes. He praised Billy & DJ's musicianship that, to be honest, compared to the other punk rock bands of the era, were several steps ahead of most players. Ray

got it and gave them ideas when they needed it, and they shined because of it. He exalted Exene & my lyrics and compared them to Jim
Morrison's. He saw the connection we had to our audience & the wild,
bohemian life we lived. Four of us—Exene, Billy, Ray & I—were born
in the Midwest and in February. He told us we could do it, and most of
the time he was right.

During our recordings Ray kept us focused on honest, real performances. The whole band recorded together and used many of the
"scratch vocals" (vocals sung as the band tracked the song) on the final
recordings. Until the third record we never seemed to have time to experiment. But we knew the songs backward and forward. We raced to
the finish line, which was dictated by our budget. But Ray always kept
his cool because he *was* cool. He wore his steely gray hair cut short but
still kept his signature wire-rimmed glasses. His clothes didn't show
off that he had money, but you could tell that he did. His "Ray suit"
consisted of a light, draped sports coat, T-shirt, and jeans. The coat
got tossed on a chair shortly after he walked in. His confidence and
ease made you think that in another fifteen years maybe you could be
where he was. His directness spilled over into every piece of the production. From the beginning he asked us to make the performances
as real as the songs. Our lyrics talked about real people, actual events,
true landscapes of Los Angeles, heartbreak, death, and, later, influences of our lives on tour. The music was tight, short, sweet, and hard.
It blended and high bred all manner of American roots music that DJ,
Billy, Exene & I had soaked up in our twenty-plus years of listening
and playing in good or shitty bands.

In 1982, with Ray's encouragement, we included decidedly unpunk rock elements after we signed to Elektra Records. Billy played
saxophone, so we put sax on a song, "Come Back to Me," about Exene's departed sister, Mirielle. This tragic event—she was killed instantly when the VW bug she was riding in was struck by a hit & run
driver—forever changed our lives. Maybe because of the tradition of
tragic-death songs in the fifties, I wrote music inspired by fifties doo-
wop for "Come Back to Me." But that writing came after the moment
when I distinctly remember standing outside X's tiny office space, a
rehearsal studio on Hollywood Blvd., when I heard the melody and

words for the chorus of the song. To make things even more unpunk, DJ played marimba, so with Ray's encouragement, we put that on the same song. Exene wrote a song about the hard times of working-class people & drinking, "The Have Nots." The music inspired by seventies rock 'n' roll echoed the sound of bar bands we had played in before X. We were inspired by Bo Diddley, the reintroduction of wolves to Yellowstone, and American Indians and made a song about Exene's and my relationship with all of those elements called "The Hungry Wolf." We finally had a better studio and time to play around. Pulling in a few more breakneck speed songs and romance in others, somehow it still remained punk rock.

But Exene's sister Mirielle's death dominated this, the saddest record we ever made. It had been three years since the car accident, and I had no idea until years later that Exene was in no way ready to sing about that loss. We wrote the songs together, went through the pain, tried to heal as best we could, and used writing about that terrible event to try to exorcise the emotional damage. Years before, we had made an unspoken promise to tell the truth about our lives. To use our lives as the source of our songs. But maybe I believed more than she did. Maybe I had a romantic ideal about suffering and confessional poets, and Exene went along because of this unspoken pact we made or my forward motion—ambition didn't allow for dissent. Regardless, Exene and I were making good on that promise, and X made good on the promise to show the world, at least artistically, what a band from "El Lay" could do on a major label. We weren't selling out, even though we had moved from indie Slash Records to Elektra.

By today's standards our tours weren't that grueling, though for us it sure seemed tough. We had graduated from our beloved Chevy step-van conversion to a full-on tour bus. The first of which broke down several times and, once, for hours in the crushing Arizona desert heat. We continued paying our dues, and with a somewhat higher salary came seemingly much higher costs—actual & emotional. This bus also included a built-in trap door in the center lounge that dropped directly to the highway. We assumed it allowed for dumping drugs or contraband during high-speed chases or escaping the authorities in some deserted parking lot. Jesse Colin Young had owned it, which always confused us.

The next bus had only one watchable VCR tape, *The Shining*, which we watched ad nauseam to the point where we could recite full passages of dialogue. "I'm sorry, Mrs. Torrance. Danny not here." We lived on tour for at least four to five months in 1983, and it began to stretch and strain our bond as a gang of misfits. We—or I—drank too much, every night. We graduated from tiny bits of "medicinal" speed to, when someone gave it to us, much larger amounts of cocaine. One "harvest season" in Humbolt County, California, nearly did all of us in. One particular dealer/friend of Billy's then wife, Denise, pulled a five-foot mirror off our motel room wall and shook out enough coke to make a half-inch line the entire length of it. He turned to DJ, Exene & I and said something like, "Help yourself." It rolled and tumbled all night long until the last day when, at our last of three shows, he said he had run out.

We lied to ourselves that this was all in the name of rock 'n' roll or research, and maybe it was. We collected and forgot so many memories that we lost track of where and when any of it happened, but we listened to songs and bands old and new, and we saw the sights of America that shaped the lyrics for the next record, which we wrote along the way. In the Midwest we toured with The Replacements, The Del Fuegos on the East Coast, or the South with The Big Boys. They all played hard and partied hard. We had to keep up and discovered the magic of classic, old-man bars in the daytime. When you use a great opening act and get high praise from the press, you better live up to it. Most nights we did because we felt a duty to spread the gospel we thought we were. Some nights we probably sucked, but some we outplayed even ourselves.

The *More Fun in the New World* record contained all those experiences with a reimagined Americana hybrid punk rock sound. Again Ray sat at our helm and, unfortunately, due to our misguided loyalty, so did the engineer from our previous two records, Clay Rose. He had become our front-of-house sound mixer and tour manager, so it seemed obvious that he would also continue as our recording engineer. Clay had talent as a sound mixer and recording engineer. He traveled well and could keep us all moving in mostly the same direction. Except one European tour, when he had become the quintessential Ugly American, like talking louder so that the desk clerk in Paris could understand him better. It got so bad that in a hotel lobby Billy lit the newspaper that Clay was reading on fire. *Wild Gift*, Clay's first, didn't sound as full and foreboding as *Los Angeles*, but the record was lighter and more fun, so we blamed that on the studio equipment. *Under the Big Black Sun* had deeper, darker sounds but didn't capture our live power, so we made other excuses. We should've listened to Billy, who objected several times about the recordings.

But *More Fun* in particular sounded thin and jumbled. Not as we made it but after the fact. It could've been due to the influence of cocaine, which had also invaded our recording sessions. Using the same producer for four records is unprecedented, but the same engineer? Unheard of. At Cherokee Studios, our new, fancy studio, I recall a kind of resident coke dealer, Sammy or Skip or Jake, who made the rounds to each room. During the same time Mötley Crüe and Oingo Boingo worked in both of the other rooms—you might ask them what his name was.

This record of ours and its subject matter might've been too big for us to capture. We were delivering "the state of the union" according to the band X. We tried to cram all the musical influences we had been exposed to or ones who influenced us from earlier days. We were full of ourselves and thought we could define "punk rock" any way we chose. After all, The Clash released double records. We listened to Marvin Gaye's *What's Going On* and George Clinton's *Atomic Dog* nonstop. Early funk and rap had appeared on Blondie and Talking Heads records for years. In retrospect, we were probably running out of ideas for songs. The evidence lies in the facts. There were more words, more parts to songs, and more chord changes, maybe too many of all three. We had moved away from tight, short, and economical. The songs were some of our best, but we could've benefited from a better engineer and less cocaine.

I started to write some songs on acoustic guitar, and Billy didn't like that very much. He said my guitar parts defined how his should go. I didn't understand that at the time but realize now that it took some of his creativity away. "I Must Not Think Bad Thoughts" was one of those moments that I misinterpreted a suggestion that Ray made about using a major seventh in a song—again, not very punk rock—but Billy used that to feature his beautiful finger picking. So on at least one occasion it actually didn't affect his huge creative contribution. Lyrically the song gave Exene and me a forum for our outrage toward the government's handling of the conflict in El Salvador and Nicaragua. Sadly the song's lyrics are as true today as they were then. We also took this opportunity to bitch about the neglect of some of our compadres (Minutemen, Flesh Eaters, DOA, Big Boys, and Black Flag) who we thought deserved more attention. We even ended it with a kind of barroom soundscape. As the band played on with more and more intensity, buried in the mix is a dialogue between Exene and me as barmaid and drunken barfly. Exene painted a striking, colorful piece of outsider art for the cover, and again we hand-lettered or typed lyrics for the inside sleeve. Elektra made good on their promise not to meddle, and no dumbass A&R guy had the guts to come down to pronounce, "I don't hear a single." It was clear that the songs "The New World," "Breathless," or "Devil Doll" could take care of that.

We maintained a steady stream of great press but still couldn't crack the elusive radio play that had begun to benefit even The Replacements. At that time program consultants programmed (determined playlists for) stations all over the country from isolated offices in Phoenix or wherever instead of local stations playing what related to their listeners. For just this reason our song "The New World," which has the lyric "Don't forget the Motor City," got little or no radio play in Detroit. This was at a time when Detroit was seeing the effects of what became a long-painful social and economic decline. Groups like Blondie, The Pretenders, Devo, and The Go-Go's had all cracked the Billboard's Hot 100, but somehow we were still stuck in dirty rock clubs. Our credibility couldn't really be assailed, but according to more hardcore punks, we had sold out. "Fuck 'em," we thought. They said we sold out when we signed to Slash Records instead of sticking with hopeless Dangerhouse. Our confusion ran deep. In Los Angeles we sold out the Greek Theater (six thousand cap) in 1982, but in the darkest depths of middle America could only draw three hundred on a good night. We didn't need or take record-company tour support for any of the three- or four-month-long tours across the US. We had changed management to work with Ron DeBlasio and Ned Shankman, both seasoned veterans of the music business. All signs pointed toward success. But the cycle of write, record, tour, write, record, tour, repeat for the last four years began to take a serious toll. Tours extended to seven or eight weeks long, and when we came home to our little white clapboard cottage up the hill from Highland Park, it took a solid week just to open the mail. Exene began to feel bullied by my constant work ethic and stifled by our constant "John and Exene" identity, losing her sense of self. How I wish I could've given her more time to herself and not been insecure, demanding or needing a twenty-four-hour, seven-days-a-week partnership. Most times we took solace in the fact that we knew what each other was going through since we went through it together. But there was no time for introspection, and I didn't fully consider the value of our creative partnership. Really, it was too much to ask of two people to spend every day, all day working, playing, partying, and socializing. At least we had some good pals—Judith Bell and Chris D., Phil and Dave Alvin, Top Jimmy and Gil T, Jill Jordan and so many more. They helped take the place of our Hollywood punk rock community from the early days. Exene and I had even begun singing with Dave Alvin to play benefits for our after-hours gallery/nightclub The Zero or Medical Aid for El Salvador. But all the activity covered up the strain that was beginning to grow inside us.

Each tour would start in Los Angeles and try to make a loop to return us home. In years past those loops would go to Seattle or Vancouver and back or we headed east to Texas and back. Now we covered half the country at a time over a six-week period or longer. I don't remember ever meeting the bus or band gear in a distant city. Seemed like we usually converged outside our rehearsal studio on Hollywood Blvd. And after waiting for an hour or three for Billy to wrap up all his stuff, we took off from there. I didn't understand then, but leaving for tour is something like dying. You feel an urgent desire to tie up all your loose ends, cleaning parts of the house that had been filthy for months or decluttering some part of the garage. At least we didn't worry much about what clothes to bring. At this stage we wore on stage what we wore on the street—T-shirts and jeans, a jean jacket if it was winter or fall. Exene always brought her trusty polka-dot dresses and leather motorcycle pants. Unlike most of our fellow bands, we had management and a booking agent, and stayed in hotels, *not* on people's floors in sleeping bags. We prided ourselves on professionalism. We showed up on time, looking like a fucking band. We also played as hard as possible, always did as many encores as asked so no one was left wondering why we were thought of as the best punk rock band from Los Angeles.

In retrospect I put too much pressure on everyone and especially Exene. It was unfair to ask of her the same as what I put out, but maybe that was the downside of our equality as band members and partners. We drank pretty damn hard back then, and Exene could drink us all under the table. Whisky was her main drug of choice, and she handled it well, except maybe every ten days or so, when she overdid it and ended up with arms around the toilet in the morning with dry heaves. Sometimes it was the same toilet she used as a desk the night before. Ingeniously she would close the seat, sit facing the wall, and use the tank as her writing desk. I wonder how many of our best lyrics she wrote on the tank of a toilet? Billy and DJ were just quieter about their indiscretions. But I recall being thrown out of a Slidell, Louisiana, bar at 3:00 A.M. for strangling a peanut machine or kicked out of a diner for snoring at the counter or peeing on the inside of the door of our hotel room because I couldn't find the bathroom door next to it.

Exene and I also began to argue, which I now realize was initiated by my expectations of what I thought Exene should be doing, I was so foolish. Secretly it broke our hearts to turn against the only person we could truly trust. But the most frustrating and stupid thing I wanted was for Exene to discuss or argue or fight back. If I was angry, then I wanted to have it out and be done with it, but Exene would clam up, probably because she had seen my explosive temper and wanted no part of it. I could be quite a mess back then. It was adolescent, childish, egotistical behavior. I broke shit. During an argument with Exene I threw a full bottle of beer against the motel wall. No wonder she didn't want to engage. I got into fights with the audience on stage and off. There was one particular after-party near Wrigley Field in 1984 when I actually counted strikes against some guy. He was drunk, and so was I. He stood in the hallway of an apartment and harangued me as I sat at a table. He said things like,

"Hey, you think you're a fuckin rock star, don't you?"

Me: "Not really." (strike one)

"Well, I think you're an asshole."

"Maybe I am." (strike two)

"I think your band sucks." (STRIKE THREE)

I jump up and, in a sort of football, shoulder-down tackle, crash this jerk through the center panel of the bedroom door he's standing in front of. We collapse into the bedroom, poorly landed punches follow, he tears the inside of my pants and bites my leg very close to my crotch. We stand up, and I slam him against the wall before other partygoers grab and shove him out the front door. A stupid aftermath, recounting of the incident happens in the kitchen, and the party is pretty much ruined. I feel like an idiot the next morning when I feel my bruised hand and see a bite mark inches away from my scrotum.

Sometime in mid-'84 Exene and I split. As difficult as it was, we didn't bicker about dividing things or money or talk shit about each other. For some foolish reason we didn't seek counseling. She moved into a condo previously owned by Jim Gordon (a great but very troubled drummer who killed his mother with a hammer). This place in the San Fernando Valley could be the creepiest domicile I've ever stepped foot in. A few months later she took up with an old friend (not a very good one), Pete Haskell. Pete could've walked out of a Jack Kerouac novel—very rough, handsome, wild, and unfocused. Around the same time while driving her 1968 Mercury Cougar, Exene heard "Wild Thing" on the radio. She suggested we work up a version, which we recorded with Elektra-recommended Michael Wagener. The metal years were in full swing these days in El Lay, and though I hated the songs or lack thereof, the production had some dark, heavy appeal. Though we didn't care for Mötley Crüe or any other hair bands, Black Sabbath, and AC/DC weren't all bad.

We didn't completely abandon Ray, but the past five years and last two records hadn't taken us where we were told we should be. Elektra whispered in our ears, held up an imaginary carrot, and we tried Michael Wagener for the single "Wild Thing." Billy's guitars were triple, quadruple, octuple tracked. DJ's drums sounded like they came from the far side of an airplane hangar. So many tracks of Exene's voice she sounded a lot like Joan Jett. And then there were the backing vocals! Michael set up a kind of choir riser and had all five or seven of us sing/shout, "WILD THING!" Then he tracked that ten times or more, so I figured there were over one hundred people shouting "WILD THING!" I don't mind admitting that in the moment the effect was thrilling, brutal, and felt like driving a stock car. IT SOUNDED HUGE, and it was wild and free. We were all seduced.

Since *More Fun* had sounded thin & jumbled, this pointed us in a new and somewhat popular direction. Beware the popular sound, however—in two years it will sound dated. We questioned whether we knew how we should sound. We doubted whether Ray could "take us to the next level." How cliché. Exene and I worked on most songs individually as we prepared to make a fifth record in so many years. Determined not to let our separation affect the band and the moderate success of "Wild Thing," we forged ahead with Mr. Wagener. The record company had gotten what they wanted. Oddly we never discussed leaving Ray, but we remained friends for years up until his passing.

Michael Wagener was decidedly German and maintained a precise work ethic to prove it. Though he laughed and joked and made fun of the stereotype German, his recording technique couldn't have been farther from our punk rock hearts and methods. We believed the bullshit people had been writing about and telling us for the last seven years. For the "demos" we recorded every note and drum fill as if it were a record but didn't spend time on the tone of the instruments. After all, these were *just* demos. The process couldn't have been farther from recording a sloppy, untamed "Wild Thing." I recall we used electronic drums. We/he recorded the bass direct to tape, with no amp sound and guitars without attention to tone, drive, or feeling. Just demos. Exene and I dutifully sang every part we could think of. Gave heartfelt performances because these were some of the most personal songs we had written. This chronicled the breakup of the only punk rock marriage— our marriage. Songs like "Burning House of Love," "I'll Stand Up for You," and "My Goodness" came from a deep and painful place, but we soldiered on under the precise and unemotional hand of Mr. Wagener.

By the time we started recording the record, half the life had already been sucked out of it. We had just sung and played every note, bridge, chorus, lead, drum fill, bass line, etc. These "demos" charted every single note to play on the "real record." But we didn't care about perfection. We cared about raw emotion, spontaneity, telling a story, and giving a true performance. No scratch vocals were used. We sang and sang, but Mr. Wagener didn't get Exene. Either as a person or a singer. His tastes leaned toward Don Dokken or Scorpions, both of whom he worked with. It was a battle to keep Exene in the game. Why should she work so hard and have so little respect paid her? Though we had separated, we still cared deeply for each other. I stood up for her and found ways to keep her engaged. Listening to the double-tracked vocals now, you can hear the strained effort and how little character both our vocals have. We had made the choice, and we were seeing it through. Billy liked the guitar sounds at first but also found the triple and quadruple tracking tedious. His guitars were huge, but they could've been a dozen other guitar slingers. Billy did play some beautifully written guitar leads and orchestrated his part with adventure. DJ developed "Pac-Man elbow" from hanging around so much with so little to do. He would see this through with us. The only scratch vocal we almost kept was for "Burning House of Love." For reference I sang a lead vocal to only the bass and drums, which were the final tracks. Once the many guitar tracks were done, I could not duplicate the urgency of that scratch vocal. I must have sang it thirty times without finding as good a moment as the scratch vocal. Finally, in anger and frustration, I managed to get close to the truth of the scratch vocal. I never had to learn that lesson again. Toward the end of recording we cast about for a usable title. Finally our dear friend Michael Blake suggested *Ain't Love Grand*. The irony couldn't have been more of a perfect fit. To make things worse, a creepy A&R man, who shall remain nameless, even coerced us/me into doing a Small Faces' song, "All or Nothing." I hated the song and our version of it, but we had let go of the reins, and nothing seemed within our control. To be fair, out of the eleven songs, only half were worth a damn. The whole affair—writing and recording—sucked out our souls, made us feel less than, and, for the first time, like we *had* sold out. "Burning House of Love" and "Ain't Love Grand" charted the highest of any X record. We don't play any of the songs live.

CHAPTER 27

SHOT GLASS FULL OF LUCK

by Terry Graham

"Go ahead," I told myself, "curse the heavens, stomp both feet, and drink all the booze you want—it ain't gonna stop the bleeding."

My time playing drums for The Bags was over, and I was not happy about it, but what could I do? Death from a thousand cuts, so died The Bags. The mortal blow was delivered on stage during a filmed performance for *The Decline of Western Civilization*. The young kids staring up at us were already infused with the nuclear energy of hardcore, suburban punk rocking, not artsy, female-driven Hollywood punk. We were the older generation, and the reaction was more than enough proof that our time as a band had come and gone. Alice Bag, Patricia

264

Morrison, and Craig Lee disappeared from my musical life in one last cloud of sticky, smelly Aqua Net. Suddenly no band, and no way to pay my electric bill. Shit. I could use a break and wasn't entirely sure about my next move, but I wasn't going to stop playing drums in a rock 'n' roll band.

By 1980 a few first-generation punk bands (X, Go-Go's, Dickies) were making enough noise to attract the attention of big record labels. I assumed, after all the sold-out shows and warm fuzzies as a member of The Bags, I could attract big too. I was in Los Angeles, after all, where the entire city could burn away or just as surely fade away on a cosmic or cocaine-addled whim. I could also get rich and famous. Unfortunately I had no divining rod with which to chart my course to stardom, but I had one great advantage: Rob Ritter was the best musician I knew at the time. He was as deft and capable at playing bass as he was at lead guitar. He agreed to join me in a search for a new band desperate enough to take us. We would sort out all that other crap— song styles, band-member temperament, and proclivity for drug and alcohol addiction—later.

Who within the local rock scene would have us? We maintained a strict club-hopping grind. On a random Tuesday night at the Hong Kong Café, surrounded by tacky Chinese décor and the sickly-sweet smell of duck sauce, Rob and I found a corner where no one could see us, nursing beers while Jeff Pierce's new band The Gun Club tortured a few patrons scattered about the joint. I'd known Jeff for over three years and never thought of him as a musician, more an unwanted ice cream truck cruising the neighborhood to the tune of "Let Me Play with Your Poodle." His head teemed with ancient noises and musical conspiracies that blared, unedited, out of his mouth for hours on end. I guess it was inevitable that Jeff made his way from the turntable in his bedroom to the stage at the Hong Kong Café. He once told me his only aspiration—if he ever became a musician—was to create an honest band with enough street cred to get him through the rest of his life playing songs that exorcised his demons and confounded the critics. The Gun Club was his third time at bat—his other two bands gone soon after a show or two. Aspirations aside, as of that night Jeff didn't have much of a rock 'n' roll pedigree, but I was happy to allow his latest creation to be background noise while Rob and I plotted our next move.

As Gun Club's rat-tat-tat from the stage grew louder, I was about to suggest we leave and come back after the set (to congratulate Jeff on a great set), but, in some sort of cosmic intervention, I heard something from the stage that I liked. I knew Jeff didn't care too much about a punk rock revolution, his perspective being much wider than that, but he left no doubts about his love of blues. Delta blues, to be exact. And here was Gun Club's puckish version of those blues spit out with a punk rock blast of fury infused with slide guitar (!) and the shrill edge of Jeff's beseeching vocals. Quite a racket, but oddly compelling, so I stopped talking to Rob and gave my attention to the band. Rob and I were skeptical bastards, but a sloppy, punk rock orchestra of dead blues guys blaring from the stage was not so easily dismissed. Intrigued, we had little choice but to reconsider Jeff and his musical aspirations. In fact, reconsider our own musical aspirations. Was The Gun Club our shot glass full of luck?

As the band punched and jabbed through the rest of their set, I couldn't quite make it all fit until they played a song called "For the Love of Ivy." Stomping through the roots-and-blues graveyard with all the grace of a drunk elephant, Jeffrey's brain was tuned to a frequency that may have been steeped in tradition but was actually quite revolutionary. He was injecting blues into the heart of punk rock, struggling to give life to something new and brilliant, even if it was old and obvious at the same time.

So was this Gun Club the embodiment of our rock 'n' roll dreams? Did it matter? I needed a fucking band. After the show I spotted Jeff alone at the bar. He wasn't smiling. "Pretty good band you got there, Jeffrey. When's the next show?" It so happened that Brad Dunning (drums) and Don Waller (bass) had quit after the show. Really? I asked Jeff for the job. I got the job. Rob got a job too. Thankfully, Brian and his murderous slide guitar were staying put. Damn, that was easy. Let the new Black Train roll.

Rehearsals in our filthy room on Selma Avenue in Hollywood crackled with the intolerance of four people who had lost their fucks and had none left to give. From Jeff's overheated brain we birthed rough, crude songs without clues as to our whereabouts on the road to rock 'n' roll perdition. Brian's slide guitar work improved rapidly and was made all the more necessary by our impudence. Something had to cover for our unabashed theft of riffs and lyrics, "exotic" timing, unapologetic trashing of sacred melodies, and the complete sacking of the house of tradition. We were slap-happy pillagers and plunderers and assumed Robert Johnson would have been proud of us. Jeff Pierce was a contentious bastard and relished the monster he—and we—were creating. It only took a few rehearsals before we decided to pull out of the Selma Avenue station and ride the Black Train all over Los Angeles.

First shows were not well received. Jeff did, however, throw a Bible on the stage floor at Club 88 in West L.A. and beat it with a length of chain during "Preaching the Blues" and "For the Love of Ivy." That got us banned from the club. Gee, really? Jeff also instigated his fashion free-for-all with a kind of Colonel Sanders, Civil War couture that endeared him to exactly no one. Even wore a headband with a spot of fake blood on it. Or maybe it was real blood. The effect was kinda funny and kinda stupid. Kinda like The Gun Club. But then, just as our yins and yangs began to coalesce into a ragged but functioning whole, we got hijacked by our grave mates, Lux Interior and Poison Ivy Rorschach, who asked Brian to join The Cramps. Yanked off the Black Train and into the Psychedelic Jungle, Brian didn't look back. Bruised—but happy for Brian—we bade him much good fortune. He hit the rock 'n' roll jackpot as far as we were concerned, and if The Cramps ever needed an opening band . . .

Like any trashy novel worth its schmaltz, we came by our new guitarist, Ward Dotson, mere days after he was turned down by, of all bands, The Cramps. His audition was liked, but apparently he didn't look good in a leg-bone necklace. Or something like that. Who cares? He had the necessary roots-rock chops and passed our audition with flying colors. Obviously he was disappointed he lost out to Brian— now Kid Congo Powers—but we couldn't have been happier to have him and his Telecaster aboard the Train. By the end of our first rehearsal Ward had given our songs the melodic underpinning they so desperately needed, which, in turn, freed Jeff to huff and puff and blow his microphone down. Gun Club was, again, good to go.

Two quick shows to give Ward some stage time and, on the heels of that, a bit of luck. We scored much-needed publicity in a review in the *LA Weekly* by our friend Pleasant Gehman. Not that she was a shill. Yes, we had a few rough spots and could use a little more time in the oven, all of which was true. But she officially christened us a "punk-blues" band, among other well-considered pats on the back. She was careful not to break our fragile confidence, and deserved or not, her generosity went to our heads.

Based on a tiny contingent of fans and single critical acclaim, we declared that The Gun Club was ready for the recording studio. Vitus Matare, a man with finely tuned ears and a true proponent of DIY, recruited us for a compilation album he was producing called *Keats Rides a Harley*. Four tracks, played live, and no unicorns to sweeten the sound. Actually, we loved the coarse, bristly, unsophisticated sound of ourselves on tape. "Preaching the Blues" and "Devil in the Woods" were my favorites. While Vitus prepped our four-song tape for vinyl release, we lusted for more and plotted a path to a full-length album. Jeffrey played Vitus's rough mix to The Flesh Eaters' singer-songwriter, Chris D., who was smitten and pleaded our case to Slash Records owner Bob Biggs, who was not smitten. But, according to Bob, we might be worthy of a full-length recording for something called Ruby Records, a subsidiary of Slash Records. Whew, how low could we go? Humbled to have been considered for any label, we accepted the offer. Thank you, Chris D.

Two grand to make a record ain't much, but if we kept our studio time to an absolute minimum, made no mistakes, and added little or no overdubbing, we just might be able to stitch together a bastard child of which we could all be proud. For a bunch of sloppy, barely rehearsed hooligans, we sure were full of ourselves. Probably a good thing too, seeing as how we had so little time to make it all work. Two different studios were booked, a single, six-hour session at each. The production duties would be divided between Chris D., who would man the controls the first night at Quad Teck (Pat Burnette, engineer), and Tito Larriva, who would step in for the second night at Studio America (Noah Shark, engineer).

The setup at Quad Teck was stripped to the bone. All of us were herded into the same room for basic tracks, including vocals. A couple of sound baffles here and there. Chris was an intense young man. He knew what he wanted, for the most part, but insisted we play like crazed lunatics, just in case. Hearing myself play like a crazed lunatic through headphones was intimidating and threatened my timing. As if Chris cared—"Shut up, drummer boy!" The mad rush of songs and the expediency required of us obliterated any lingering awkwardness. We went through a couple of takes for each song and, just inside the six hours allotted us, spit out the first half of our album. We'd not sounded that good, ever. How did we manage to pull it off without major meltdowns?

A fantastic singer, songwriter, and guitarist for The Plugz, Tito Larriva was an open-minded and freewheeling boss behind the glass at Studio America. Anything we could think of doing he was willing to try, within our time constraints. Jeff brought along a cassette-tape recording of frogs and insects he made at a drainage ditch near his mother's house in Reseda. Tito loved the idea of using it as background on "Cool Drink of Water." Tito played the violin on "Promise Me," another spur-of-the-moment idea. We all sang backup vocals on "Jack on Fire," including my wife, Lois. All in all, our session at Studio America was a repeat of the few hours at Quad Teck—a couple of takes for each song, a bit of cursing, a smattering of threats and vows to never talk to one another again, and, ultimately, eleven songs and an album called *Fire of Love*. Together we delivered a bastard child of which we were all, indeed, very proud.

Anxious to probe the unknown parts of the world, we left Los Angeles behind with a knapsack full of recorded songs and two or three unrecorded encores. Unfortunately, as the tours, attention, and good reviews ratcheted up, our fearless leader began to shapeshift. Though subtle about it, Jeff mused aloud on the possibility of different musicians for a song or two, an entire album, or even for the pure hell of it. The rest of us were replaceable on a whim? Has Jeff started drinking? And by drinking, I mean more than nine, ten shots a day. When Jeff voiced such opinions we suggested he go fuck himself. Nervy bastard.

I was well aware that his musings could crackpot and fray at any moment, but I wasn't giving up my seat in the band. Ward wasn't so sure and, as the fraying turned to frazzle, began to plot a possible path to the exit. We all knew Rob wasn't a Gun Club lifer; we just didn't want to admit it and hoped he would stay on in spite of his inner gagging. In 1982, emboldened by a tattered, mutinous but functioning esprit de corps, we kept right on rollin'.

My biggest fear after the release of *Fire of Love* was that we would be locked inside the dreaded "cult band" prison. I believed in Jeff and his punk-blues theory of relativity. It was, at worst, an entertaining ruckus and, at best, an archaeological dig into the buried remains of country and western twangers, Delta blues hellhounds, and raspy archetypes of rock 'n' roll pioneers and originators. Can't get that kind of education at no goddamn Juilliard. Underscored by a brazenly selfish attitude, Jeff bartered for himself—and the band—a palpable and irrefutable list of things truly worth remembering: his songs. That's why I played drums for the guy. I loved the music. I loved the fans. Ward's bathroom breaks during live performances were pretty memorable too.

As 1982 stumbled forward, Rob became more and more agitated with all things Gun Club. Rob was never too quick to laugh, but if he stopped laughing at all, I knew he wasn't long for the band. Well, he stopped. A new album, *Miami*, was on the docket, and a new label, Animal, had acquired our services. On our way to New York to begin recording, Rob confessed he had bet his last dollar on his new band, 45 Grave, becoming a reality. What did Jeff think of that? Not much. His raison d'être for all things was the rate at which he could devour the increasing attention. Let bandmates come and go—Elvis from Hell was preaching blues, blood, and blarney for as long as his liver and tolerant musicians would allow.

Rob's relationship with the rest of us disintegrated before our eyes the moment we wrapped the basic tracks. He never came back. A year ago we lost Brian to The Cramps, and now Rob has left to join 45 Grave. Anyone else? Billy Idol approached me after a show at the Peppermint Lounge in NYC and offered me a spot behind the kit in his new band.

They were slated to record a new album soon. Hmm, interesting. But I declined. No, I'd rather play small clubs, make chump change, put up with Jeff, and live in L.A. Would someone please kill me?

Back in Los Angeles, now without a bass player and our guitar player ready to jump ship, Jeff's hairdo grew into a mushroom cloud of possibilities. Who to play bass? Jeff even suggested a second guitarist—himself. New songs and fashion cues were demanded by Jeff to keep Jeff interested in Jeff. Ward, after much introspection, a long round of drinks, and bit of begging on my part, decided to stay the course for the short, foreseeable future. Another tour, but not another record. The roulette wheel of reinvention was spinning in earnest.

I didn't believe The Bags' Patricia Morrison would have the inclination or stomach for a ride on the Black Train. She was far too smart and had too much self-respect. But if I didn't ask, I'd never know. The thought of who Jeff might drag through the rehearsal door to sow discord and undermine the fragile trust upon which this train huffed and puffed was a harrowing thought. In a bit of inspired lunacy, fueled by fantasies of ratted-out hair, short skirts, and torn fishnets, Jeff took a liking to Texacala Jones of Tex and the Horseheads. Yikes. Damage control! Ward and I got on our knees and prayed fervently to the clouds for a yes-vote from Patricia. Maybe she would, at least temporarily, satisfy Jeff's need for a female band member. I didn't tell Jeff that if he thought Patricia was going to be subservient at all, he was in for a shock or a boot up his ass or both. Patricia agreed to attend a rehearsal with her bass and amp.

A shock, followed by rapid relief: Patricia said yes. She could play, she could laugh, she could dismiss the eccentricities of our singer with a shrug. Patricia changed the band dynamic for the better—the much better, thanks to charm, guts, and commitment. She would need all that and a full helping of patience to learn our songs and get used to Jeff, but she put her seat belt on and braced *hard*. A week of rehearsals—go! A quick spate of shows in California and elsewhere, enough to give Patricia—and the rest of us—confidence that the new Gun Club was in proper working order. We had to make ready for soon-to-come American and European tours. Sparked by her presence, the newest version of The Gun Club soon jostled with the witty banter and caustic parodies of old. I became a fan of my own band. For about five minutes.

Before we pushed ourselves down the track another inch, a funny thing happened. Ward quit. Seizing his opportunity while in Los Angeles, Ward planted his flag behind the Orange County Curtain and vowed to never board the Train again. *No!* I saw it coming, of course. I surely did. Without Ward, the soul of The Gun Club would suffer a terrible blow. Back to the drawing board for a new guitarist.

While we were retooling Jeff's magical misery tour, I got a phone call from Kid Congo: "Interested in joining us for a couple of shows and a five-song recording session in the studio?" Us being The Cramps, of course. My answer being yes, of course. A show in Detroit and Chicago and a day inside a big room at A&M Studios in Hollywood. Damn, I could live off that high for weeks. Kid was a friend, too, and a soulmate inside the rock 'n' roll graveyard. When do I start? Both live performances and every minute of my six hours in the studio with Lux, Ivy, and Kid were the most fun I'd had in many months. Ivy and Lux were gracious and supportive and patient with me. I kept as close as possible to Nick's drumming for each song. Why fuck with a great thing? Simple and to the point. No frills. Thanks to Kid's grinding feedback, Lux's spastic fantastic stage antics, and, of course, Ivy's exquisite picking, I could manage the drum kit with far more fun than fear. The recording sessions were a bit of a toss, nothing meant for vinyl. But damn, was it ever fun! "Five Years Ahead of My Time," "Sinners," and "Call of the Wighat" were my favorites. I didn't care what they planned to do with the finished material—it was enough that I recorded with The Cramps.

Out of the jungle and back onto the Train. Jeff has been strapping a Telecaster over his shoulder for a song or two at rehearsal, and he's slowly getting better, but he's not yet a full-time singer *and* guitar player. By way of cosmic happenstance (again) Jim Duckworth, late of The Panther Burns, found his way to us. Shows were booked, rehearsals extended, and a new guitarist met his fate. Let the brainwashing begin. I had fight in me, but perhaps for a different war? I quit the band by allowing my conscience to beat me with a cat-o-nine-tails. If

Ward was gone, then I must follow. Seemed the right thing to do. I was confused.

The Gun Club hired Dee Pop to beat the skins. He was a good drummer, so I didn't feel too bad about it. I did feel bad about quitting. Stay, go? No, yes? My conscience was being a total asshole. I had no idea what I was supposed to feel *good* about. I was clueless, unhappy, and smoked an extra pack a day to spite myself. I was in full-on fuck-it mode. After getting high with The Cramps and low with The Gun Club, I got even lower with myself. I wasted weeks wrestling with ideas for new bands, all of which sucked. Got a job at Bleecker Bob's Golden Oldies Record Shop on Melrose Avenue. Everyone who knew me asked the same question: "Why aren't you playing drums?" Why, indeed.

After a couple of months at the store I was ready to kill myself, kill Bob, or join a low-rent carnival as the resident punk rock freak. As luck would have it, I got another phone call. Jeff Pierce, lead singer for The Gun Club, called to declare that he actually needed me on drums. The 1983 European and American tours were a bit of a Waterloo for Gun Club. Afterward Dee quit the band. Jim stayed. The Gun Club needed a drummer. Would I perchance care to reboard the Black Train? Translation: more shows were lined up, with no time to find a new drummer. Between the lines: Terry is dumb enough to do it. I did it. Rolling the dice, I concluded that no matter how obnoxious Jeff might be or become, I will always like the songs, respect his vision, and enjoy his contrary attitude from the stage. Sheesh, I can always join the carnival.

Our intrepid booking agent, Bob Singerman, arranged for us to travel to the bottom of the earth where people live upside down under. Australia for ten or so dates—who's counting? At the San Francisco airport while waiting for our long, long flight, Jim and I faced a foreboding, angst-ridden Jeff Pierce pacing the empty terminal. He looked spit out of a reverse washing machine—wrinkled, disheveled, and sweaty. After so many defections, Jeff had settled into his role as bellwether of belligerence. Again, I can't quite put my finger on the cause of his peevishness. His alcoholic intake hadn't subsided—maybe it's worse? I don't know, but I know this: I hate flying, and the thought of twenty-plus hours in a metal tube with a mucho-disgruntled Jeff

was damn unappealing. If I had no interest in the tour, I'd be okay with
the rats gnawing away at my conscience. Stay? Go? Before slithering
off to the boarding ramp, our fearless leader harangued Patricia, who
sat nearby trying to be invisible. Was she going? He then turned on us
all with a helping of sour-puss asides and half-baked insults. I think he
was drunk. "Either I'll see you in Australia . . . or I won't." Jim looked
at me. I looked back. No fucking way.

Jim had a twinkle in his eye, and it was contagious. We hatched a
devilish conspiracy to escape this wreck in progress by renting a car
and driving back to Los Angeles. Patricia was beset with fears and
not so anxious to jump off the Train and join us in our mutiny. A bit
hasty for her. We understood and suggested that if she wanted to go
down under, we would love her no matter what, hoping she would
live through the ordeal. We bade Patricia a fond farewell. Two Gun
Clubbers went to the bottom of the earth, and two went to the bottom of California. Motoring south on Interstate 5, Jim and I discussed
just about everything but what we just did—delivered the fuck you to
Jeffrey Lee Pierce. Interchangeable musicians we may be to Jeff, but
not without enough self-respect to call him on his bullshit. God damn,
did he need that! Hardly mattered to Jeff—he picked up enough musicians to finish the Australian tour (plenty of good players in Oz). That
gave the myth inside Jeff's head a few more weeks to live. From Los
Angeles Jim and I parted ways. I really looked forward to playing a
lot of shows with him, but not to be. I guess I had more quit in me. I
floated peacefully for about a week before I realized I would never play
"Preaching the Blues" again. That hurt.

Turned out that Kid Congo had just been released from The
Cramps. Not only that, he was back in The Gun Club! Wait, Kid was
booted from The Cramps? Why on earth? Many reasons came to mind,
and none of them the fault of Kid Congo Powers. What a strange, incestuous universe we live in. I wasn't at all sure Kid would be happy
shoveling coal back into the belly of the Black Train, though I suppose
The Gun Club was as much his band as Jeff's, so they've come full
circle, back in each other's arms. Yet another phone call from the lead
singer of The Gun Club: "Shut the fuck up and get your drums ready.
You're back in the band." In an incestuous universe, does it matter

how many times I quit and reboard the Black Train? Without time to think it all through, I dusted off my kit and prepared for Armageddon. In 1984 Jeff, Kid, Patricia, and Terry were suddenly in—or back in—The Gun Club.

Four survivors from L.A. punk's earliest days gave post-punk rock 'n' roll a run for its money. We had a third album—*Las Vegas Story*—to record and, after a spate of performances here and there, declared ourselves studio ready. Jeff's new songs were well worth a third album, and we included "Walkin' with the Beast," a favorite from the old days. We secured a producer, Jeff Eyrich, and a studio, Ocean Way, that afforded us much better opportunity to create a layered, more intricate Gun Club than in the past. We tried hard to create a stress-free zone in the studio, though Jeff's alarming alcohol consumption continued unabated and unaddressed. *LVS* was the most difficult to record so far, but with Kid back in the band, I was pretty fucking happy. The personality parade was much more harmonious than it had been in the past. Jeff even made noises between sessions that sounded like laughter.

Our 1984 tour of America with the new lineup was the closest we'd ever come to a well-oiled machine. Meanwhile we hadn't cracked any commercial playlists, but we discovered a lot of new fans. We had a lot of songs to play this time out, very few from *Fire of Love*, now relegated to encores. That's okay, but the reaction was pretty mixed. Every new fan wanted to hear "Sex Beat" or "Ivy." As always, I played drums *off* of Jeff, not the guitar or bass. Jeff's phrasing and song timing required an almost psychic connection between me and him. We were bound together by a musical tightrope—always scary, always an adventure. Good thing I didn't drink before a show. On rare occasions we would trot out a song like John Coltrane's "A Love Supreme" for laughs. Fans didn't get it, but playing songs like that were our opportunities to celebrate *and* destroy the roots of rock. The Gun Club revolution at work, brought to you by Marilyn Monroe from Hell. Our dedication to comedy may have fallen on deaf ears, but it always brought a cackle to the members of The Gun Club.

The 1984 tour came to an end in the States without incident and nearly made it across Europe but for one big incident: I quit the band for good. The weight of the past and lack of clarity for the future was taking its toll. Not sure I could justify more time as The Gun Club's drummer, now four years on and little to show for it. My biggest mistake was to think—or hope—I could somehow avoid the dreaded "sell-out" while earning enough coin to pay my way out of penury behind the kit of a politically correct rock 'n' roll band. So silly. Not only was political correctness an exercise in eventual self-destruction, but there was nothing PC or financially solvent about The Gun Club. I didn't really give a fuck about correct or incorrect anyway—I needed money to survive, and I wanted lots of it. The Gun Club's hand-to-mouth reality and Jeff's nonstop substance abuse put a truncheon to my idealism. And my bank account (I didn't have one). Just as vexing was Jeff's penchant for musical suicide as the leader of a band with a lot of fans and a unique roots-rock history. As the Train ride got smoother, he was determined to blow the tracks up. He confounded critics, all right, and made sure fans were just as confused, frustrated, or ignored. Our gradual drift from the blues roots that made The Gun Club so interesting was a wrench in my works. For Jeff, however he chose to interpret himself—there was no turning back.

The Gun Club was a shot glass full of luck, all right. I nursed it all the way through three albums, ten tours, and almost five years, with plenty left to drink. If only Jeff Pierce had nursed it—instead of swallowing it whole and eating the glass—he'd still be making music. And I, like an idiot, would probably be making it with him. I was relieved when my time ended. But, yeah, I feel pretty damn lucky it began.

CHAPTER 28

HARDCORE TO SPOKEN WORD: A CONVERSATION WITH HENRY ROLLINS

by John Doe

Since Black Flag were at the forefront of punk rock, Henry Rollins is uniquely qualified to talk about how "hardcore" took over most people's definition of the scene and the genre. Rollins is a force of nature, a righteous guy who lives for music and communication. We talked on the phone as friends and comrades.

JOHN: In the first book there were people from the original Hollywood punk rock scene that said, "We had this great scene, and then hardcore came and fucked it all up." I know you came in a little bit later, but I think you felt like, "I'm not fucking anything up—I'm just doing my thing. Don't blame me." I'd like to get your perspective on that.

HENRY: I grew up on the East Coast, so West Coast punk rock was an import item in that I would mail order singles like yours from Dangerhouse Records, like Black Randy, The Weirdos on Bomp!. In July 1981 there was a quick audition, and then I'm suddenly the singer in this legendary band Black Flag, and I go from my ice cream scooping job into a van, and several days later I'm delivered to the scalding streets of Hollywood, California. I did not know anything of the politics or the machinations or how the Hollywood scene was built because I'm just an outsider, a fan. I asked a fellow member of Black Flag, who laughed and went, "Well, here's what the politic is: the beach bands, as they were termed, have ruined the Hollywood scene." I said "How do they do that?" These young kids came in from the beaches into the enshrined Hollywood clubs, which I guess would be the Whisky, the Starwood, etcetera, and started smashing into people. I saw those Orange County, Huntington Beach guys, and they were no picnic. It was like *A Clockwork Orange* with a snare beat behind it. It was terrifying. All I wanted to say was, "Oh dude, I didn't start that. I have your records."

JOHN: So you were encountering Nazi punks at the same time that we were.

HENRY: Yeah. *The Decline of Western Civilization* cast had made its stain on the Hollywood scene, and everyone had their fill, like, in one weekend. By the second weekend I think everyone went, "Oh, this is the new normal? I'm going to have to reset everything because this is not good."

JOHN: Did you clock it at a particular time, being misunderstood as a skinhead?

HENRY: Well, I got the "Black Flag is not cool in this town" thing very quickly. But we rarely played in town [Los Angeles]. I had short hair, but I did not consider myself a skinhead in that there was inherent misogyny, racism, some kind of odd nationalism—I had none of that. All my friends from Washington, DC, like Ian Mackay, also had none of that. We just started cutting our hair off in response to, I don't know, everything. As a youth will do. Like, I don't want your glamour. I don't want any of it. For me it was, "I didn't want your beer, I didn't want your drugs." Taking the hair off, you just isolated yourself by such an intense look—me with no hair, big cheekbones, and big eyebrows . . . everyone's like, "Whoa." I saw that look and went, "Okay, this definitely parts the waters." However, doing shows across America, you would have skinheads coming up and saying, "All right, so what's the plan?" I'm like, "Whoa, I'm not one of you." Or you'd be in New York, and there were these boneheads, and they're like, "Hey, so you're with us, right?" I'm, like, "Nope." And that's when, by '82, I stopped cutting my hair until '86. With full transparency I never heard any of those quote-unquote hardcore bands that I ever really liked. Besides maybe Minor Threat, who got called a hardcore band, but I don't know whether they would have called themselves that. They were just ridiculously good. I mean I didn't like being lumped in with it because all these people are calling themselves hardcore. I thought what Black Flag was doing was extraordinarily hardcore. Like here's a seven-minute song that goes at the pace of the first Black Sabbath album on codeine. *That's* hardcore.

JOHN: I totally get that, okay. We took Chuck Berry at 45 [rpm] and, you know, went up to 78. Then other bands took that and said, "Okay, let's go to 105." What was the template, or was there one?

HENRY: Here's the missing link. Because the people who took it from those who took it from Chuck Berry and cranked it up a notch—they never got the Chuck Berry idea and the beat never swung. The first time I saw Bad Brains, me and Ian saw them June '79 opening for The Damned, and they're playing at this hyperspeed. But the drummer Earl is swinging. *Chooka packa, chooka packa.* We're like, "What is that?" Because all of our fast punk rock drummer friends are *oompa oompa oompa*, as we called it—it's like *oompa* music at 78. It's really uptight. But here's what I think happened. You have bands like Minor Threat and The Necros from the Midwest. I think everyone bought those records and made a band. They didn't hear X or The Weirdos or The Germs necessarily. Minor Threat was one of the most influential bands of the last century in American independent music. I just think they incorporated what they learned from Bad Brains covering "12XU" by Wire. I thought that was a Bad Brains song until we heard *Pink Flag* by Wire. So we got the Chuck Berry, but Wire still traded through Bad Brains.

I think what hardcore became was this marvelous distillation of youth, anger, not a lot of talent needed necessarily. "Let's start a band Thursday." Which is a beautiful paradigm punk rock ethic but without any "Here's my other eighty records that made me want to be in a band." They didn't have the eighty records; they had two. Some band comes to town, like a Minor Threat, and they go, "Okay, that's it." And they're trying to emulate a drummer like Jeff Nelson, who was really good, the best that *oompa* gets. It wasn't swinging; it was just this kind of weird tripling that did a great thing. I think that's why one band becomes viral. It just becomes a cloning thing. Whereas I think your early New York scene like No Wave, you get Lydia Lunch, Alan Vega, and James Chance, you have a lot of that in the Hollywood or L.A. punk rock scene. You know X, Weirdos, The Screamers—forget it! One of the best bands in the history of music. Full stop. The Screamers. I never saw them, but I have every bootleg I've ever seen. There's not a bad song in the bunch. I hear those *Live at the Masque* tapes and wonder: How the hell did anyone sleep after seeing The Screamers play? You guys had a very potent scene. I mean, it was coming from a high-, high-calorie thing.

JOHN: Yeah, The Screamers had a complete experience in mind. They didn't want to just come up and be a band and play some songs; they wanted to affect every piece of it. What were you and Black Flag listening to at that time, and what was influencing you? Because obviously you have more than two records.

HENRY: Okay. What you might not know is what they listen to and what I listen to. There is a lot of where those two circles, Circle A and Circle B, intersected into the big fat C section.

JOHN: Yeah, what's the Venn diagram of this, Henry?

HENRY: I came into the band younger than everyone, and I'm coming in with all my British punk rock. The Damned, The UK Subs, and all of that. Whereas Greg Ginn and Chuck Dukowski, your leaders of Black Flag, almost completely disregarded British punk rock. They thought it was the biggest possible container of crap. You'd play The Clash, and they'd say, "Okay, just stop. 'Cause that's a bunch of posers." I'm, like, okay I'll just have to wait around for an invention called the Walkman because I can't play my tapes in the van because I'm just getting teased. Early on I was told, "Here's a handful of bands that you have to like to be in this band because we're coming from this." Chuck gave me the tapes, and luckily I took to it like dropping a fish in water. Stooges, MC5. Before I was in the band Chuck would call me. He'd go, "Hey, have you bought *Fun House* yet? I told you to buy *Fun House*." I'm minimum wage, so I'm like, "Okay, Dad," and I never did it. Stupid. So he goes "Well, you didn't do it, and now you're in the band, and here's your *Fun House* tape— play it." After one listen I went, "First off, that's my favorite record. And second off, I'm never gonna do anything that good." Then they gave me the first Stooges album, *Raw Power*, *Kick Out the Jams* by the MC5, and the first four Black Sabbath albums. That's where those guys were coming from. And early Ted Nugent. Where it's just like this from-the-bone-marrow Detroit—you know: *rock*. This was before Nugent was, you know, *talking*. It was *Great White Buffalo* and *Stranglehold*—kind of unimpeachable music. Or *Master of Reality* by Black Sabbath. And, to their credit, those guys liked all of the L.A. punk bands, even though the L.A. punk bands didn't necessarily like them back. They liked X, Weirdos, Germs, The Alley Cats, who they did play a lot of shows with. All of this has stopped right around the time I joined the band. I lived in Hollywood for a minute, but then we got kicked out by the cops. Someone said that one of us robbed a local with a shotgun, which is just not true. So we retreated back to the beach, and that was all new to me, and suddenly I'm a Hermosa Redondo resident until Black Flag broke up. It was just weed and beer and your friends were surfer-stoner types—really mellow.

JOHN: SST was at least as eclectic as Dangerhouse, but somewhere in the mid- to late eighties it became a little bit more uniform.

HENRY: I think that was in a way the Black Flag/SST masterstroke. If you listen to early Black Flag, it's not riff rock. Look at the bands that Ginn and Dukowski signed. The Minutemen, who are just all kinds of fantastic, but how do you sell that record? Saccharine Trust, another amazing band. Who's going to buy these records? I'm not saying they're bad; I'm just saying these are tough sells. The first Meat Puppets record. Good luck! Then they signed a stoner heavy metal band that is now iconic, Saint Vitus. Whereas now that's a go-to band, all your bands like Sleep and all these stoner bands, you say, "Who's the big woolly mammoth?" They go, "Oh, Saint Vitus." That's a beach band! They would keep sending us their flyers. Greg I think literally went up to them after the show, because they knew who he was, and said, "Great, let's make a record." So if you look at the first five years of the SST catalog, it's, like, how do you go broke? Sign all these bands. What's going to keep the money coming in? Black Flag never stops touring, and the records are getting somewhere. But finally the label signed Hüsker Dü, you get the *Metal Circus* record and just these fantastic records one after another that are barely classifiable. I think that's a product of Ginn and Dukowski. I don't know that they were looking for sales; they just had an interesting ear.

JOHN: At the time could you appreciate the effect that you and Black Flag and the rest of those bands were having on punk rock? It became, "Okay, guys, you're on a major label, but this is where the real network is being made. We're out there touring our asses off, sleeping on people's floors, but we are developing the network." Before that there wasn't a network. The first time we toured we went from L.A. and drove straight to New York and played four shows and then fucking drove home.

HENRY: Bands like Dead Kennedys kind of blazed the trail because they were big fish immediately. They were really good, and with a name like that, you know the priests are coming after the show with the cops and the governor. But D.O.A. from Canada—I mean, those guys were just killing themselves out there. They were sleeping on my floor before I was in Black Flag! They're going out every night, sweating through their flannel shirts, and just killing it. Black Flag had that same kind of ethic. Ginn and Dukowski, they should get the credit; they would bring SST bands on tour just to get the label happening. We'd let some local band open, and they do the punk rock thing for thirty-five minutes, and then we'd have an SST band open, and quite often that was Saccharine Trust, which is Joe Baiza on guitar—they broke the mold on that guy—and Jack Brewer, amazing singer-poet. The audience was, like, "Whoa, whoa, wait a minute." I think Black Flag was one of those bands that just kind of ramrodded eclecticism into the brainpan of a lot of their fans. I think it did have some results, and it did help.

JOHN: Did you feel like it was political, like traditional governmental politics, or just social politics that you were trying to change?

HENRY: With Black Flag we never wrote about Reagan, and a lot of bands were Reagan and Thatcher, you know. I don't dare speak for all of us, but our politics were really local. As far as I can stick my arm out and touch something, that's my politics. That would be clashes with law enforcement. I'm not the law-breaking type. I worked for minimum wage, went home with my aching swollen feet from standing all day. I'm not trying to break into a building. So cops have nothing to say to me 'cause I'm not the problem. I got out here with Black Flag's reputation preceding me, and within three days I'm in the *L.A. Times*. We go off on Darrel Gates, and you know that love affair. I become this recognizable face to members of not only LAPD but Redondo Beach PD. Hermosa Beach PD were like, "Oh, you're the Black Flag guy—insert expletive." All the sudden I'm getting cops in my face, yelling at me. Terrifying. Well, not all cops are bad. But, "Bad enough for me. Bad as every experience I've had in the last five months. Screw it, kill 'em all." I think our politics was us vs. law enforcement people trying to close our shows down. "Well, you're Satanists." Really? We're four starving vegetarians in a van. You have no idea what you're talking about. None.

JOHN: We experienced some of the same kind of prejudice. "You represent freedom. You represent nonconformity. So therefore you're the enemy. And you think you're so fucking cool, just doing your own thing. I don't like that, and I actually have a billy club and I can do something about it."

HENRY: Right. If [police] were obeying the law, they wouldn't make me stop walking to band practice, twist my arm behind my back, and pat me down. The command was "Left hand on your head, right hand behind your back." Then they get behind you and bend your index finger back. "Where you going?" "Band practice. Officer, you stopped me yesterday a block before—same question." "Shut up." That was my take on cops. I don't get to break the law, but you break the law. So for me it was all very personal, and we never wrote about a president because we never met the guy. We met cops. We met psycho religious groups picketing our shows with signs, "Save the Children." HUH? What are you people talking about? Go back to your job. You know what I mean? We would get these wacky groups or, like, the Channel 7 guy coming down to our show. "I need to talk to someone in Black Flag. Henry? Go. So why do you guys like Satan?" That would be the first question, and you can't answer out of that. Our reaction: well, there's a Black Flag song called "Spray Paint." It's a great one. It's, like, a thirty-one-second song. It comes from how we would show our displeasure. We called it voting. One of the things we would do when the owner of the club would call the cops on his own show to get us off stage—this happened—you whip out the spray paint and you find his car, and that car gets some beautiful new racing stripes. It kind of looked like a swastika, but they're racing stripes. This is not magic marker in his backstage dressing room—it's spray paint on not only your venue but the two shops on either side. It's more than a middle finger. Thankfully we didn't have Molotov cocktails.

I joined Black Flag when I was twenty, so by the time I was twenty-two I kind of came at everything from a fighting crouch. I'd say we didn't go on tour, we went to war. Those aren't songs, they're battle hymns. Law enforcement would sometimes meet us at the county line, waiting for our van to pull into wherever. Everyone out of the van. All your stuff gets thrown on the grassy median strip, just thrown out. All the gear gets taken out, and they just look at it and they go, "Okay." And you have to pack it all back in. This kind of thing happened all the time. Black Flag lived in this craziness that came with us everywhere because of the reputation.

Then some opening band has the temerity to say, "Why'd you grow your hair long?" And I'm like, "Hold me back before I rip one of this kid's ears off and eat it in front of him." I couldn't have been a more irrational, more angry person. Again, it's not an excuse, but I don't know of any band who's doing 160 shows a year releasing a record every eight months who is so in that fray.

JOHN: I had no idea that you had become such a target. Not you personally, but as a band.

HENRY: Oh yes. After a while you start reacting like the bear that's been poked too many times. Someone says, "Good morning," and you just leap at the person. That's the stuff I'm still walking back. By '86 I was just, you know, PTSD. Someone's, like, "So is your band playing tonight?" WHAM! "Why'd you hit the guy, Henry?" "He moved. He spoke." I won't make excuses. I won't go, "Well, I was young." I'll just go, "Yeah, write me off." I don't know what else to say except I wonder what you would have done if you were there in my shoes. That would have been interesting to see how you would have rocked that house party.

JOHN: When did you start transitioning from Black Flag lyrics to doing spoken-word stuff?

HENRY: In 1983 our pal Harvey Kubernik was doing those great shows at the Lhasa Club. We'd get, like, twenty-five people. Everyone gets three minutes. I'd go with Dukowski into Bright Lights Big City Hollywood to watch him do his five minutes on stage with his Orwellian apocalyptic terrified stuff. One night Kubernik came up to me and said, "You got a big mouth. How about you do five minutes next week?" "What am I going to do?" He said, "It pays ten bucks." "Oh, I'm in." I saw an omelet coming my way. So I got up and did my five minutes. I read a thing I'd written, and then I told a quick story about how Greg Ginn had nearly been run over by a neo-Nazi in a car that ran up onto a lawn because we let Mexican guys hang out at our band practice. They said, "Hey, this is our neighborhood. We're going to come and watch you practice." We're like, "That's great." Our gear is in your neighborhood at night. Greg was walking to the liquor store to get some orange juice, and some white-power guy tried to run Greg over, yelling about being a particular epithet lover. I told that story, and the audience was aghast. That's just a Wednesday in the world of Black Flag. People came up to me after and said, "When's your next show?" I thought they meant Black Flag. They said, "No, no, the next show where you just talk." I said, "Oh, never. I just got this ten-dollar bill. You know, I won."

JOHN: You figure that's all you're going to get, you might as well quit while you're ahead.

HENRY: I got that ten-dollar bill, and I got food. It was more than the five-dollars-a-day per diem I got on tour. I realized almost immediately after walking off stage I really liked that format. I had no fear or trepidation, and I wish I could have had another fifteen minutes. Harvey said, "Okay, you're a natural. Let's put you on a show opening for one of my poets, and I'll give you ten minutes." After several of those shows some of those poets were opening for me. By '85 I was doing shows internationally, and by '89 I'm doing a full nineteen- to twenty-one-country tour of talking shows, as I call them. "Spoken word" always sounded too stuffy to me. A bit too NPR for my liking. I do multiple nights at the Sydney Opera House now. I go on stage, and I tell you where I've been, what I saw, what I thought about it, and try and make that into a story that communicates. I took to it way quicker and way more naturally than I ever did with music. By '87 it's how I financed the Rollins Band's picks, strings, drumsticks, and salary when the band was in the red every year until things got better.

JOHN: You were out of Black Flag by '87?

HENRY: Summer '86. Maybe July was the last show in Detroit, and by October I was in the studio making my first solo record, and April '87 I'm in rehearsal with my new band. As I said at the beginning of the interview, Black Flag had their music, and I had mine. By '84 I was listening to Diamanda Galas. I was going to KCRW, learning basically how to do a radio show, which I have now. I'm into Laurie Anderson, Birthday Party, Einsturznede Neubauten, and picking up the spoken-word records of William Burrows. Mike Watt of The Minutemen is turning me on to Albert Ayler, etcetera. I became this sponge, like I want to hear all of it. So that's kind of where I started fissuring off from Black Flag. My bandmates, they weren't really on board with all that. They maybe had a respect for it. For me that became kind of my steady diet.

JOHN: Part of this book has become about legacy. Looking back on what you guys did, can you see the seeds that you sowed into what became of punk rock?

HENRY: I don't think you can point to any one band. But I think labels like SST and Dischord, they started a consciousness that said, "Wait a minute—I can do this." All of a sudden here comes this highway that was deep woods when I first got there. By Lollapalooza time it's a four-lane highway, with rest stops every seven miles. The reason you and I got to do what we did and do is because Iggy Pop got his lights punched out by bikers in the Midwest. There's always someone ahead of you clearing the lane as you clear the lane further.

I think what happened in the eighties going into the nineties was a lot of bands saw immediately there's an alternative to being on the radio, being on MTV, and being on a big label. Once, I called Dischord and Ian picked up the phone. "How do you make a record?" "You call these people and you send them your tape and they make the records and send it back in two weeks." "Oh." That's the early Dischord Records. All of a sudden everyone has that phone number, and by golly I'm making a record. That was a consciousness that gave the major labels quite the hip check. They had to play catch-up. I think one of the bands that started that was X being on Elektra. That was a big thing. Like, well, wait a minute, look at that. They got there. And those are beautiful records. Then Hüsker Dü went to Warner Brothers from SST, and R.E.M. went up the hill. Some of the brighter talents are being plucked. The cynical part of me went, okay, the majors are looking at the farm teams and they're just plucking the Michael Stipes. The more "we can sell that" kind of bands. They're letting all these bands kill themselves in vans for ten years and do their own A&R, and so the majors just go, *pluck!* They don't have to pay for any of that nurturing. I resented that. I said no. You told these bands to go screw themselves for years. When they sent you the demo tapes you laughed them out of the office. So you see a consolidation of labels communicating, pioneering college radio as a viable tool to sell records and get the word out. So things changed. Labels like Slash and Dangerhouse, SST, Alternative Tentacles, Thermidor, Dischord, and Touch and Go—it's a connecting of dots from coast to coast that became this fantastic network that ran this parallel universe to the majors. Where the real music is happening is where it's always been happening—in the clubs. But that distribution system, that execution is a gleaming machine now.

JOHN: The indies have always been where it's at, but now they actually can have a real impact and make some money, and it makes me glad that the major labels ignored everything and failed on their own. I don't have one ounce of sympathy for them because they had a great opportunity and they said, "Oh no, we can't do that, and oh no, you're stealing my music." Good, I'm glad you failed because you were fucked up and stole from artists to begin with.

HENRY: They deserve to lose what they lost because of their hubris and their sense of entitlement, like, "We invented this." Actually you didn't. Hey, can I tie something up?

JOHN: Yes, sure.

HENRY: As far as hardcore, we're talking all your Murphy's Law, Cro Mags, that big New York CBGB's matinees scene, and all your midwestern hardcore. It's a great distillation of "I want to be in a band right now." But beyond that, it's youth and masculinity without having been tempered by eighty dates, thirty breakups, and trying to understand a woman's point of view. A lot of that stuff is incredibly puerile. Like, "All the women hate me." Because you're seventeen and obnoxious, as we all were. Hopefully you'll meet the right gal who will straighten you out. I saw a lot of kind of cool and articulation with city bands because everyone's, you know, *voulez-vous*'ing at the club later on. A lot of Midwest bands, there's like a stiffness in the playing, like, "Oh, that's just nine tons of testosterone with nowhere to go." I mean, the intensity—you don't want any part of it. It's so full-on. The anger is real; the playing isn't bad. It's not misguided; it's just coming from a really limited worldview. I remember being surrounded by a bunch of skinheads in New York summer '84 with my Meat Puppets tie-dyed shirt on. I was in town to make a movie with Lydia Lunch and Richard Kern. Suddenly I'm surrounded by skinheads. One guy's swinging a chain in front of my face. He's like, "I hear you don't like us." I went, "No, I don't, actually." They all deflated because they didn't think I was going to say that. They're like, "Well, why?" I said, "Because I remember you guys. You were at my show at the Ritz the other night, and you guys were like pulling chains off people and beating up on gay folks. We had to make you leave. So, no, I don't like you." And they all went, "Oh." They all shook my hand and kind of moped away. I think they wanted to beat me up. I've got my long, curly brown hair and my tie-dyed T-shirt, and I'm like, "No, I don't like you. I don't like what you do. Mugging people at a show? Like, who are you people? You got to get more holes poked in your can, man. You need more ventilation."

It's good to know that there is someone out there like Henry Rollins who thinks and cares about big issues and won't shy away from confronting and understanding what it all means. We are all fortunate and maybe a little better off for that.

CHAPTER 29

EVERYTHING BECAME POSSIBLE

by Allison Anders

If there had never been the DIY reaction in music in the seventies known, for better or worse, as punk rock, there would never have been the American independent film movement in the eighties.

I was living in the Valley in 1978, the SFV, specifically Van Nuys. There was absolutely nothing to do. Especially not for a twenty-two-year-old single mother of two little girls on welfare with no car. To relieve the boredom there was Wednesday-night cruising on Van Nuys Blvd. Yeah, everyone came out in their cars—all kinds of cars: low-riders, Chevy vans, surf wagons, motorcycles, fifties pickups—and drove down the length between Vanowen and the turn-around spot to Chandler. I lived right at that turn-around in an apartment with my little girls.

I had been attending classes at L.A. Valley College before I had my second baby. Finding childcare for a one-year-old was rough, so I had been taking a little break till her second birthday and I could get her into the daycare center at the college, which was amazingly good, and, like, my tuition, was free. Yeah, those were the days . . . the Jerry Brown years the first time around.

Like everyone else in the Valley, my boredom was not just centered in my unfortunate address. It was cultural. The pop culture malaise, which had infected my ears and eyes, had been there since around 1973. The only saving grace were a handful of filmmakers who had cut their teeth working for Roger Corman and were now getting studio support—Scorsese, Coppola, who also produced a hit film that summer for very little money directed by George Lucas: *American Graffiti*.

The reason *American Graffiti* was more important than any of the rest was the focus on youth culture, their meandering narratives, the cruising in cars, and the endless soundtrack of early rock 'n' roll. It was not roots music; it was not daring. It was a collection of radio hits from the late fifties, early sixties culled together sometimes inaccurately by Kim Fowley for this single night in 1962.

It may sound strange that a movie so not edgy and a soundtrack of a bunch of oldies could have signaled a new direction for me. But I think it was a starting point of getting back to basics, getting back to simple songs, simple stories on film, and putting music and film together. In fact, in Los Angeles *American Graffiti* had a larger effect: K-EARTH, a radio station, emerged playing "oldies" from the fifties and sixties, and Art Laboe had a club on Sunset Strip (which had been Ciro's and is now the Comedy Club) where revivals of artists from those years performed. Big Joe Turner was the house band. This existed in L.A. in a world of prog, The Eagles, and Pink Floyd.

Before having my first baby in Pacoima in 1974, I had lived in London and worked as a barmaid at the Hope and Anchor Pub in Islington. In the pub, bands were trying to get back to early rock 'n' roll—our house band was Brinsley Schwartz with Nick Lowe and Ian Gomm. Above the pub lived Dave Robinson, Brinsley's manager, who would come down around 2:00 P.M. in his bathrobe for his wake-up pint before the mandatory afternoon closing. The governor of the pub, Fred, told me, "Dave's building a recording studio up there. He's going to start a record label." I scoffed, "Dave, who doesn't get out of bed until two?"

By 1978, when I was living in Van Nuys, that record label of sleepy Dave's became Stiff Records. Some friends from high school, Michael Uhlenkott and Laurie O'Connell, had started an art zine, *World Imitation*, and a band, Monitor. Other than them, I had no connection to the music scene happening over the hill in Hollywood until another high school friend invited me to a show at the Whisky a Go Go. The opening act was The Bags. It was like nothing I'd ever seen before, yet there were elements of things I knew very well.

For example, Alice wore a sexy tight black 1950s sheath dress and black high heels, like my mom's friend Judy Arthur used to wear, or Kim Novak. Only, her black hair was cut short and in peaks on her head as she moved around the stage with the most self-possessed energy I'd ever seen in a woman performer. Patricia on bass: first of all—to see a woman bass player was incredibly rare before this scene. Sure, we can point to exceptions like Fanny and the Runaways, but I can't impress upon people enough how shocking it was to see a woman own that instrument like it was part of her. Porcelain skin, red lips, black-cat eyeliner, teased black hair falling around her shoulders, in her white satin gown to her pointy shoes—stunning. On guitar Craig Lee wore some old-man suit, had a wild look in his big round eyes and a fuzzy head of red hair. Terry Graham, wearing sixties mod clothes, was one of the cutest boys I'd ever seen.

After their set the headliners came on stage, The Dickies, and to my shock the lead singer, who was eliciting female sighs and even a "Leonard, I love you" from one punk girl down in front, was someone I knew: Leonard Graves, one of my regular customers at Corky's Coffee Shop on Van Nuys Blvd. In 1974 I worked the graveyard shift while my sister Luanna babysat. Leonard and his friends came in and ordered loads of coffee and French fries and stayed long hours in a big Naugahyde booth. It didn't take long till I realized—which he later confessed—he had a big crush on me.

I shattered his dreams one night when he asked, "Hey Allison, what do you think of Genesis?" I was quick with my thoughts: "Oh god, I hate them!" His friends exploded in laughter while Leonard deadpan slowly sank in his seat nearly to the floor. I went on and on how very much I hated that band, right down to Peter Gabriel's stupid haircut. Then I said, "Why do you ask?" Leonard sat up quickly, clearing his throat: "Um, well, I happen to be in that band." I tisked and shook my head and walked away to coffee other customers.

Years later he told me he had finally got up the nerve to ask me out and was going to take me to see Genesis. Oh gee. Four years after I dashed his dreams he was on this stage with no shirt, a skinny black silk tie, and legions of local fans, even a smattering of screaming girls, in a band with some of those same boys he'd loiter with during Corky's after-hours.

I left that show completely changed. Somehow these people who were not rock stars were rock stars. Somehow this look, these musicians and fans, had was familiar and yet twisted into something new, vibrant. Somehow this music was back to something authentic, and yet it was its own frequency—scary, exhilarating, hilarious, outrageous, and a challenge to everything I knew up to that point in my life.

There was finally something to do in L.A.

Thank god, 'cause in 1978 there was nothing at the movie theaters worth the hassle and cost of getting a babysitter. The state of mainstream movie theaters sucked just as hard as what the radio was offering up in terms of music. And like the music business in the late seventies, any filmmaker who didn't have a foothold already in the movie business and/or had a truly independent voice was not only not welcome but locked out completely—there was no way in.

It didn't help that 1978 was deeply entrenched in the new movie model—the blockbuster. Steven Spielberg's *Jaws* had launched what would become the impenetrable trend in 1975 and George Lucas's *Star Wars* sealed the deal in 1977. It's crazy ironic that this same filmmaker who got me back to basic rock 'n' roll—American International Pictures teen movies of the fifties and sixties, a radical meandering narrative, and independent spirit straight out of Roger Corman's AIP years—had now made a movie so successful at the box office that a little personal film like *American Graffiti* could not possibly get made in the new movie system. That had all happened in five short years.

There was not only no way someone like me—and a woman—was going to get to make a movie in that system. There was fuck-all I wanted to go see in most movie theaters.

Before the musicians who created this new scene of independent music emerged, they had, in their despair, turned back to listen to music of the past, be it sixties garage and psych through Lenny Kaye's *Nuggets* LP or records brought home from a thrift store 'cause the album cover was so insane. Likewise, those of us who would become filmmakers in the American indie movement were reconnecting to movies of the past, and the beauty of it all was that we could do it for free! Long before cable, these movies were on TV. The local channels played movies all night long. In L.A. Channel 5 KTLA was your go-to station. In retrospect it was the most radical movie programming ever. 'Cause even though there was no dirty language or nudity, you could see absolutely everything else: film noir (a rich catalogue of the RKO Films years were among my favorites), fifties teen exploitation films from AIP, heists, horror, and rock 'n' roll movies. The latter comprised films made from 1954 all the way through the late 1960s. Many of us recall seeing one of the greatest concert films of all time: Steve Binder's brilliant mid-sixties doc, *The T.A.M.I. Show*, for the first time in the 1970s around 2:00 A.M. on KTLA.

So you can talk to any filmmaker of my generation—and our forefathers John Waters and David Lynch—and we were all watching backward to the more exploitation, independent movies of the forties, fifties, sixties and listening to the same records our brothers and sisters in the emerging independent music scene were listening to, just as they were watching the same movies we were.

Luckily revival movie houses had emerged in the early seventies in L.A. So theaters like the New Beverly Cinema, the Nuart, and the barely there but not forgotten Fox Venice were playing double bills of classics by a single director of the French new wave or Orson Welles or Hal Ashby. It was at these theaters that I was able to play catch-up on what I'd missed—the early films of the New German cinema of Wim Wenders and Rainer Fassbinder and Werner Herzog, which was life changing for me as a filmmaker.

Wim Wenders's films spoke to me and influenced me more than any other filmmaker's work I'd ever seen. I'll never forget seeing how, in his movies, characters would play a record of the past in present day. Until I saw Wim do it, no one else had. Records were always used to set up a time period. In Wim's early films characters who lived in the 1970s also listened to Kinks' records from the sixties, played a 1968 Canned Heat song on the jukebox, maybe sang along to Chris Montez's "The More I See You." And in *The Goalie's Anxiety at the Penalty Kick*, during a one-night stand, a girl introduces herself as "Gloria. G-L-O-R-I-A." I know it's hard for people to imagine, but no filmmaker had ever done this before: made music a living fabric of his film characters' lives. He did something else no one was doing: he hired a band, Krautrockers Can, to compose his scores on several movies. I took note.

Once at UCLA film school I walked into the first day of Robert Rossen's class at Melnitz Hall, and with a big smile, he introduced a double bill of *A Hard Day's Night* (which I had already seen over fifty times in the theater) and *Beyond the Valley of the Dolls*. The exhilaration I felt from this single afternoon in Bob's class, watching these two films together, cemented the path my work was going to take.

But the ideas, while they came easy, were too ambitious for what I could do in film school. Inspired by Alan Betrock's killer book on sixties girl groups, I wrote a little script about a band like The Shangri-Las, a kind of dark side of a girl band in the years after they'd disbanded, and began a script about a King/Goffin songwriting team at the Brill Building. But to do it right, I needed more money and more experience, and they were probably features. A decade later I'd make *Grace of My Heart* from the seeds of these two early ideas.

In 1983, during my second year at UCLA film school, I took a quarter off to study with Wim Wenders on *Paris, Texas*. I had pursued him—some might say stalk, but that is way too simple—with letters after seeing his film *Lightning Over Water*. Had I not followed my gut, going against all my friends' advice, and included a mix tape of my favorite sixties girl-group songs with that first letter I sent to him, he would never have become my willing mentor, and we would not be friends to this day. On *Paris, Texas* I saw Wim directing a local Texas girl punk band, The Mydolls, in a scene, playing live, and also watched him direct musician John Lurie in one of his first acting roles. I filed it all away for future use.

I made music integral to my first two films I made at UCLA. The second film was literally music driven: the main character was a record collector. I used record stores, jukeboxes, and record players and cast Keith Mitchell from Monitor in a few scenes and a few scenes with Rockin' Ronny Weiser of Rollin' Rock Records, who put out the first Blasters record.

When Kurt Voss, Dean Lent, and I screened our second film projects at UCLA, all of which Dean had shot in 16mm reversal black-and-white, a lot of our classmates and professors felt there was something new here, even within the school. But it was one person, one who worked in the department and was a filmmaker we seriously looked up to, Billy Woodbury, who encouraged us to take it further. Billy made a feature with $25,000 some years previously called *Bless Their Little Hearts*. It was like a Cassavetes lyrical poem set in South Central with an all-black cast. Sounds great, doesn't it? It's beyond great—it's genius. Billy was working in the film school, checking out equipment to the students. All cameras, lights, everything you needed to make your film project—you went to Billy.

Billy saw our three films and said, "You guys need to make a feature. Pull together some money and just start. I'll help you with the gear." With our idol's push and with DIY culture telling us we could just go make a movie, we did just that. Kurt had $2k as a graduation present and was willing to invest it to get us going. The three of us went on a little trip to Baja, CA, to stay in a trailer on the beach owned by the new lady friend of an old boyfriend of mine. There we proceeded to hash out what sort of story we'd make. Kurt was into a guy alone, hiding out in Mexico in a trailer on the beach. I liked the idea of a couple on the run, hiding out in Mexico in a trailer on the beach. Dean said, "No, no, it's two guys on the run hiding out in Mexico in a trailer on the beach." We all brought our own romantic longings to it, you might say.

Our first draft of *Border Radio* was a dark film noir, a man who'd left behind a wife and child while hiding out in that Baja trailer on the beach. And there was another man who was perhaps more obsessed with his friend on the run more than his wife, who he was sleeping with. This sounds like the movie we ended up making, but believe me, this first version was so very far in tone from the movie we actually made. However, had we never had that original dark film-noir tone, we would never have *Border Radio* at all. Why? Well, 'cause that was the movie Chris D. signed up to make. And without Chris D. I probably never would have met John Doe.

Kurt was a huge fan of The Flesh Eaters and, in particular, the onstage presence of Chris D. Kurt and I were living together (we'd become a couple at LAVC in 1981, and both incredibly got accepted to UCLA's super-competitive film program for 1982), so being a very good girlfriend and hoping to breathe in some of the L.A. music scene we loved into our movie, I said, "Hey, what about Chris D. as Jeff?" Kurt mulled it over: well, how could we get to him? We didn't know Chris D. As many shows as Kurt and I might go to of X, The Blasters, The Gun Club, we were outsiders. We were from the Valley, and while my lifestyle was raucous enough, motherhood and the Canterbury would never have gone together. There is another reason: the scene was very insular. To protect that energy that was germinating and exploding and including so many races, gender, styles, and voices, maybe the instinct to contain it was vital to its survival. I had managed to get Wim Wenders to UCLA to see my *Super 8* movie—I think we could do this. So we went, script in hand, to a Divine Horsemen show at the Music Machine in West L.A., near where we were living in UCLA's married student housing.

We didn't have any real plan, and I think we were both pretty nervous to approach him even though we'd been going to his shows for years. I saw a friend, Craig Roose, and solicited his help: we want Chris D. to be the lead in our movie . . . could he please take the script to him for us? He walked over to Chris, who had just finished his set. We could see him take the script in his hand and look over at us, wary, giving us the once-over. Then he took the script and walked off. Craig came back and said Chris had asked, "Do those people even have any money to make a movie?"

What we didn't know was that Chris D. was a deeply savvy film scholar. He knew film noir better than anyone we'd ever met. And when he agreed to make the movie, he gave his character Jeff a last name, Bailey, to reference and nod to Robert Mitchum's character in *Out of the Past*.

We wrote the script to shoot in locations we could access—the trailer in Baja and Dean's apartment in Echo Park primarily. As the story evolved, we added locations—stole some, negotiated the rest . . . for free. Every dime spent had to be on the screen. Except the beer we were perhaps a little too generous with for the cast!

Looking back on it, Chris was amazingly trusting of us, three film students he didn't know from Adam. He was great with his costars Luanna and Chris Shearer. I can't remember how it came about, but Chris D. brought John Doe and David Alvin into our movie. While it's hard to pick favorites of all the great bands in L.A. at this time, I can only say that X spoke directly to me in every way. The band visually were such unique personas, John's voice continues to be one of my favorite voices, and I love hearing him and Exene sing together. The songwriting was pure storytelling, rich with characters, atmosphere, triumphs, disappointments, and flawed joy.

Unlike a lot of the punk songs we enjoyed sweating to at the Hong Kong Café, you could have conversations about an X song. Even after we were making *Border Radio* with John Doe, I remember Kurt, Luanna, and I discussing "Drunk in My Past" and wondering: Who is the drunk in his/her past? I thought it was literally someone in the past, and Kurt thought it was the narrator of the song himself or herself, they were the drunk. Luanna thought it was maybe someone in the narrator's life he/she couldn't get rid of. Kurt finally said in irony, "Gee, I wish we knew these people. We could call them up and find out!"

Luanna and I had seen X more times than I could ever count and never once met them, no matter how many times we'd been inches away from the stage. But she and I will never forget the day we got to meet John Doe at UCLA's Melnitz Hall. He was interested in being in our movie. I think we were going to show him some footage we'd shot. Luanna and I sat on a bench outside, and like Wim Wenders before him, John descended down the stairs from the street above and into my life. And neither have left since.

John was way ahead of grunge in that time period—his jeans were ripped, he was wearing a flannel shirt, and his hair was longer than it had been in the early X days. When we saw him at the top of the stairs, we sisters slapped each other, and Luanna said under her breath, "Oh my god." And then he came and sat down on the bench with us and smiled, "Hi girls!" Okay. You got the part!

We began production in 1984 and finally finished the film in 1987. Our crew mainly was the three of us: Dean shooting, Kurt recording sound, and me doing everything else. We all three codirected, which is not as rough as it sounds. Since we were all busy with other duties making the movie, it's not like we were all sitting back in directors' chairs at video village, scratching our chins over each take and bickering over how a scene should be played. We would work the scene until we got it how we all liked it, and we genuinely had a shared vision.

The reason it took so long was mainly financial. We would get some dough and buy film and shoot till we ran out of film. Then we'd take it to the lab and leave it till we raised money to get it out, and then we'd begin to edit that material. All this time we were still students. Kurt was now in graduate school, and Dean and I were still undergrads. We'd edit late at night after-hours at UCLA. During the day the editing rooms were crowded, but after-hours—empty. We would bring my daughters to the editing room with us, and they would sleep in sleeping bags on the editing room floors while we cut *Border Radio*.

When you work on a schedule like this, you have time to set up beautiful shots, work on scenes—all the things that are so hard to do when you're on the clock on a financed movie. Believe me, the irony is maddening. But another thing happened: the film began to evolve. Partly we all realized film noir was really hard to pull off! Not only did we lack that skill, but we also lacked that inside of us. We were having fun, and we wanted our characters to take themselves very seriously in a ridiculous situation. That ended up being the movie we finally made.

Other inspirations would come in too. One of the most important influences on the film's structure was seeing Michael Apted's 28 Up at the Nuart. We realized we could do interviews with our characters both to fill in information important to the narrative but also to be rather unreliable witnesses so the audience is actually ahead; they know the characters are not always telling the truth. Having met Iris Berry when she was waitressing at Duke's Coffee Shop at the Tropicana Motel on Santa Monica Blvd., we cast her to give a scenester perspective—she, too, unreliable. In all these interviews the truth is somewhere in the middle. Except in the interview with my little daughter Devon, who plays the daughter of Chris D. and Luanna—she is entirely honest.

Chris D. had a poetic filmmaker soul and came up with some great visual ideas, like burning a piñata in the shape of a guitar on the beach in Baja. Dean waited for the right light, and Chris set it on fire—it was stunning. We also saw wild horses running on the beach, and Dean whipped his camera around to grab it. Chris added the next beat: he crouched in the beach sand, wearing this great Mexican mariachi shirt, smoking a cigarette, and his gaze matching the cut exactly to where the horses had been roaming. Some of my favorite scenes visually in any movie I've ever made are in *Border Radio*—much of it chance, with Dean seizing the moment to grab something gorgeous unfolding.

The very first film we shot with John was of him walking out of the house where he's hiding out in Antelope Valley, which was actually the house of some college friends of ours in Canyon Country. All those great scenes with him and Luanna at that house were shot on his very first day as an actor. It pleases me to no end all these years later.

The film ended up financed through a series of packets of funds. Kurt's parents were friends with the character actor Vic Tayback, who was Mel on *Alice*. He had given Kurt an initial investment of $2,000 with the understanding that he would have first right of refusal to invest further. He exercised his right to refuse when Kurt went back to him, imploring him to invest, 'cause now we have real stars—we have John Doe! To which Tayback replied, "Tell me you got Charlton Heston, and I'll be impressed."

The final financing came full circle back to our inspirations—Wim introduced us to Georg Alexander from WDR, a German TV station, who had just put some money into Jim Jarmusch's *Stranger Than Paradise*. The first cut we showed him was not convincing, but the second one he got behind. It was enough to finish the movie. The next godsend was Enigma Records, who wanted these artists they could not otherwise have on their indie label: John Doe recorded an acoustic version of "Little Honey," Los Lobos gave us a very rare early cover of Mexican folk song "Maria Chuchena," Chris D.'s "Divine Horsemen," Tony Kinman's country acoustic version of The Blasters' "Border Radio," and Green on Red, who were in the movie playing on camera at the Hong Kong Café in Chinatown. Plus, there was the amazing score by Dave Alvin and Steve Berlin. The advance Enigma gave us for the soundtrack rights helped us then get the film blown up from 16mm to 35mm.

We had seen these bands who inspired us because they not only created new music and style but also promote their gigs with homemade flyers, created or revived their own venues, created their own fanzines and magazines, and, yes, even made records independent of the music industry. Now we were doing the same. But none of us knew about each other. It wasn't till we were already shooting that we heard about *Stranger Than Paradise*, where Jarmusch, like us, had cast musicians as his stars. We had to go all the way to Torino, Italy for a festival to see a poster for Gregg Araki's *Three Bewildered People in the Night*, and I said to Kurt, "Oh my god. This looks like our film! And he lives in L.A.!"

Border Radio was picked up for distribution by a company who released it in five theaters and then somehow ripped us off. Later, Monkee Michael Nesmith's company Pacific Arts picked up the video rights and was good to us. Cut to many years later: the film rights reverted to Kurt, Dean, and me, and Chris D., who was now programming movies at the American Cinematheque, struck up a friendship with Criterion Collection producer Susan Arosteguy and asked her about the possibility of releasing *Border Radio* on DVD. That is how we got that beautiful release on Criterion.

These days, in the internet and computer age, it's no big deal to make your own fanzine or record or movie. But it was an outrageous thing to do in the seventies and eighties. Maybe if there were a little less outrage today and a little more outrageous creative energy, we'd feel a little less despair and a whole lot more vibrant. Maybe there will never be a time like the punk and postpunk period again. Maybe the internet has killed that necessary private incubation period any art movement needs to flourish and form and cultivate and protect its power.

But within that incredibly unique time everything became possible, 'cause we didn't ask. We just did it.

CHAPTER 30

FALLEN SOLDIERS

by John Doe

Fallen soldiers? . . . we didn't even know that we were an army or in some kind of war? It had been a war of attrition, where the punk rockers or those associated with punk had not fared well. We all had different reasons for being in the trenches, but all did it with fire and blood. For it's a life that can beat you down, drink by drink, tour by tour, gig by gig, until even the blur gets blurry. The lifestyle becomes addicting, and then the addiction creeps up behind you, puts its arms around you in a warm, tight embrace, and it becomes one very long night on a nationwide—and then worldwide—tour. But regardless of the value, scale, or goal in the campaign, all the players deserve recognition and honor. And not just because they were there but because, for some time, long or short, they influenced or inspired someone.

The early deaths—like Darby Crash, D. Boon, and Exene's sister, Mirielle—made us deeper with sadness and hardened us against what we hoped could be a long career that included the occupational hazard of living a hard, fast, and loud life. Some of us—like Country Dick Montana, Jeffrey Lee Pierce, and Top Jimmy—chose lifestyle over life and checked out after many battles, a few victories & too many losses. But what the rest of us couldn't have anticipated was the long haul. What happens after the first blush fades. You don't measure up to either someone else's or your own standards. The money goes up, sometimes way up, and then stagnates or comes down, maybe way down. But our contribution grew from our collective effort through songwriting, gigs, words, touring; images through photos, movies, posters, art, performance art; radio play and dedication to search for a different way to say something that might already have been said.

Early on, we knew that some of us—like Jeffrey Lee, Texacala Jones from Tex and the Horseheads, Dee Detroit from UXA, or Top Jimmy—would struggle. Maybe they'd make it, but probably not. (Tex and Dee D are thankfully still with us.) We accepted the adage that sometimes "The wages of sin are death." But some of us were and are still determined to fight the good fight, and maybe somewhere down the line we'd be recognized as doers who stood for something. Here is where the roots rockers and hardcore stand together. Though the music may have been far apart, the desire to offer an alternative to the blandness unified us and gave respect to the music that started the whole punk rock thing in Los Angeles five years prior.

Finding origins can be tricky, and everyone wants to point to their contemporaries as ground zero. Thousands and thousands of music lovers may not know Lone Justice, Rank and File, or Green on Red, but it's likely they've heard of Neko Case, the Avett Brothers, and Wilco. They may not have listened to The Gun Club or House of Freaks, but they sure as shit know The White Stripes. Or, if not for the Big Boys from TX and Fishbone, who knows if funk would've found such a heavy core in The Red Hot Chili Peppers' mix? Your basic punk rocker may not have Flipper or Circle Jerks on their playlists, but they can probably name half a dozen Green Day or Rancid songs.

I'm not saying that those who came later than these pioneers I've mentioned did anything sneaky or underhanded. They simply got inspired and moved the needle forward with their version of a musical continuum, which is twisted music for people who feel a little more twisted than your casual consumer. What Neko, Jack White, Billie Jo, and Jeff Tweedy have in common is that they all got inspired by some kind of music that included the scene called "cowpunk" or "Paisley Underground" or "hardcore." Then maybe they went back even farther to the originators and then turned it into Americana, alt-country, funk-punk, country, or truly financially successful punk rock.

The "soldiers" from the eighties worked hard, played hard, toured hard, drank hard, partied hard, or sometimes sat around and did nothing but dream and drink and fuck off. But they tried and they did something. Some, like Tomata du Plenty and Biscuit Turner, enjoyed successful second acts as fine artists and received the attention that their bands, The Screamers and Big Boys, deserved. Others who are still with us—like Mike Ness, Jane Wiedlin, Dave Alvin, Penelope Houston, and Maria McKee—moved forward with solo careers, while some others concurrently hold down straight jobs.

Regardless of whether they have stuck around, checked out, stuck with it, or changed directions, they all deserve honor and congratulations for taking that emotional, creative, and physical risk.

They all deserve credit for where they went and how. Credit for all the crappy, cold dressing rooms or hot, bubbly audiences ten times bigger and better than expected. Credit for the hundreds and thousands of miles, day and night, riding in vans, saying stupid or brilliant shit to people you've known forever or have just met. Credit for getting paid less and still sending money home or being stupid and just blowing it on cowboy boots that don't even fit right. Credit for setting up and tearing down the stage and loading and standing by the gear so it doesn't get stolen. Credit for carrying on when all your shit *does* get stolen, and strangers from another band or music store lend instruments so the songs get played that night. Credit for all the shitty border crossings, where everything you have with you is pulled out and scattered across a parking lot, and you're strip searched in cold exam rooms. Credit for still paying attention and writing down a phrase that becomes a chorus. For sliding across and spinning around, three hundred and sixty degrees, through two or three highway lanes on ice and snow. Credit for fighting off the blackness when a bitter reviewer says your last performance or record was inspired and this one wasn't or when the insipid A&R guy says, "Can't you write more songs like 'Wild Thing'?" Credit for the band who never really leaves their hometown but breathes fire for two or three years. Credit for simply putting up with all the transcendent moments and complete bullshit that invariably happen in rapid succession.

Nowadays, when the news arrives that another comrade has crossed over, I greet it with a tight grimace and a light shake of my head and go on with my day. But the shadow lingers. That small sadness makes a little pocket inside with all the other brave soldiers who went down before. And I'm grateful for those of us who are still here to sing another old or new song, still here to tell an old or new story and to continue to be brave for those coming up behind us.

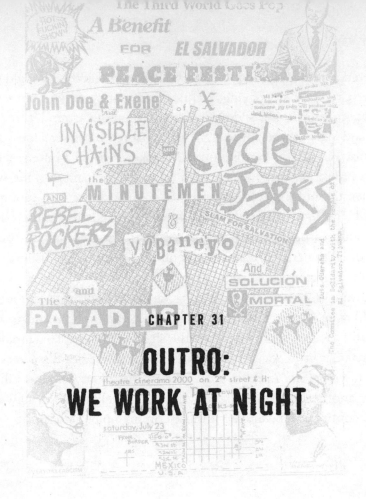

CHAPTER 31

OUTRO:
WE WORK AT NIGHT

Over the years I've made several offhanded comments to friends, ac-
quaintances, or strangers that have resonated deeply with them long
after I've forgotten the moment. Sometimes I cringe at the drunken
advice I offered that they took to heart; other times it's a smart-ass re-
mark they recall. But on occasion it turns out to be sort of profound.
We all hope to influence or inspire someone, to change their perspective, to open a door just a crack. Don't we all wish we could do that on
a weekly basis?

Thinking about this and our previous book, *Under the Big Black
Sun*, it struck me that this time in American art was about more
than just the music; it was about individuality, diversity, and self-
expression. About not giving a damn what people said and doing

stuff anyway. The fact that we inspired people without realizing we were doing just that kept the era . . . pure. No one thought about what would happen decades in the future; we were living in the here and now. At times we were optimistic; at times we were desperate. We just wanted to do shit, make shit, and change things. Through individual heartache and triumph, support and adversity, I believe we did just that.

In this book we've included people/artists who may not have directly contributed to the Los Angeles music scene, but they found a spirit there they could use to move forward and make their own mark in a different discipline. By doing that, they have inspired us or someone else to follow a totally impractical pipe dream and create something that didn't exist before. The people in these pages are ones who have made a mark, big or small, and have thrown seeds for others to pick up & spread further.

X has weathered many battles, successes, and failures and, to this day, remain a working, touring band—one who celebrated a fortieth anniversary in 2017 by playing over one hundred dates in the US. In those forty-some years Exene and I married, divorced, and stayed friends; Billy Zoom beat cancer twice, quit the band, and rejoined ten years later; and somehow DJ Bonebrake continues to be known as "the nicest man in rock 'n' roll." We can't play casinos or state fairs because we never had a bona fide "hit." If you ask Joan Jett or Blondie, they may say that can be a double-edged sword. I'll admit that sometimes we wish we had the bank account or luxury to reach the masses like they have. But at every X show I see some twenty-something or younger in the front row, losing their shit and getting schooled in original American punk rock. In that way it's the best job anyone can have. It's reassuring to also know that many of our contemporaries, who are more or less popular, experience something similar, gig after gig.

We see ourselves as part of a continuum. We learned from each other, got inspired by, or stole outright from those who came before us. We "stood on the shoulders of giants" and believe we can give others a leg up. So, in turn, they can do the same in the future.

As the great Mike Watt says at the end of every show as he holds his bass in one hand, high over his head: "START YOUR OWN BAND!"

yrs, John Doe
fin.

ACKNOWLEDGMENTS

John Doe special thanks:

KT, Amelia, Elena, Veronica, Freddy, Maud, Leila, Ben, Uncle Joe, Cousin Tim, Billy, DJ, Exene, Cindy, Stuart, Dave, Kevin, Jesse, Howe, Rouse, Cerneka, Leahy, Guralnick.

Tom DeSavia special thanks:

Joel Amsterdam, Tyler Barstow, Ken Bethea, Joyce Caffey, Kevin Coogan, The DeSavia Family (Tony, Terry & Natalie), Brian DiGenti, Gia DiSantis, Richard Edwards, Kim Frankiewicz, Murry Hammond, Lisa Johnson, Cathy Kerr, Erica Krusen and MusiCares, Matt Messer, Rhett Miller, Francois Mobasser, Jenny O., Philip Peeples, Jeff Sosnow, Shane Trulin, Skating Polly, The White Family (Nicky, Corey, Ethan & Aaron), Jake Wisely.

John and Tom special thanks:

John and Tom offer their deepest thanks to all the authors and photographers who bared their hearts & souls for this project; our agent Lynn Jones Johnston of Lynn Johnston Literary; all at Hachette/Da Capo (especially Ben Schafer, Michelle Aielli, Justin Lovell, Kevin Hanover, Matthew Weston, Quinn Fariel), Michael Barrs, Damon Booth, Natalie DeSavia, Melissa Dragich-Cordero, Marty Glosser, Stacie Havemeier, Debbie Deuble Hill, Christine Marra, Heidi May, Scott Sherratt, Richard Scheltinga, Jeff Slate, Brian Speiser, Anna Statman, Seth Venezia, Lissa Warren, Victoria Yarnish; all at Penguin Random House Audio (especially Heather Dalton, Brie Garcia, Donna Passannante, Katie Punis, Louise Quayle, Dan Zitt).

Perpetual extra special thanks to Krissy Teegerstrom, who joined the project as creative consultant. Your intuition, uncapped thinking and encouragement lead us to a more expansive and inclusive book. You effortlessly served the roles of muse, organizer, teacher, and referee. We honestly couldn't have completed this book without you, Krissy. Thank you, from the bottom of our hearts.

John Doe and Tom DeSavia would once again like to thank each other.

THE CONTRIBUTORS

Dave Alvin

Dave Alvin is a GRAMMY Award–winning songwriter, singer, producer, and barroom guitarist. He cofounded the legendary roots-rock band The Blasters with his brother, Phil Alvin, in 1979, and then left the group in 1986 after four albums. He has released several solo albums since 1987, including *King of California*, *Eleven Eleven*, *Ashgrove*, *Blackjack David*, and *Public Domain*. Many of his songs have been used in a wide variety of films and television shows during this time. In 2014–2015 he reunited with his brother for two highly regarded blues albums, and in 2018 Dave Alvin released another critically acclaimed album, *Downey to Lubbock*, with Jimmie Dale Gilmore. Dave lives in California and on the US Interstate Highway System.

Allison Anders

Kentucky-born, L.A.-raised Allison Anders is an award-winning screenwriter and film and TV director whose work includes *Border Radio*, *Gas Food Lodging*, *Mi Vida Loca*, *Grace of My Heart*, and *Sugartown*. She's directed episodes of *Sex and the City*, *Orange Is the New Black*, *Southland*, *Riverdale*, *Murder in the First*, and recently *Sorry for Your Loss*. She was nominated for an Emmy for Best Director for the Lifetime movie *Ring of Fire*, wherein she cast John Doe as the Father of Country Music, A. P. Carter. She's a MacArthur Fellow and won a Peabody Award for her film *Things Behind the Sun* and is a Distinguished Professor of Film at USCB. She resides in Altadena, California with Mattie, her adorable dog who's a retired actress.

Charlotte Caffey

Charlotte was born and lives in Los Angeles and remains a member of The Go-Go's. She continues her intense passion for songwriting, composing for artists, and theater. She has been married to Jeff McDonald since 1993, and together they are the fiercely proud parents of Astrid McDonald, songwriter and lead vocalist for the L.A. punk band Side Eyes. *Head over Heels*, a theatrical musical based around the songs of The Go-Go's, opened on Broadway in 2018 to rave reviews.

Peter Case

Peter Case moved from Buffalo to San Francisco at age eighteen. A founding member of The Nerves and The Plimsouls, he's a singer-songwriter, performer, and producer, with thirteen solo albums to his credit, including his self-titled T Bone Burnett–produced debut, the GRAMMY-nominated *Let Us Now Praise Sleepy John*, as well as *HWY 62*. He is also the author of a memoir, *As Far as You Can Get Without a Passport* (Everthemore Books) and a contributor to *Your Golden Sun Still Shines* (Manic D Press). After thirty years of L.A. living he has returned to San Francisco.

Tom DeSavia

DeSavia, an L.A. native, is a longtime music industry A&R rep/music publisher, sometime journalist, and occasional podcaster. He uses humor as a defense mechanism, is Italian, a Libra, and stands five-ten and has flat feet. Thanks to John Doe, he is now also GRAMMY-nominated. He likes L.A. punk rock a whole lot.

John Doe

John Doe—musician, actor, writer. Born in Decatur, Illinois. Splits his time between Austin, Texas and interstate highways. As a founding member of X, proud to have celebrated their fortieth anniversary in 2017. Has released several solo records in addition to collaborating with The Sadies, The Flesh Eaters, Jill Sobule, and The Knitters. Appeared in many, many films & TV shows. Coauthored *Under the Big Black Sun* with Tom DeSavia and friends in 2016.

Shepard Fairey

Shepard Fairey was born in Charleston, South Carolina, and later received his bachelor's of fine arts in illustration at the Rhode Island School of Design. In 1989 he created the "Andre the Giant Has a Posse" sticker that transformed into the OBEY GIANT art campaign, changing the way people see art and the urban landscape. Raised on a steady diet of DIY, punk-rock, and skateboard culture, Fairey uses his art as a megaphone for the voiceless and a tool for positive propaganda. In 2008 he created the now-iconic "Hope" portrait of Barack Obama as a tool of grassroots political support. His works are in the permanent collections of the Museum of Modern Art (MoMA), the Victoria and Albert Museum, the Smithsonian's National Portrait Gallery, and others.

Norwood Fisher

Norwood Fisher, bassist extraordinaire and founding member of Fishbone, took funk, ska, and metal bass and ran it through a punk-rock blender. Using bass as a lead instrument, he leant his songwriting talents to every Fishbone record. He has composed, produced, and contributed to countless productions, including *Trulio Disgracias* and *Mr Green All-Stars*. He's acted in several films and TV shows. When he's not touring the world with Fishbone, he devotes time to creating the Watt's Conservatory of Music. He's a proud father who lives in Santa Monica, California.

Pleasant Gehman

Pleasant Gehman is a Hollywood icon and true renaissance woman: author, musician, dancer, actor, show producer, and well-known psychic. Her forty-five years of multidisciplinary creative output shows no signs of slowing down. She's the author and/or editor of eight books, singer and founder of three bands, and has been featured in numerous feature films, videos, and documentaries. Currently she is the coproducer of two ongoing productions: occult burlesque show *Belle, Book & Candle* and *War Stories*, a rock 'n' roll storytelling show (coproduced by Theresa Kereakes) with a revolving cast of punk icons. She lives in Hollywood with four extremely spoiled cats. www.pleasant gehman.com.

Terry Graham

From 1977 to 1987 Terry Graham sat behind the kit for numerous bands, including The Bags, The Gun Club, and The Cramps. He is a member of the Writers Guild of America, an author (*Punk Like Me!*), and a screenwriter living in Los Angeles.

Sid Griffin

Born in Louisville, Kentucky, Sid Griffin moved to Los Angeles in October 1977, fibbing to his parents about grad school at USC. Instead of a master's degree, he immersed himself in the fierce local music scene, starting with Death Wish, followed by The Unclaimed, then the groundbreaking Long Ryders, then back to obscurity with his "alt-bluegrass" Coal Porters. He is the proud author of four books and a BBC TV documentary on Gram Parsons and the father of two fine kids. Since 1992 he has lived in England, where he frequently appears on the BBC discussing popular culture.

Jack Grisham

Jack Grisham is a writer, photographer, punk provocateur, and actor. He is currently playing the part of a father, ex-husband, and recovering alcoholic while living in Huntington Beach. The reviews have been mostly favorable.

Tony Hawk

Now the most recognized action-sports figure in the world, Tony Hawk was nine years old when his brother changed his life by giving him a used skateboard. By fourteen he'd turned pro, and by sixteen he was widely considered the best competitor. In 1999 he became the first skater to ever complete the legendary 900, a trick that had eluded skaters for a decade. Tony has created numerous brands throughout his career, including Birdhouse Skateboards, Hawk Clothing, and the Tony Hawk Pro Skater videogame franchise. His autobiography was a *New York Times* best-seller, and his Tony Hawk Foundation has given over $7.4 million to 609 public skatepark projects throughout the world.

Chip Kinman

Chip Kinman, with his brother, Tony, kickstarted the punk-rock revolution with their first release, *I Hate the Rich*, in 1977 and never stopped. The Dils, Rank and File, Blackbird, Cowboy Nation, and Ford Madox Ford are their shared folly as well as their contribution to the never-ending party.

Maria McKee

Maria McKee is an American singer, songwriter, multi-instrumentalist, film producer, and actress. She began her professional career as the front person for critically acclaimed L.A. band Lone Justice and has since released a number of solo projects as well as writing hit singles for herself and others. Her song "If Love Is a Red Dress (Hang Me in Rags)" remains one of the memorable sync usages from Quentin Tarantino's modern classic *Pulp Fiction*. She has produced and starred in three major independent film features via Shootist Production company, which she owns and operates with filmmaker Jim Akin.

Angelo Moore

Angelo Moore, aka Dr. Madd Vibe, musician–vocalist–composer–poet– satirist–performance artist. Moore began his career in high school, when his career path started as part of the creative force, lead vocalist, and saxophonist of the legendary band Fishbone. Since the late seventies Moore has been a pioneer of alternative music, fusing punk rock, funk, ska-reggae, gospel, and rock 'n' roll, making him an inspirational icon to many. Fishbone has released over twenty studio and live recordings and are the subject of a feature length film *Everyday Sunshine: The Story of Fishbone*. Dr. Madd Vibe has released eight recordings. Fishbone and Dr. Madd Vibe continue to tour worldwide.

W. T. Morgan

W. T. Morgan is the writer and director of *The Unheard Music*. Other credits include *A Matter of Degrees*, *Columbus*, *500 Nations* (with Kevin Costner), *Spirit*, *Obama in Indian Country*, *American Epic*, and some video games, Disney adventures, and the forthcoming *See How We Are*. He developed movies and television with Michael Blake, author of *Dances with Wolves*, and is a longtime member of the board of directors of The Actors' Gang theater company (led by artistic director Tim Robbins). He lives in Los Angeles with the incomparable Alizabeth Foley.

Chris Morris

Morris, one of the contributors to John Doe and Tom DeSavia's *Under the Big Black Sun* (2016), has been writing about music in Los Angeles since 1978. He was senior writer at *Billboard* (1986–2004) and music editor at the *Hollywood Reporter* (2004–2006); he currently contributes to *Variety*. He served as the music critic at the *Los Angeles Reader* (1978–1996) and *L.A. CityBeat* (2003–2008). Morris's writing has also appeared in the *Los Angeles Times*, *Rolling Stone*, and other national publications. His book *Los Lobos: Dream in Blue* was published by the University of Texas Press in 2015; *Together Through Life: A Personal Journey with the Music of Bob Dylan* was published by Rothco Press in 2016.

Keith Morris

Keith Morris is a singer, songwriter, political activist, author, and Southern California native. Known for his role as front man of hardcore bands Black Flag, Circle Jerks, and Off!, Morris has also appeared as a guest vocalist on several albums by other artists. In 2016 Da Capo Press released his autobiography, *My Damage: The Story of a Punk Rock Survivor*, to national critical acclaim. Keith has battled diabetes, drug and alcohol addiction, and the record industry and lived to tell the tales.

Mike Ness

Not only is Mike Ness known as a legendary member of the early Southern California punk movement with his band Social Distortion, he has also become a rock 'n' roll icon with an impactful career in music that spans four decades. Ness is an artist who encompasses the true essence of an Americana original while continuing to hold firm roots in punk and glitter. Each step in Mike's career has portrayed and encapsulated a variety of musical styles that reflect his soul, which is apparent on every record.

Louie Pérez

Louie Pérez is an American songwriter, percussionist, painter, prose writer, and guitarist for the multiple GRAMMY Award–winning band, Los Lobos. Pérez is the group's principal songwriter and lyricist. His side projects include the Latin Playboys, songs for several stage productions. His prose has been published in the *Los Angeles Times* magazine, *LA Weekly*, *Dinosaur* magazine, and the New York arts journal *BOMB*, to name a few. Pérez has shown his paintings and sculptures since 1975 in countless museums and galleries. *Good Morning, Aztlán: The Words, Pictures and Songs of Louie Pérez* was published in October 2018 by Tia Chucha/Northwestern University Press.

Tim Robbins

For the past thirty-seven years Tim Robbins has served as artistic director for The Actors' Gang, a multi–award winning Los Angeles–based ensemble that has performed in over one hundred cities and on five continents. The Actors' Gang's nationally recognized education programs and Prison Project have received the support and praise of the White House, the Department of Justice, and the California governor's office. As an actor, Robbins has won an Academy Award, Golden Globe, Sag Award, and the Prix d'Interprétation masculine at Cannes. His credits include *Marjorie Prime, Mystic River, Shawshank Redemption, The Player, Bull Durham*, and *Jacob's Ladder* and, as a writer/director, *Dead Man Walking, Cradle Will Rock*, and *Bob Roberts*.

Henry Rollins

Born in Washington, DC, Henry Rollins moved to California in the summer of 1981. For over three decades Rollins made albums with Black Flag and The Rollins Band, wrote over twenty books, and performed in bands and on his own all over the world. He continues to write for magazines and newspapers; publish work on his imprint, 2.13.61 Publications; and speak to audiences in up to twenty countries a year.

Jane Wiedlin

Jane Wiedlin is a founding member of The Go-Go's. The band was the first-ever successful all-girl group to write their own songs and play their own instruments. Jane has released six albums of her own. Besides being a song-writer, guitarist, and singer, she is also a playwright, the world's first atheist minister (licensed to perform weddings), a comic book author, an actor, and an animal rights activist.

Annette Zilinskas

Annette Zilinskas is the original bassist for The Bangles and lead vocalist with roots-punk outfit Blood on the Saddle, whose juiced-up anthems inspired the cowpunk genre and paved the way for the No Depression movement and its related alt-country/Americana revivals. Zilinskas later led the dream-pop group Weatherbell and the punky all-girl garage-rock trio 3 Hole Punch as well as collaborated with the experimental noise-pop auteur and Medicine leader Brad Laner. She's a noted spoken-word stylist and longtime member of the spoken-word/music troupe The Ringling Sisters, whose debut album on A&M Records, *60-Watt Reality*, was produced by the legendary Lou Adler. She's currently compiling a short-story collection with the working title *Walking After Midnight*.

Billy Zoom

In addition to cofounding X and bringing his own brand of fiery rockabilly to punk rock, Zoom has played guitar for everyone from Gene Vincent, The Blasters, Etta James, Big Joe Turner, to Mike Ness, and countless others. Born in Savana, Illinois, Zoom is a longtime, proud resident of Orange, California, where he runs Billy Zoom Custom Shop, designing and repairing guitar amps and effects. In 2008, in honor of his contributions to both the world music community and the legacy of Gretsch guitars, Gretsch unveiled the G6129BZ Billy Zoom Custom Shop Tribute Silver Jet model.

INDEX